W9-CCX-099

# HARD DRIVING

# HARD DRIVING

## The Wendell Scott Story

### The American Odyssey of NASCAR's First Black Driver

Brian Donovan

Steerforth Press
Hanover, New Hampshire

Copyright © 2008 by Brian Donovan

ALL RIGHTS RESERVED

For information about permission to reproduce
selections from this book, write to:
Steerforth Press L.L.C., 45 Lyme Road, Suite 208,
Hanover, New Hampshire 03755

The Library of Congress has cataloged the hardcover edition as follows:
Donovan, Brian, 1952–
Hard driving : the Wendell Scott story : the odyssey of NASCAR's first Black driver /
Brian Donovan. — 1st ed.
p. cm.
Includes bibliographical references and index.
ISBN 978-1-58642-144-1 (alk. paper)
1. Scott, Wendell, 1921–1990. 2. Stock car drivers — United States — Biography.
3. Automobile racing drivers — United States — Biography. 4. African American
automobile racing drivers — Biography. I. Title.
GV1032.S36.D66 2008
796.72092–dc22
[B]

2008024287

ISBN (paperback): 978-1-58642-160-1

FIRST PAPERBACK EDITION

*For Ellen, always my inspiration*

## Contents

Everyone who accomplishes greatly is obsessed with one purpose and nearly blind to all else; he can only with difficulty tear his mind away from the one thing that is important to him to consider lesser matters — and everything except his purpose in life is a lesser matter.

*All But My Life,* a memoir and biography of the racing driver Stirling Moss, by Moss and Ken W. Purdy

Among the Negroes there is a saying: "Up North they don't care how high up you get as long as you don't get too close. Down South they don't care how close you get as long as you don't get too high."

*Norfolk Virginian-Pilot*, September 26, 1954

## Preface

The day I first met Wendell Scott, he didn't act like somebody who'd played a noteworthy part in changing America's moral landscape. He seemed to lack the self-importance that journalists learn to expect from many such people. I wanted to talk about his former career as a racing driver and the troubles he'd faced in challenging racial prejudice. But Scott kept changing the subject back to old auto radiators.

He'd collected a pile of them outside of his weathered shop in Danville, Virginia. He was loading them into his truck, figuring he'd sell them to the local junkyard. He hoped the price would be worth his time, because he was running late on repairing some cars for customers from his modest neighborhood. This visit from somebody who wanted to write his biography didn't mean he could interrupt his customary routine of long workdays. He was friendly enough, but we'd have to talk while he ran errands and fixed grungy cars. "Got bills to pay," he said.

Except for a couple of his old race cars rusting in the weeds nearby, Scott could have been just another struggling small-town mechanic: sixty-eight years old, showing every year, dirty overalls, work-worn hands, limping on a bad leg. I wondered if anybody else who had raced in seven Daytona 500s woke up that morning worrying about the salvage price for junk radiators.

I'd come to Danville intrigued by the little that I knew about Scott's role as a sort of lone wolf among the nation's integration pioneers. He'd broken the color barrier in southern stock car racing in 1952, a time of fiercely entrenched segregation. In contrast with some other courageous figures who confronted discrimination, he had no organized support system behind him, just family and friends. Unlike Jackie Robinson, Scott integrated an all-white sport without the backing of any powerful white patron in its hierarchy. Unlike Rosa Parks, Scott had no connections in the civil rights movement, no lawyers and organizers to publicize and challenge the injustices he faced. Although his difficult years as NASCAR's first black driver took place during an era of historic racial conflict, the mainstream news media mostly ignored him.

For me, the idea of writing a book about Scott pulled together several threads from my past. As a boy, I'd been awed by the racers who drove Indy 500–style cars on the one-mile dirt oval outside my hometown of Syracuse, New York. The predatory howl of the Offenhauser engines in those rocket-like machines resonates in my memory still. As a teenager, I'd built a '32 Ford hot rod before I was old enough to drive. As a newspaper reporter, I wrote many stories about prejudice and our stumbling, often reluctant progress toward equality.

In my thirties, I became an amateur racer, driving smaller, slower versions of those open-wheeled cars I'd loved as a kid. I could understand Scott's obsession with racing. Even small-time race cars go fast enough to serve up the potent cocktail of addictive excitement that nourishes a driver's passion for this sport — one whose appeal baffles many people with stronger instincts for self-preservation. Finally, like any reporter, I felt the pull of a story about an underdog bucking a sometimes hostile environment, and I had a vague notion that Scott's experiences promised at least a small new window into those turbulent years that changed our country.

At one point that afternoon, fortunately for me, Scott needed to break loose a rusted bolt. Without being asked, I handed him a wrench of the correct type and size. For the first time, he gave me a sharp, narrow-eyed look of evaluation, signaling that, well, okay, maybe he could find some time after all to work with this stranger on a book about his life.

As I interviewed the many people who shared their thoughts for these pages, I began to get a sense of what may have been Scott's most meaningful accomplishment. It wasn't something he set out to do, but it happened anyway. I heard this same observation again and again: During the 1950s and '60s, as civil rights conflict roiled the South, the first black person that many white southerners came to admire was the driver who'd integrated their beloved sport of stock car racing.

Week after week, year after year, Scott showed NASCAR audiences an example of skill, courage, a tenacious work ethic, and the character to persevere despite disappointments. His dogged pursuit of his dream refuted racial stereotypes. For the first time in their lives, numerous NASCAR fans found themselves rooting for a black man to defeat white men. By the mid-1960s, only a few superstars like Richard Petty got louder cheers and applause from southern speedway crowds than Scott. At a critical time in the nation's history, Wendell Scott helped to change the way that many thousands of ordinary Americans looked upon black people.

To be sure, he wasn't always exemplary. He had his flaws and blind spots, and he did some things he shouldn't have. Nevertheless, the record of the civil rights era should include the improbable fact that those pioneers whose lives contributed to undermining the national embarrassment of segregation included a stock car driver whose credentials, incidentally, included some misadventures on the wrong side of the law. In certain circles of our culture, a few rough edges can help.

A close look at Scott's story also provides some previously unexamined episodes from the history of NASCAR, which has grown in recent years into a major national sport and cultural phenomenon. For NASCAR's celebrated founder, Bill France Sr., the arrival of a black driver posed some business, political, and moral decisions, and in important ways what France chose to do, and not to do, shaped Scott's fortunes.

As for those radiators Scott sold to the junkyard, he didn't want to talk about how much he got paid. Apparently it wasn't much.

## Prologue

They drove all night from Virginia to Florida, three black men crowded into a scruffy GMC pickup, towing a stock car through the segregated South of 1963. As usual, Wendell Scott had a loaded pistol under the seat and at least a dozen problems on his mind.

With two friends as his volunteer crew, Scott was heading for a speedway in a tough, shabby white neighborhood on the outskirts of Jacksonville. He would race against twenty-one white men in front of a white crowd. As NASCAR's first black driver, Scott had been in this sort of situation many times since he'd begun racing eleven years ago. But these days, with civil rights turmoil inflaming the South, racial hostility seemed to worsen by the week. Lately, his roughneck sport had served up one nasty surprise after another.

After midnight, Scott's friends took turns driving so he could get some sleep. He'd been laboring over his battle-weathered race car all day. His eyes felt gritty, and he leaned back and tried to relax. At forty-two, Scott was wiry, light-skinned, almost six feet tall. Already his narrow face showed the worry lines of an older man. He wore frayed coveralls. His hands were nicked and grimy like old wrenches. He had a thin mustache, touches of gray in his hair, deep squint lines around his shrewd blue eyes, and unsatisfied hopes that gnawed at his guts.

To many casual acquaintances in NASCAR, he seemed amiable and unpretentious. They liked his country-flavored speech and the quiet, uncomplaining way he went about his business. Few realized that this unassuming exterior, carefully calibrated, served Scott as a protective shield, concealing parts of his real self that some white people might find unacceptable.

That night, Scott's worries ranged from the shortcomings of his vehicles to the odds for someday realizing his ambitions. His old truck wasn't much good for towing. Even with his eyes shut, he could feel it trying to wander out of its lane. At home, overdue bills covered his bedroom dresser. Trips like this one, into the Deep South, were getting more dangerous. His career wasn't where he wanted it to be. His pistol was illegal — no permit.

His race car wasn't fast enough. He wondered when his next attack of ulcer pain would leave him throwing up by the roadside.

The green 1956 pickup rolled south through the Carolinas and Georgia, past the places where he and his friends could not buy a meal, rent a motel room, or take a sip of water from a drinking fountain. WHITES ONLY, the signs warned, or sometimes, NO NIGGERS. When they needed a bathroom, they looked for bushes near the highway. They brought their own food, which they ate in the truck. When Scott drove his first race at the Danville Fairgrounds speedway in 1952, black southerners were still expected to step aside for whites on the sidewalk, and the civil rights movement was still in its infancy.

Now, with the movement gaining strength, racial violence racked the South. During the past couple of years, the furrows across Scott's forehead had deepened. They gave him the look of someone peering into the near future and spotting trouble. Just in the past six months, five southern blacks had died in racial killings. After a recent race in Birmingham, he'd had to flee when he learned that white men were plotting to seize his race car and burn it. Before every trip to a racetrack, Scott made sure his .38-caliber revolver was cleaned, loaded, and stowed under the seat of his truck.

Those who knew Scott best understood something that few competitors and fans recognized: His low-key humility was partly genuine, partly camouflage for a driven personality and high-horsepower ego. Under his veneer of modesty, he saw himself as deserving a niche in history, one at least as eminent as that of Jackie Robinson, who had broken the color barrier in modern major-league baseball in 1947 and whom Scott regarded with considerable rivalry. Privately, Scott believed without reservation that he had the talent to be one of the country's top racing drivers, if only he could land the sponsorship to get into a competitive race car. Three years ago, he'd moved up to NASCAR's top-level series, the Grand National circuit (known today as the Sprint Cup). In the minor leagues, he'd won dozens of races and two championships, but he still didn't have a single Grand National victory. Every day he thought about how badly he needed that first major-league win.

His race car, a pale blue 1962 Chevy, rolled along behind the truck on a tow bar; Scott didn't have a trailer. The Chevy, past its prime, was faded and patched in spots. Scott had bought it from a driver who'd moved on to a lucrative sponsorship deal. In a series whose elite teams had large professional crews and generous backing from Detroit's auto manufacturers, the lettering on the Chevy's front fenders spelled out Scott's place in the financial hierarchy: MECHANIC: ME.

As often happened on the way to a race, Scott's ulcers doubled him over with nausea during the trip to Jacksonville. They made some quick stops so he could run to the ditch. But something beyond the pain and the money problems kept Scott wakeful — a sharpened sense of anticipation about this particular race. He had a feeling, against the odds, that Jacksonville could be the race that turned his career around. Toward dawn, he gave up trying to nap. He couldn't get his mind to slow down. There were rewards to a life driven by the obsessive passion for racing, but the gift of letting go and relaxing wasn't among them. He'd raced many times on little sleep or none at all.

The sun was up on the morning of December 1 when Scott and his friends, Winston "Wild Horse" Chaney and James "Brother" Robinson, pulled into Jacksonville Speedway Park and started getting ready for the hundred-mile race that would be run that afternoon. This wasn't one of the circuit's high-profile events. Jacksonville's run-down half-mile dirt oval was much smaller than the major speedways at Daytona Beach, Florida, and Darlington, South Carolina, where NASCAR's most prestigious competitions took place. The Jacksonville track's poorly maintained surface often broke up during a race into bumps and ruts. For exactly those reasons, though, Scott figured that this track offered his best chance for a surprise victory that might bring him some support from one of the auto companies. He'd won many races on tracks just like this one. Even with his mediocre Grand National cars, he'd twice finished third on half-mile dirt tracks, beating cars with much more power. Last season, he'd outqualified the entire field at Savannah's half-mile oval. Sometimes on a dirt track, especially a bumpy one, the best driver could outrun the best car.

If he could win today, he might move closer to the big break he'd been hoping for — sponsorship from the Ford Motor Company. One of Ford's top executives, Lee Iacocca, was creating the most ambitious racing program in the auto industry's history. With Henry Ford II's enthusiastic support, Iacocca was pouring millions of dollars into teams competing in NASCAR, the Indianapolis 500, and elsewhere. This year, factory-backed Fords dominated Grand National racing. For a black driver in a southern sport, corporate sponsorship remained a long shot. But the past decade had brought some historic changes in the country; maybe his time was coming.

The day was sunny, breezy, and cool. About five thousand fans filed into the crude wooden grandstands and bleachers as the drivers ran their practice session and began their individual qualifying laps to determine the race's starting lineup. All the spectators, even those in the top rows, knew they'd be showered with dirt as the cars sped past. The roar of the unmuffled engines shook the windows of the small houses in the neighborhood around the track. Some of those homes sat on unpaved streets. Some had no electricity.

NASCAR was still a largely southern sport in the '60s, and its races drew a mostly blue-collar crowd. Only one journalist showed up to cover the Jacksonville race, Gene Granger of the *Florida Times-Union,* the local newspaper. The civil rights conflicts roiling the South, Granger recalled, had stirred up considerable anger among local white people, including many spectators at the track. "There were some real rednecks there — I mean some fightin' rednecks. That wasn't the friendliest part of town. There were hot feelings there."

When Scott's turn came to run his qualifying laps, the track surface was already breaking up. His stiffly sprung car handled badly, bouncing from one pothole to another, losing traction, sliding erratically. His qualifying speed left him with a poor starting position for the race: fifteenth of twenty-two cars. He jacked up the Chevy and crawled underneath, studying the chassis, looking for some adjustment to make the car less clumsy. Abruptly, an inspiration struck: a simple, radical idea to soften the suspension drastically. At this point, he had nothing to lose by taking a chance. Nobody at Ford would be sending Iacocca a memo about a driver who'd qualified fifteenth. Working hastily, he removed one of the two shock absorbers at each corner, giving the wheels more freedom to bounce.

The change worked even better than he'd hoped. A few laps into the race, Scott realized he probably had the best-handling car in the field. "That thing knew where to go!" he would recall. "Working! Just working with that track. I was passing 'em as fast as I could catch 'em." Broken wheels and axles took out several drivers. Others crashed. Many struggled with cars that were difficult to control.

Scott stayed on the lead lap, pacing himself, trying not to punish his car. Late in the race, he found himself challenging for the lead. He was storming around the bumpy track in second place, sliding the heavy car around the rutted turns, his rear wheels spitting dirt. He listened to the melody of the tires skittering along the rough surface, and he breathed the bouquet of hot oil and rubber, and he couldn't remember when he'd ever felt better in a race car. Maybe never. Time unfurled slowly, and the car seemed part of his mind, and he knew in his nerves and bones why he was addicted to doing this. The bellow of the big V-8 engine rose and fell in a rhythm, booming in the Chevy's gutted-out interior, singing to Scott that his luck might be changing at last.

Not far ahead, the first-place car slid around the turns, a bright blue, factory-sponsored '63 Plymouth, number forty-three. Scott liked the Plymouth's driver, a friendly, talented young man who was quick to flash his wide grin. But Scott knew that Richard Petty, for all his charm, could be risky to pass. The previous year in a race in Georgia, he'd run Scott into a guardrail. Today, though, luck was on Scott's side. With twenty-five laps to go, Petty's car slowed abruptly; the rough track had damaged a steering arm. Scott swept past Petty into the lead.

Suddenly the NASCAR officials running the event had a problem they'd never faced before. Apparently, in just a few minutes, a Negro driver would win the race. Then he'd go to victory circle and step up for his trophy. If custom prevailed, he would kiss the race queen, a white woman, in front of the white crowd.

Black men had been lynched for less.

On the next lap, Scott glanced at the scoreboard and registered a quick surprise: His number was no longer there. All through the race, NASCAR had posted the numbers of the cars in the top five positions. Now, for the first time, all of the numbers had disappeared from the scoreboard. He waved at his crewmen in the pits, pointing at himself and at the scoreboard, trying to find out if they knew what was happening. They didn't understand. On his next lap, they held up the gas can — did he need fuel? Scott waved that off. Next lap, they held up a tire. He waved that off, too, and kept on charging around the track.

He didn't know what to think. Years ago, the top man in his sport, Bill France Sr., the charming autocrat who ran NASCAR like a czar, had assured Scott that his color didn't matter, that NASCAR always would treat him like any other driver.

But why had the scoreboard gone blank?

On what should have been the last lap of the race, Scott roared across the finish line, looking for the checkered flag. The NASCAR official in the flag stand just watched him go by. Scott ran another lap and crossed the finish line again.

Still the flagman stood motionless.

Scott kept on driving hard, every little rattle in the car sounding ominous now. The euphoria of driving was fading, and he was slipping back into the everyday world. For years his memory would return to the two thoughts that ran through his mind right then. This was the moment he'd anticipated for so long, his chance to show Iacocca's people what he could do, the payoff for all his work and troubles, all the times he'd been treated wrong and had to swallow his anger — so what the *hell* was going on?

At the same time, Wendell Scott was thinking that he knew perfectly well what was going on, knew it like he knew his own skin.

# 1

## "Didn't no black kids have no bicycles."

More than anything, Wendell Oliver Scott wanted to be his own boss.

Even as a young boy, growing up in the 1920s and '30s, he vowed that no matter what, he wasn't going to wind up like so many people in his neighborhood: stuck in a dull, regimented job. He didn't want to work for The Man. He'd say this so vehemently and so often that his younger sister, Guelda, knew better than to question the idea, and sometimes she thought that if anyone in the family besides herself had a chance to escape to an interesting life, most likely it would be Wendell.

For the working folk of Danville, blacks and poor whites alike, the local economy didn't offer many career choices. Two industries, textiles and tobacco, dominated life in Scott's hometown, a hilly city of about twenty-five thousand in south-central Virginia, just above the North Carolina state line. From miles away, travelers heading for Danville could see a huge, illuminated sign that proclaimed the most important economic fact about the city since the late 1800s: DAN RIVER COTTON MILLS. These cavernous mills, turning raw cotton into threads and fabrics, were the biggest structures for miles around, five stories high with acres of floor space. They crowded the banks of the Dan River, fat columns of smoke pouring from their stacks.

Inside, thousands of workers toiled in a clattering din as thirteen thousand looms shook the floors. Black employees got the most menial jobs. All of the workers breathed air full of cotton dust; some died from brown-lung disease. Employees shopped in company stores, sent their children to company schools, worshiped in company-subsidized churches, got haircuts at the company barber shop. Many white workers lived in the "mill village" of company houses. Dan River Mills essentially controlled Danville: its economics, its politics, and City Hall. During the 1920s, the company experimented with a workers'-rights scheme called Industrial Democracy.

It foundered, but not before the white workers passed a measure banning black workers from all of the better jobs.

Outside the city, tobacco fields stretched out for many miles. Tobacco jobs were even tougher than mill jobs. Workdays lasted as long as fourteen hours. Laborers worked the fields for subsistence pay. Children worked alongside adults. Some workers died from heatstroke or bites from disease-bearing insects. Tobacco warehouses and processing plants dotted the landscape. Like the cotton mills, they were stifling and stuffy inside, their pungent air full of lung-damaging dust. Black workers had to conceal their resentment that white co-workers got better pay.

"Being black, you could work alongside a white fellow, doing the same thing that he's doing or more, and you could never get his salary," Scott's cousin Alonza Carter recalled of his years as a tobacco worker. "He could get twelve to fifteen dollars a week. The most you could get was about nine."

The idea of life beyond Danville was inconceivable to many. Scott's sister, Guelda King, said: "In the community that we grew up in, in our age group, I cannot think of a single person who went to college but me. Everybody, when they finished high school, they got a job in a tobacco factory or the cotton mills."

Scott swore he'd avoid that kind of boss-dominated life. "I'll never go work in those mills," he told a boyhood friend. "If it gets to where I can't make a living, I'll get me a mule and a plow and raise corn. That mill's too much like a prison. You go in and they lock a gate behind you and you can't get out until you've done your time." Across the South, towns like Danville supplied many of the men who would be drawn after World War II to the new sport of stock car racing. A career in which you risked your life and labored for long hours over wrecked cars seemed much more attractive if your other choices were the mill or the tobacco industry.

During Scott's boyhood, his prospects for any kind of decent future sometimes looked doubtful. Besides the insults of segregation, growing up often seemed for Scott a process of being buffeted by one unhappy personal situation after another. His parents broke up. His father disappeared. His family ran out of money. At school he did poorly. Other kids mocked his stammering speech.

Scott was born in Danville on August 29, 1921, in a bedroom of his family's house at 243 Keens Mill Road. Back then, black children often were born at home. Danville Memorial Hospital delivered only white babies. His parents were William Ira Scott and Martha Ella Motley. They got married in 1919, when he was forty-two and she was twenty-five. Each already had a young daughter: Ira Scott, from William's previous marriage, and Willie Elizabeth from Martha's. In 1923 a fourth child, Guelda, was born. Wendell Scott wasn't the first in his family to look to the automobile as an escape from the bleak options of Danville industry. His father, a handsome man with an adventurous streak, avoided the mills and tobacco plants by becoming the mechanic and driver for two prosperous white families who jointly owned one of Danville's first cars.

Will Scott was stubborn and tough. One cold winter day he washed his hair, and Martha told him he shouldn't go outside with his head still wet. Immediately he went out and worked in the yard until little icicles froze in his hair, just to make the point that he'd do as he pleased. Once, when a power saw tore a deep gash in his leg as he was cutting a load of firewood to sell, he ignored the bleeding wound and kept on working for hours until he got all the wood cut and delivered.

Wendell idolized him. As a little boy, he would sit beside his father while Will Scott worked on cars. Wendell would pass tools to his father and try to anticipate what size wrench his father would want next. Quickly the boy learned to glance at a nut or bolt and pick out the right wrench before his father asked. Their father's daring behind the wheel impressed Wendell and his sister. "My father was something with a car," Guelda said. "He frightened people to death. They say he'd come through town just about touching the ground. After Wendell started racing, all the old people would say the same thing: 'He's just like his daddy.'"

Danville's mill owners failed to modernize their machinery while times were good, and by 1924 the company began losing money. Five years before the Great Depression, Danville already had fallen into a deep slump. During those hard times, Scott's father decided to take a new job. Will Scott, Martha, and the four children moved to Pittsburgh, Pennsylvania, and he went to work as a mechanic at a Studebaker factory. The family's new home was near a firehouse. Young Wendell spent a lot of time there, fascinated by the noisy, exciting trucks.

Wendell found another quality to admire in his father — Will Scott had the nerve to cross racial barriers, regardless of white reaction. "Daddy was the only black mechanic there," he said. "The shop foreman died, and they made my daddy the foreman. Just about all the mechanics, they quit because they didn't want to work under no black man." The boss backed up Will Scott, telling the mechanics to come back or be replaced. After a week, some of them returned.

After two years in Pittsburgh, Scott's parents separated. Martha and Will Scott had clashing personalities and different attitudes toward life. Will Scott liked fast living as well as fast cars and fast driving. He gambled heavily. Guelda remembered him as "a carefree, happy-go-lucky person" who just wanted to enjoy himself. Martha Scott, a serious, religious woman, became worried that her husband set a poor example for their children. She had been a dedicated schoolteacher before marrying Will, and her relatives in Danville included some prosperous black businessmen. She wanted her children to become college graduates. Her husband's lifestyle, she felt, would not teach them to put any priority on education, culture, concern for others, or playing by the rules.

It was Will Scott's compulsive gambling, finally, that broke up the marriage. After many fights over his numbers betting, Martha told him to leave. "My daddy, he just mess his life up, messin' with them numbers," Wendell Scott said. "That's what my mother thought. He was writing numbers and playing numbers. She kept telling him she was going to leave him."

As a boy, Wendell didn't understand why his mother was so upset over gambling. Wasn't taking chances part of what made his daddy special? Wendell thought his mother was too hard on his father, and he was frightened of losing him. His mother not only wanted Will Scott out of the house — she wanted him to have nothing further to do with the children.

One night after the separation, though, Martha Scott permitted Wendell to spend the night with his father. "He had a room that didn't even have a bed in it. It had a mattress laying on the floor. He bought me some bananas, and I stayed in that room and laid on that mattress with him that night, and I was the happiest person in the world."

Wendell was seven. That was the last time he would see his father for years.

Far from home and broke, Martha Scott had to fall back on family charity. Fortunately, her sister Lavella Pope in Louisville, Kentucky, was comparatively well off. Lavella agreed to take them in, and the Scotts moved to Louisville. Martha Scott tried to pass on to the children her respect for education and culture. She was only halfway successful.

Guelda flourished. She took ballet and acrobatics lessons and starred in recitals in local theaters. People in the audiences gave her flowers and threw money onto the stage. But book learning and culture didn't appeal to Wendell.

Overshadowed by his little sister, angry with his mother, wounded by the loss of his father, young Wendell developed a bad stammer. He couldn't say his last name: The best he could do was *Sot*. Other kids gave him the nickname Wella-wella, mocking his efforts to speak. "I was ashamed," Scott said.

Back in Danville, Scott's maternal grandmother, Lottie Motley, ran a small neighborhood grocery. When Mrs. Motley's health began to fall, Martha Scott moved back to Danville with the children in 1931. Wendell was ten. They all lived in the same small family-owned house where Wendell had been born. Mrs. Scott helped her mother run the store, and the children spent their afternoons there, playing, doing chores, watching their mother and grandmother eke out a fragile independence in their neighborhood of blacks and working-class whites.

When the children started school in Danville, one of Wendell's first lessons was in the workings of segregation. In Louisville, his school had both white and black children — "so it wasn't until I came back to Danville to live that I realized I was different," he said. After his first day in the four-room Negro school, which housed grades one through twelve, he told his mother, "There weren't any white kids in school today, and not one white teacher."

His mother looked at him for a long moment. "There aren't going to be any," she replied.

Wendell had light skin and blue eyes, so he found segregation puzzling at first. His father had been light-skinned, too, and his mother and Guelda were even lighter. If white Danville didn't like people with dark skin, what did that have to do with his family?

Learning the new rules didn't take long. At the movie theater, Negroes could sit only in the balcony. When Wendell came in one day and sat downstairs, the manager assumed he was white and raised no objection. Then a white boy who knew the Scotts spotted Wendell. He ran to the manager, who promptly threw Wendell out. The lesson was clear: Any trace of black ancestry earned you the same treatment as the darkest Negro in town. Later, Wendell learned that his mother's father had been a white man who had children both with his white wife and with Wendell's grandmother.

The Ku Klux Klan was growing in Danville during Scott's youth. Hundreds of whites packed a local theater for Klan rallies. But in the Scotts' racially mixed neighborhood, Crooktown, most people got along. The Depression left everybody struggling. As providers of food and arbiters of credit, Wendell's grandmother and mother were people of stature in Crooktown. White customers addressed them as Mrs. Motley and Mrs. Scott. Many customers had no telephone at home; they depended on the phone in the Scotts' store. Neighbors of both races would hang around to chat and catch up on local gossip.

For adolescent boys, race relations weren't so harmonious. At the swimming hole near Wendell's house, groups of black and white boys regularly threw rocks at each other. Many of Wendell's peers had as little to do with whites as possible. "If we went through their neighborhood, we had to walk in a gang, ten or twelve of us," his cousin Alonza Carter said. "Otherwise you'd have to be a good runner." Wendell walked the tightrope of racial diplomacy more easily than many of his friends, however. He learned that even strongly prejudiced white people sometimes made distinctions between his race as a whole and individuals in it. They talked of good niggers and bad niggers. One could associate with them in a reasonably friendly way, he found, if one observed racial etiquette and did not show interest in white girls.

Scott's lifelong habit of hard work started with his impassioned desire for a bicycle. He earned the money to buy his own. "I used to ride bicycles with the white boys," Scott said. "I was the only black boy that had a bicycle in Crooktown. Having a bicycle then was a big thing, almost like having a car today. Didn't no black kids have no bicycles. They had old wagons, homemade wagons. But I worked." Wendell set up a little bike shop in a spare room off the store. He fixed flat tires quicker than any of his bicycle companions. Looking for more speed, he learned to adjust the ball bearings for the least possible friction. His sister would watch him conjure up working bicycles from what looked to her like piles of junk.

His talent for fast riding on the streets of Crooktown, which were mostly dirt back then, won him respect. Soon he could ride faster backward — sitting on the handlebars and pedaling while facing the rear of the bike — than many kids could ride forward. On roller skates, too, Wendell was speedy. He taught himself to leap and spin like a figure skater. Among the neighborhood boys, skating down the steep hill at the Rock Hill Playground was the litmus test for courage. When Wendell sailed down the hill on one skate, the feat clinched his reputation as Crooktown's leading daredevil. He had found something that set him apart, something that made him special — going fast, taking risks.

His stammer began to fade away. Soon, he could say his name as well as any of the other kids.

## 2

### "I don't never want to punch no clock."

For the Scotts and their neighbors, labor strife at the textile mills made the Depression years of the early 1930s particularly harsh. The owners refused to bargain with workers trying to form a union. The workers went on strike for months. Demonstrations, brawls, and bombings roiled Danville. The governor called up the militia. Union activists fled the city, defeated. With no paychecks, some families became destitute.

At their store, Scott's mother and grandmother carried families on credit for months, sometimes collecting as little as fifteen cents a week on a seventy-dollar tab. As the hard times dragged on, the store wasn't bringing in enough money to support the family. Martha Scott had to find outside work. She cleaned and cooked at white people's homes for four dollars a week. Rising before dawn, walking two miles to work, she started her chores at 6 AM.

While still a child, Wendell had to do his part. Before his teens, he got used to working long hours and contributing money to the family. On a patch at his uncle's farm, he grew sweet potatoes and tobacco to sell. During summers, he put in hard days at a fish market, where sometimes he had to take part of his pay in fish. He worked at a drugstore, where he made a dollar a week more than his mother by putting in seven days a week. "I'd be at work at seven o'clock in the morning and get off at eleven at night," Scott said. "I like to killed myself working that job." In high school, he worked a night shift at the P. Lorillard Tobacco factory. He was out of school at three o'clock, at work by four, and on the job until midnight.

He bought his first car for fifteen dollars, a decrepit Model T Ford. As with bicycles, the car quickly became a central passion. Its mysteries absorbed him, and he began teaching himself how to work on it, trying to get it running. He'd talk friends into pushing the car up a nearby hill so he could get behind the wheel and coast back down. In class, his mind would wander, and sometimes his feet would follow. He'd slip out of high school, the teacher would call home, and Scott would be down at the junkyard, scavenging parts.

Soon after Scott got his driver's license, he learned that his father, whom he hadn't seen or spoken with in nine years, was living in Rock Hill, South Carolina. One day he drove there, found the address, and knocked on the door.

"Who is it?" his father shouted. Will Scott wasn't a man who opened doors without knowing who was on the other side.

"Open the door," Wendell replied.

"My son!" his father cried out.

They had a pleasant reunion, but it didn't lead to a resumption of their relationship. Wendell's mother still wanted Will Scott to have nothing to do with her children. Apparently he was comfortable with that situation. Scott would have little contact with his father for the rest of his youth.

A teacher who Scott respected advised him to become a mechanic. A skill like that, the teacher said, could give him more control over his life than an industrial worker had; maybe someday he could become his own boss. "I don't never want to punch no clock," Wendell often told Guelda. He wouldn't act on the teacher's advice for a while, but he kept it in mind.

His mother begged him to finish high school, but Wendell had made up his mind to leave. Guelda, clearly, was college material, and Wendell felt he wasn't. Soon the family would be facing Guelda's tuition bills — all the more reason, he told his mother, for him to make more money. He quit school in eleventh grade and became an apprentice bricklayer. As with any work involving his hands, he learned the craft quickly. But once the challenge faded, the work became repetitive, and he didn't like spending his days under a supervisor's scrutiny. Sometimes he felt like one of the bricks, hemmed in, rooted in one place. After a pay dispute, he left for a job that seemed to offer more freedom — driving a cab.

He drove for the Danville Taxi Company at first, but as soon as he could afford it, he bought his own cab. He learned all the back roads and shortcuts and how to speed through them like his father. He learned where to go when a fare wanted moonshine whiskey or other goods and services not listed in the yellow pages. By 1939, at age eighteen, Scott was known around Danville as the cabbie who could get you anywhere in a hurry. A Danville policeman, John Broomfield, soon became Scott's nemesis. Out of thirteen speeding tickets Scott collected during those years, Broomfield wrote eleven.

Scott liked driving a cab. He made his own hours, seeing life on a broader canvas and learning to find ways in which the caste system of segregation could be bent a bit in his favor. The white man's respect for his skill behind the wheel, he saw, gave him a little more freedom to be himself. He didn't have to put on quite as much of the deferential manner that white people usually expected. They seemed to accept that a cabbie was likely to be an independent character.

At age twenty, Scott had his first tangle with the law. On March 22, 1942, Danville police arrested him and two acquaintances, charging them as accomplices in a yearlong scheme to steal and sell motor oil. Detectives said their arrests "solved the mysterious disappearance of approximately $1,000 worth of oil" from a local warehouse company, the *Danville Register* reported. One of the defendants carried out the thefts while working at the plant, according to the detectives. Scott and the other defendant, they said, bought and sold the stolen oil. In April, a grand jury indicted Scott for grand larceny, a felony. He pled guilty to a reduced charge, petty larceny, and was sentenced to sixty days on the city's prison farm.

Scott had grown into a handsome young man, and as he got involved with girlfriends, he became a sharper dresser. He wore leather jackets and high boots. He remembered how his father could toss back his loosely curled hair with a shake of his head. He wanted what he called "good hair" for himself, so he attacked his own tight curls with a women's product called Finger Wave, sometimes leaving them in an unmanageable mess. He'd developed a much more confident — sometimes aggressive — manner than he'd had during his boyhood. When he spotted Guelda dancing with a teenage boy he disliked, Scott strode onto the dance floor, separated them, took her arm, and walked her home, ignoring her protests.

One Sunday night, Scott spotted a pretty black girl waiting at the cabstand of the Trailways bus station in Danville. He pulled up in his cab, and Mary Belle Coles got into the backseat. She was nineteen, just back from a weekend with her family. They lived in Chatham, about twenty miles north. She was the third of ten children. Her father drove a city dump truck, and the family farmed. Mary worked as a live-in maid for a white lawyer's family in Forest Hills, Danville's most exclusive section. She had a room in the basement. During the day, she got a few hours off to attend beauty school.

Scott launched into a flirtatious patter, and Mary noticed that he seemed to be making the short trip to the lawyer's house last as long as he could. She paid the thirty-five-cent fare, and they sat and talked awhile at the curb. Finally, she let herself be persuaded to go riding. Afterward, they stopped for supper.

Scott was working hard at being charming. Mary liked his humor and, as a serious, churchgoing girl, she liked that he didn't smoke or drink. She casually dropped an important fact — she had just broken up with her boyfriend. What a coincidence, replied Scott — he'd just broken up with his girlfriend. Mary thought this was probably just a line, but she was pleased to hear it anyway.

It was late when Scott dropped her off. That night she kept thinking about him. "I guess he had swelled my head by then," she said. "I knew I was hoping to meet him again." Mary wasn't allowed to take calls on her employer's phone, but Scott had asked enough questions about her daily routine to make sure he knew how to find her.

Most days when Mary left the house to catch a bus to beauty school, the young cabbie with the leather jacket and shiny boots would be waiting at her bus stop in his taxi. He seemed more serious and ambitious than other young men Mary had known. He talked about opening his own garage someday.

As with many courtships in those years, theirs was accelerated by World War II. Scott was drafted in 1943 and sent to Wyoming for basic training. They got married in Danville on July 10, 1944, while Scott was on leave, and a few weeks later he left on a troopship to Europe. Their first child, Ann, was born while Scott was overseas.

In the segregated army, Scott felt like a prisoner. "I hated every moment of it," he said. Most black soldiers, like Scott, served in labor or other support units. His unit, the 3116th Quartermaster Service Company, moved across Europe with General George S. Patton's Third Army. He worked as a mechanic for the black trucking outfit known as the Red Ball Express. The restriction of black troops to support roles didn't shield them from danger. Scott came under fire, and when German planes blew up a fuel depot, several of his friends were killed.

But the quartermaster corps, the army's supply branch, did have its fringe benefits. One day near Cherbourg, France, Herman Dodson, a white soldier who'd ridden bicycles with Scott when they were boys in Danville, was maneuvering his jeep around a bomb crater in a highway when he heard someone call him.

Back home everybody called Dodson by his nickname, Catfish. But because Dodson had a colonel in his jeep, the soldier who'd hailed him didn't use Catfish. "I heard a fellow holler, 'Hey, Mr. Dodson, hey,' and I looked over, and it was Wendell."

Scott invited them to join him for supper. They were glad they accepted. Soldiers in the Red Ball Express who hauled the supplies off the ships had access to fresh food that most other soldiers hadn't seen in weeks, months, or years. Scott gave Dodson and the colonel each half a dozen eggs. For a long time, they'd been eating only powdered eggs, and the appeal of fresh eggs proved stronger than any barriers of race or rank. "The next night, the colonel said, 'Let's go down and see cousin Wendell again.'"

Scott reached the rank of technician fifth class, the same pay grade as a corporal, but he still hated army life as much as he had as a buck private. The experience strengthened his conviction that "I don't want no bosses — I can't stand a boss." He wrote to Mary about how much he longed to come home. For the rest of his life, he would remember the exact amount of time he served: a miserable two years and thirteen days.

For many of World War II's black soldiers, their years in Europe were enlightening. Few blacks lived in Europe, so there was no entrenched culture of segregation. Many Europeans welcomed the black GIs as liberators, seeing their color as exotic rather than a stigma. For the first time, many black soldiers got a sense of what it might feel like to be the equal of whites.

Danville seemed a small, backward place to Scott when he got back from the war. The city refused to renew his taxi license, saying he'd gotten too many speeding tickets. This irked Scott — one day he was a victorious war veteran; the next day, unfit to drive a Danville cab. He got more trouble from the police: an arrest for gambling. He pled guilty and paid a fine and court costs of $33.75.

He decided to move to California. He had no real plans; he just wanted a drastic change. But James Hughes, who ran Danville's black funeral home, made him an offer. "He told me he'd like for me to work on all his cars before I go," Scott said. "I lined brakes, tuned up motors, I worked on all of 'em. He said, 'Wendell, why don't you just stay on here? I'll build you a shop right back here.' So he talked me into staying, and he built me a shop, a nice cinder-block place."

Scott soon discovered, not for the last time, that realizing a dream brought a new tangle of problems and obligations. He took in a friend as his partner. "He was a pretty fair mechanic, but he was careless," Scott said. "Back in them days, to take a transmission out, you had to take the floorboard out. He would never put the screws back in the floorboard, or put the floor mat over it right. He was just a messy mechanic."

Scott's second child, Wendell Jr., had been born by then, on July 5, 1946, so Scott watched the shop's finances closely. He'd been conditioned since childhood to watch every dollar, but he realized his partner didn't share that outlook. "We bought a lot of equipment, and we were supposed to be working for a salary every week. We was supposed to put all the money in the bank, take us a salary, pay our bills at the end of the month. But he was going with a girl, trying to show off big, and he'd get his salary and then he'd borrow ahead on next week's pay. He kept doing that until we didn't have no money, and we got way in debt."

One day when Scott was home sick, his partner was spot-welding a loose rear fender on a customer's 1935 Ford. A neighborhood alcoholic known as Bro C. was trying to help out. When Scott's partner finished, he told Bro C. to throw water from a bucket onto the car to put out some smoldering fender welts. They didn't realize, until too late, that the bucket actually was full of gasoline.

The fast-moving fire destroyed the Ford and part of the garage as well. They had to pay the customer for the car. Scott decided it was time for his partner to go. He bought him out and paid off all the debts by himself. "Took me a long time," he recalled. Being his own boss hadn't turned out to be quite as liberating as he'd expected. To a young man who'd been halfway around the world and survived history's biggest war, a lifetime of fixing other people's cars in Danville began to feel intolerably dull. He needed more money, he wanted more excitement, and he believed he saw a way to get both. Scott decided to take up a new pursuit as his second job, a trade that had long beckoned to men who were looking for a way up from the lower rungs of southern life and didn't mind taking some risks.

# 3

## "A hard, nasty business."

Just one county west of Danville, in remote hollows of the Blue Ridge Mountains, bootleggers have brewed whiskey in clandestine stills for generations. The moonshine trade has flourished there since before the Revolutionary War. It's a cash business whose entrepreneurs don't believe the government has any right to tax what they see as a basic human need. In the 1940s, the potent brew was popular in Danville and all over the South, from ghetto saloons to the parlors of the wealthy. The operators of these stills turned cornmeal, sugar, water, yeast, and malt into a white liquor, usually 100 proof. A well-made moonshine delivered the powerful kick that inspired its other nickname, white lightning.

The moonshine distillers sold the whiskey by the carload to drivers who were willing to take the risk of delivering it to the marketplace, and that's where Scott saw his opportunity. He became a moonshine runner, one of the industry's middlemen who picked up carloads of illegal whiskey in the mountainous backwoods of neighboring Franklin County and drove them to market, usually at night, in Danville and other cities. A whiskey runner needed fast cars and the right mix of recklessness and calculation to outrun police and federal agents. For Scott and some other drivers in NASCAR's first generation, running moonshine would serve as prep school for stock car racing. Prominent early NASCAR competitors with moonshine experience included Junior Johnson, Curtis Turner, Jack Smith, Buck Baker, and the Flock brothers: Bob, Fonty, and Tim.

For Scott, this was an education with a major in car building and driving, and minors in duplicity, betrayal, and stress. He continued operating his repair garage during the day. At first, he didn't tell his wife he'd become a whiskey runner. When she figured it out, she was "scared to death" but decided that arguing with her strong-willed husband would be futile. "I probably would have been told to shut up," she said.

Scott would remember those years as a period when he grew more accomplished as a driver and mechanic, when he became a harder man and a smoother liar, and as the time when ulcers first dug their claws into his stomach.

The money, though, often made it all seem worthwhile. Some weeks he made as much as twelve hundred dollars in the whiskey trade. He could double his money in a few hours by driving a load of moonshine down to Charlotte, North Carolina. That city was in a "dry county" that banned all liquor sales, making it a particularly thirsty market. Scott bought the liquor in cans at 55 cents a pint and sold it in Charlotte at $1.10. A cargo of twenty-two cans was typical for a moonshine run. The whiskey presented no personal temptation for Scott; throughout his life he rarely drank anything alcoholic.

The risks, like the profits, could be substantial. The South, whose electorate included a substantial bloc of religious temperance crusaders, was awash with moonshine whiskey in those years, and even politicians who enjoyed drinking it were obliged to rail publicly against its immoral influence. Wiping out illegal whiskey became a priority for federal and local law enforcement agencies. Almost daily, the Danville newspapers ran stories about moonshine arrests. Moonshine cases clogged the courts, and the county prison farm was full of moonshiners serving their time before returning to the business.

A sizable share of Scott's profits went into building the highly modified cars that a whiskey runner needed to escape his pursuers. The cars Scott built looked like drab, ordinary sedans, but with their souped-up engines and stiffened springs, they could outrun police cars even while hauling heavy loads. Sometimes Scott had to abandon them and flee on foot, so the cars' registrations had to be murky enough to provide no clue that he was the owner. Some carried stolen license plates.

Scott stashed some of his whiskey cars in rural spots around Danville, where they sat on blocks like old junkers, without wheels, until the time came for a midnight run. He kept other whiskey cars in the mountains, where he picked up the liquor. He would drive his everyday car up to a prearranged spot where his whiskey car, already loaded with moonshine, was waiting. As part of their deal, his supplier kept the whiskey car tuned up for him. Scott would sell the liquor both to individual customers and to other middlemen. After a successful run, he'd return the whiskey car to the mountains and drive his own car back to Danville. Moonshining got its name from its nocturnal delivery schedules, and some nights Scott wouldn't get home until dawn.

As in any criminal enterprise, the players often didn't trust one another. Although Scott picked up many loads of whiskey from the operators of backwoods stills, he'd never know the exact location of the still. The distillers didn't want that information to become a bargaining chip if the driver was arrested. Scott would meet his suppliers in a wooded area off the road, some distance away from the still. Before he turned off the highway, he'd lay down wooden planks so his car would leave no tire tracks as he drove into the woods. Moonshiners knew that agents often looked for such tracks as a clue that a still could be nearby.

Besides the quick profits and the excitement, the illegal whiskey business had another appeal for Scott: It was an equal-opportunity employer. If a black man had the savvy, nerve, and driving skill to run moonshine, he didn't have to worry about the racial barriers that separated him from a good education or a well-paid job on the right side of the law. He could sell to both black and white customers.

Rodney Ligon, a former white moonshine runner who knew Scott during those years, said that black and white bootleggers around Danville did business as equals. "We were rednecks, but if you were in the liquor business, and you bought ten cases of liquor from me a week, and you kept your debts paid, I didn't give a damn what you was." Scott's cousin Alonza Carter said: "There was no segregation in moonshining. Anything illegal, not too much segregation. Same thing as the numbers racket — there was no segregation in that area, either."

At home, Scott's new occupation brought a different rhythm to family life. In some ways it was a preview of the unconventional lifestyle the family would lead for the next twenty-five years. The children learned that Daddy came and went at irregular times, and that he was involved in something dangerous, something other fathers didn't do, something that absorbed him deeply and sometimes made him tense and abrupt. Their family continued to grow, and they needed the extra money. Over the next several years, Ann and Wendell Jr. would gain four more siblings: Frank in 1947, Deborah in 1950, Cheryl in 1952, and Sybil in 1954.

One day in the 1950s, Wendell Scott Jr. recalled, his father agreed for the first time to take him along on a late-night moonshine run. Happy and excited, the boy could hardly wait for sundown; he'd asked to do this many times. Secretly, he hoped the police would chase them. He'd heard the stories for years about how Daddy, in his powerful whiskey cars, would outrun the police on the back roads late at night, coming home with another thrilling tale and a roll of cash. Sometimes Wendell Jr. would see bullet holes in the trunks or back fenders of those cars.

That night after dark, Scott drove downtown with his son to the garage where he kept a moonshine car hidden. His decision to include Wendell Jr. had provoked angry words between Scott and his wife, something that wasn't unusual at that time. "His words to Mommy were, 'I'm going to take my half of my boy with me. You can do what you want, but I'm going to teach him about life,'" Wendell Jr. recalled.

Sometimes his father's teaching style was brusque and domineering. They pulled up to a general store in Roxboro, North Carolina, a load of moonshine in the trunk. The woman who owned the store was a regular customer. Scott told his son to hide a jar of moonshine behind each of the three brick columns that held up the rickety porch. He'd find a jar with the money, his father said, behind the third column.

As they headed for the next stop, Wendell Jr. counted the bills in the jar. "I said, 'Daddy, she done paid us too much.'

"Daddy said, 'Put it back in the jar.'

"I said, 'Sir?'

"He said, 'Put it back in the jar!' He may have cursed. He was emphatic about it.

"I said, 'Yes sir.'"

Scott made a U-turn and drove back to the store. He told Wendell Jr. to put the money jar back under the porch. His son obeyed, then said, "Daddy, you want me to get the stuff?"

"He said, 'Come on over here, boy!' That's one fear I had of him; he would snap at you.

"So I got back in the car, and I asked about why he didn't take the money — what were we going to do about our money?"

His father replied in a tone that made it clear no further explanation would be granted. Emphasizing every word, Scott told his son: "You can't do wrong when you're doing wrong."

The police never came to chase them that night, but for quite a while afterward, Wendell Jr. felt anxious anyway. He hadn't really understood what his father meant, and he hated to fall short of what was expected of him.

Several times during whiskey runs, police got close enough to Scott to blow out one of his tires with a shotgun. The tactic cost him some good cars, but he managed to run away in the dark. "Cop named Clark, he was death with a shotgun," Scott said. "He'd lay that gun out the window and shoot down that tire. One night they were behind me with no lights on, about four in the morning, and I didn't know it. They cut the lights on and shot at the same time."

For daylight deliveries around Danville, when gunfire wasn't a risk, Scott occasionally used his family as camouflage. On a Sunday, in the early evening, the family would get into the car and ride around Danville, with the children in the backseat and the moonshine liquor in the trunk, Mary Scott said. Her husband would tell the children, "If you see anybody, just wave and be nice."

The ulcer pains that Scott would suffer for years began during this period. "When I'd make it one week and didn't get caught, then I'd always worry and wonder what it was going to be like the next time. It was really a nerve-wracking thing."

The moonshine trade has been glamorized and stereotyped in dozens of movies and books. Usually the moonshiners come across as dashing adventurers, the lawmen as rustic buffoons, their clashes as mostly comic. The reality, of course, was rougher. As author Derek Nelson wrote in his history of the illegal alcohol business, "In actuality, the game has rarely been a game at all; it has always been fraught with peril and tinged with disaster . . . Honor among thieves was the exception rather than the rule. Bribery, corruption, a hamstrung legal system, lethal gunfire, car wrecks, murder, piracy, amateur and professional hijacking — these were just a few of the things that drained the glamour away, leaving a hard, nasty business behind."

At first Scott had a partner, Clarence Dixon. They had an inside-man, outside-man arrangement. Dixon worked with suppliers and planned the runs; Scott did the driving and dealt with customers. They had a dozen or so customers initially, but Scott said his own efforts built the business up to about sixty-five customers. One of them, a local politician, had Scott deliver his moonshine to the golf course at his country club (a segregated establishment, of course).

Eventually, Scott said, customers tipped him off that Dixon was cheating him. Dixon was sending an accomplice named Billy around to some customers with whiskey ahead of Scott, paying Billy a dollar a case to make the deliveries and pocketing the rest of the money. When Scott found out, he offered Dixon what he considered a fair plan for breaking up their enterprise.

"I said, 'Man, let me tell you something. The customers that you had when I started hauling with you, I ain't going to sell none of them no liquor. My customers what I worked up, if they want to buy liquor from you, it's all right with me. But if they want to buy from me, I'm going to sell 'em liquor.'" Before long, Scott said, he was grossing about a thousand dollars in a good week, much more than Dixon. As Scott's reputation as a moonshine runner grew around Danville, some police officers pursued him so zealously he became convinced that their dedication was inspired, at least partly, by the fact that he was black. They'd park behind billboards or buildings along the highway and wait for hours in the dark for Scott to drive by in one of his liquor cars. The story of one such chase became an often-told favorite in the Scott family.

Late one night, Scott rolled into Danville with a load of moonshine in his souped-up 1940 Ford. He didn't realize that a police car was right behind him until a shotgun roared and a rear tire started losing air. He floored the gas pedal, managed to get one turn ahead of the police, and pulled the Ford's hand throttle all the way open. Then he dove out of the moving car, rolled into some tall grass, and hid behind a rotting log near the bank of the Dan River.

Scott hoped his car would keep on rolling down the road far enough to draw the police away. But the Ford swerved and crashed almost immediately, and the police pulled up just a few yards from his hiding place. They were so close that he could hear them talking on the radio, calling for a wrecker and a bloodhound.

Cold and wet, Scott lay in the weeds for what felt like a long time, listening to the police curse him, using racial slurs. They were gloating about how tonight, at last, they'd catch him. When the dog finally arrived, it ran around sniffing the ground and quickly found Scott. He and the dog stared at each other. As Scott related the story, what happened next seemed miraculous: The dog did not bark, and when the police began walking toward the log, the bloodhound led them off in another direction. "Daddy said he'd swear on a stack of Bibles that the dog just plain let him go," Wendell Jr. said. For the rest of his life, Scott always had dogs of his own.

During the late 1940s, Scott got news about his long-absent father. Complications from a leg injury suffered while working on a chicken farm had left Will Scott in precarious health. The elder Scott, now in his early seventies, was thin and frail. Although Will Scott had hardly given his son a model for how to behave — particularly as a father — Wendell still had strong feelings for him. He brought his father back to Danville and moved him into their small house. Their reconciliation eased an old hurt for Scott. But it also gave him substantial medical bills to pay and another person to support, at a time when he was still paying for his partner's share of the garage business and the costs of the fire. Fortunately, there was always somebody who wanted more moonshine.

## 4

**"Judge, it couldn't have been me."**

One Christmas morning, a customer knocked on Scott's door. He'd run out of liquor and wanted two cases, which Scott didn't have on hand. But he knew a man out in the country with a supply, and he told the customer he'd go get it for him. Scott, the customer, and one of the customer's friends climbed into one of the Scotts' family cars. The blue 1946 Ford was just an ordinary passenger car, not one of Scott's whiskey-running machines. The customer's friend was on crutches. Ordinarily Scott would never have gone on a moonshine run with two unnecessary passengers, especially one who couldn't run if there was trouble. But they weren't expecting problems on a quiet Christmas morning.

On the way out of Danville, Scott passed a Danville police car parked at the roadside. When he drove back with the moonshine, he got an unwelcome surprise. The two policemen were still sitting there. Scott tried to look nonchalant as he cruised by. The police pulled out and followed him, hanging back at first. He watched his mirror as they slowly drew closer.

They pulled alongside Scott on the narrow road, also trying to look cool and indifferent. Then the officer at the wheel swerved in front of Scott, forcing him to hit the brakes and slide to a stop. When one officer started to get out of the car, Scott drove off backward. The officer jumped back in the car, and they tried to follow him, also in reverse. But at the tricky art of driving flat-out in reverse, the policeman was no match for the former neighborhood champion of backward bicycle riding. Scott easily sped away down the winding road, while the police zigzagged so erratically that they had to stop and turn around.

Scott swung his car into a grocery store parking lot, slammed it into first gear, and took off toward nearby Route 360, opening up a good lead on the police car. But the police had radioed for help. As Scott pulled onto the highway, a second police car sped past him, then slowed, trying to block him while the other car caught up. Scott didn't wait to be trapped in the sandwich. He shot past the second car, dodging the officer's attempt to run him off the road, and got away from both of his pursuers. He drove out into the country and hid the liquor.

Scott then raced back to his shop. Working frantically, he pulled the engine out of the Ford, faster than he'd ever pulled an engine in his life. He left the motor hanging from the chain hoist, still hot and dripping oil. He jumped into another car and sped away to spend the night in North Carolina. He thought the police would pick him up eventually, but he figured some delay and confusion couldn't hurt.

The next day, the officers came to his house to arrest him and take him to court. Between the beefy Danville policemen, who were still irked over having been outdriven, Scott looked small, almost frail. In the courtroom he assumed an air of wounded innocence. "I said, 'Judge, it couldn't have been me. That car they say they run, Judge, the motor been out of that car ever since last week, and I still haven't fixed that motor.

"'Now, the *po*-lice say they got my tag number when they was runnin' me, Judge, and I know you goin' to believe them *po*-lice and ain't goin' to believe me, but that *po*-lice right there'" — Scott pointed an accusing finger — "'just come in my shop and wrote my tag number down.' Boy, that *po*-lice lit out after me — they had to grab him to keep him from beating me.

"And the judge said, 'Did y'all take his tag number while y'all was running him? Or in that shop?'

"They said, 'We took his tag number while we was running him.'

"I said, 'Judge, they weren't running me — my car's been broke down over a week.'

"Judge said, 'Next time, y'all catch him. Case dismissed.'

"He got confused — he really thought I was telling the truth, and I was telling the biggest lie I ever told in my life."

The police department took the officers' car away and put them on foot patrol, walking a beat that included his shop. They made a point of watching the place closely. One Saturday evening, Scott worked until after dark. He stepped outside and was locking up when he remembered he'd promised to help Mary wax floors at home. They'd need some rags. He went back into the shop, leaving the door open, not bothering to put the lights back on. Suddenly, as he reached into a box of rags, two flashlights caught him in their beams. The cops had been hiding outside, watching him. When they saw him doing something in the dark, they assumed it involved illegal liquor. Their instincts were on target: Sometimes Scott did store large caches of moonshine under a tarp in the shop's grease pit.

"They had pistols. They said, 'Run and I'll blow your damn brains out.' They called me nigger and all that stuff. So I got my hands up.

"'I ain't gonna run.'

"'What you doin' in here?'

"'Ain't none of your business. I'm in my own place.'

"'Why'd you come back in here?'

"I said, 'None of your business.'"

The police turned the lights on and began searching. "They tore my shop all to pieces," said Scott. Luckily, the grease pit was empty that night. "Them *po*-lice — boy, they rode me. As long as they was on my beat, they rode me."

Years later, Scott recalled, one of those policemen came back to see him. The officer, long retired, was in poor health, not far from dying, but still brooding over how Scott had outfoxed them.

"He said, 'Scott, what did you go back in that shop for? And wasn't that you we was runnin'?'"

Apparently, they hadn't gotten his license number after all.

"I said, 'Man, you know that wasn't me.' I never did admit to it."

Scott's worst trouble with the law began after his ex-partner Clarence Dixon dropped by for a chat in the spring of 1949. "He tells me, 'Scott, I want you to stop selling liquor, because I started you to haulin' liquor, and if you get caught, I'll feel like I was the cause of it, and I don't want nothin' to happen to you.'"

This transparently phony approach annoyed Scott. Dixon still seemed to think he was easy to fool. "I said, 'Clarence, let me tell you something. I'm a grown man, I'm going to do what I want to, and don't you come in here no more telling me what you want me to do. You want me to stop hauling liquor because I done built up a good trade, and now I've got just about everybody that I built up, and you still ain't sellin' no liquor.' So he left."

At this point, Scott would later conclude, Dixon decided to use a time-honored method for getting rid of a rival criminal. A friend of Dixon's, Jack Anderson, persuaded Scott to deliver two cases of moonshine, telling him he needed it before dark.

The same day, a burly Danville policeman with a bulging belly and a shady reputation visited Scott, saying he wanted to borrow some money. If Scott didn't cooperate, the cop warned, he would be sorry.

"I said, 'Well, I'm going to be sorry then — I ain't got no money.' Because I never paid a cop in my life, and I didn't intend to pay no cop then."

Soon after talking to Anderson, Scott drove out into the country on April 30, 1949, to get the whiskey. He used the most expensive car he owned at the time, a plush, tan 1946 Packard Super Eight. A police officer spotted him returning to Danville and gave chase, but Scott easily lost him.

Scott began to suspect trouble when he got to Anderson's house and found that Anderson no longer wanted any moonshine, saying he'd bought some from Dixon. As Scott drove away, a police car appeared in his rear-view mirror, red light flashing. He realized he'd been set up.

He hit the gas. The neighborhood was hilly, full of tight turns. With the clumsy handling of his luxury sedan, Scott couldn't take advantage of its superior power. Siren howling, the police car fell back only a bit as Scott sped up a hill. Just one more sharp turn, Scott knew, and he'd reach the open highway, Route 360, where his car should be able to pull away from the police. He barreled over the blind crest of the hill and raced downhill toward a T-intersection, setting up for a right turn.

Suddenly he realized his plan wasn't going to work. In the street he'd chosen for his escape route, some drunken Saturday-night revelers were staggering around. He recognized a couple of them as his moonshine customers. Another was one of Scott's cousins. Scott tried to turn left, but the Packard plowed across the road and crashed into a house at 193 White Street.

Inside the house, the people partying in the living room scrambled to hide their own moonshine as the police jumped out of their car and came for Scott. "Boy, they wanted me," Scott said. "They were hittin' at me with that blackjack. I said, 'Don't hit me, turn me over to the federals.' The federals, they were civilized. Them Danville *po*-lice would beat your brains out."

The next morning's *Danville Register* ran a big photo of the stricken Packard, its grille crushed against the house, the trunk lid open to display the contraband. "It's Bootlegged Whisky, Police Charge," said the headline. The officers "arrested Wendell O. Scott, 27-year-old colored resident of Keens Mill Road, as he started to slip from under the steering wheel of the car which, police said, was carrying 22 half-gallon fruit jars filled with bootlegged whisky," the story reported.

The Danville police charged Scott with reckless driving and turned the moonshining part of the case over to federal authorities. A friend bailed Scott out of the lockup that same night. On his way out the door, one officer warned him: "I don't want to catch you no more tonight."

"I said, 'Don't worry, y'all won't catch me.'"

But Scott's night wasn't over. He still owed some moonshine to one more customer. As a matter of pride, he was going to make the delivery. He realized the police would be watching for any cars they knew were his, so he borrowed a friend's station wagon, which turned out to be a wheezing junker. "I had done left some liquor out on the side of the highway. I got that old station wagon and put that liquor in it. I had that thing on the floor, but it wouldn't run but about thirty-five, forty miles an hour. Like to scared me to death! You talkin' about scared, that was as scared as I ever been hauling two cases of liquor in my life. I was so glad when I got that liquor off that thing, I didn't know what to do."

On September 12, 1949, a federal grand jury indicted Scott, along with fifty-one local defendants in other cases. "As usual, the majority of the cases concerned whisky charges," the *Danville Register* noted. The lawyers for many of the defendants, including Scott, already had made plea-bargain deals with the prosecutors. His day in court came the next day, a busy one for Judge A.D. Barksdale. Scott, who pled guilty, was among thirty-one moonshine defendants who shuttled through the judge's courtroom. Barksdale gave jail sentences to the repeat offenders with prior moonshine records, including four of the Doolin boys, members of a locally notorious bootlegging family. Scott, and the other defendants with no previous moonshine arrests, got off with probation — three years in his case.

Moonshining, which was supposed to have been a lucrative side job for Scott, had now left him with considerable financial troubles. The government kept his Packard, and he had to go into debt for legal fees and other costs. He took out a twenty-five-hundred-dollar mortgage against his house two days after his arrest. He borrowed another $1,150 from a finance company. He fell behind on those payments and his property taxes. Later, Scott often complained to family members that the cost of his criminal case had included nineteen hundred dollars in payoffs, money he had to borrow from his mother. The details of those alleged payoffs remain unclear, but Wendell Scott Jr. said: "Daddy talked about it his whole life, calling them crooked sons of bitches."

Still, Scott wasn't ready to quit running moonshine. Now he needed the extra income even more. His father's health was failing; his bad leg developed gangrene and had to be amputated. The finance company filed a claim against Scott's house. Trying to fend off foreclosure, Scott had ownership transferred to Mary. A local court, however, declared that move "a fraudulent conveyance" and ordered the property sold at auction unless Scott paid his creditors. He had to take out a new mortgage for $2,492 in mid-1950 to save the house. His father died later that year. Scott kept on making moonshine runs at night while running his garage during the day, and he never got caught again. The moonshine money eased his financial burdens, and by 1952, even with his growing family, he found he had some extra cash.

He also had a new preoccupation. Since the late 1940s, stock cars had been racing on the dirt speedway at the Danville Fairgrounds. Scott began going to watch the races, sitting in a corner reserved as the Negro section. Few blacks came to the speedway; often Scott and a bricklayer named Joe Ross were the only ones. Some of the drivers, like Roy Doolin and Bob McGinnis, were also local moonshine runners. After several years of intense involvement in the whiskey trade, with all of the problems it had brought, Scott was ready to cut back on moonshine running and try something new.

"Joe asked me one time, if they would let me race, would I race? I said, 'Yeah, I wish they would.'"

Somehow, Scott resolved, he was going to get out on that track.

# 5

## "Let me see how you doin' them turns."

On May 23, 1952, the day that Scott began his racing career, he walked up to Bob McGinnis in the Danville Fairgrounds Speedway pit area. They knew each other, mostly by reputation, from the moonshine trade. Among the local whiskey runners, not many could make an old Ford fly down a country road like the lanky, laid-back McGinnis.

In just a couple of hours, Scott would be starting in his first race. Speedway driving required different skills from those he'd polished while running moonshine. He hoped that McGinnis, one of the region's top stock car racers, would give him a lesson during the day's first practice session. "Wendell said, 'Bobby, let me ride with you around the track,'" McGinnis recalled. "'Let me see how you doin' them turns.'" Climb in, McGinnis told him.

They rolled out onto the half-mile oval in McGinnis's '37 Ford two-door sedan. Scott crouched behind McGinnis in the space where the backseat used to be. The car's floorboard ended behind the driver's seat, so Scott braced his feet against the rails of the frame and gripped the roll bar with both hands. He could see the dirt surface of the track moving past under his shoes. Then McGinnis floored the gas pedal, and the dirt turned into a blur.

As they approached turn three, the Ford was hitting eighty miles an hour, engine howling, dusty air blasting in through the open windows, pebbles flying up from the tires and ricocheting inside the cut-back fenders. McGinnis, relaxed as a sunbather in a beach chair, gave the steering wheel a little twitch and threw the Ford sideways into a full-throttle slide around the turn. He flashed a quick grin into the mirror at Scott. He ran six laps that way, pushing the limit, power-sliding every turn, with Scott hanging on tight behind him.

As things had turned out, while Scott had been watching the Danville races and wishing he could get involved, the promoters had been wondering where they could find a Negro driver. Their idea wasn't to pose a moral challenge to segregation — they just needed to attract more fans.

The Danville races were run by a group called the Dixie Circuit, one of several regional racing organizations that competed with NASCAR in its early years. The Dixie Circuit raced at several Virginia and North Carolina tracks. Its logo featured two crossed flags — one checkered, one Confederate. Danville's speedway always made less money than other Dixie Circuit tracks. The circuit's races elsewhere drew as many as twenty-five hundred spectators, but Danville was lucky to get half that many. When the promoters counted the money at other tracks, they'd always see some twenty-dollar bills, sometimes even a fifty. In Danville, they'd usually see nothing but singles. "We were a tobacco and textile town — people didn't have the money to spend," said Danville businessman Aubrey Ferrell, one of the circuit's organizers.

The Dixie Circuit promoters wanted some sort of gimmick or novelty act to bring out more Danville spectators, and they came up with the idea of pitting a Negro driver against the good ol' boys. To their credit, they wanted a fast black driver, not just a fall guy to look foolish. Martin Rogers of the Dixie Circuit asked the Danville police if they knew of any likely prospects. "The police told him he ought to talk to that darkie they'd been chasing over the back roads hauling liquor," Scott said. "The promoter looked me up, and that's how I became a race driver."

The day before the event, the promoters announced to the *Danville Register* that a Negro would be driving in the amateur race, the class for entry-level drivers in inexpensive cars. As they'd hoped, the publicity brought out a bigger crowd, including black spectators who'd never come before. Scott, unsure how he'd be treated, decided to leave his family at home. For the race, he'd borrowed a '35 Ford four-door from his brother-in-law. The Ford had been one of Scott's modified moonshine haulers. He'd had to get rid of it when the car became too familiar to the Danville police.

The Ford was fast, but — as Scott was about to find out — it wasn't ready for the rigors of racing. He started thirteenth and quickly began passing cars. He'd worked his way up into the top five when the troubles started. First his seat came loose; he put his left elbow out of the window and tried to clamp himself in place with his arm. Then the gas pedal broke; he began using the hand throttle with his right hand. Then the transmission began jumping out of gear.

For several laps, Scott tried to steady the steering wheel with his left fingers while his right hand first worked the throttle, then held the shift lever in place, then jumped back to the steering wheel in time for each turn. "That thing was whipping me to death," he said. "I didn't know the race was almost over, so I pulled in two laps from the end. I couldn't go no longer."

As the debut of the first black driver in southern stock car racing, Scott's effort was comically unimpressive, and as a milestone in the integration of sports, the event went unnoticed outside of Danville. Considering the racial climate, however, it was remarkable. This was a time when southern Negroes were still expected to be servile. The Supreme Court was two years away from ordering the integration of southern schools. Martin Luther King Jr. was a graduate student in Boston. Elvis Presley was a junior in high school. A first-class stamp cost three cents. Harry Truman was president, and American troops were fighting in Korea.

Few could have foreseen during this era that racial slurs and stereotypes would someday become highly controversial. Two years later Truman's successor, the popular Dwight Eisenhower, would explain to Chief Justice Earl Warren of the Supreme Court that opponents of school integration "aren't bad people. All they are concerned about is to see that their sweet little girls are not required to sit in school alongside some big overgrown Negroes."

Danville, small and conservative, a city that still celebrated its history as the Confederacy's last capital during the final eight days of the Civil War, wasn't a likely setting during the 1950s for any sort of pioneering development in integration. Nevertheless, in the spring of 1952, a group of local stock car racers, the sort of people sometimes labeled as white trash, had not only sought out and recruited a Negro driver but also given him a lesson on how he might outdrive them. For its time and place, this was an improbable event. They had invited a talented black competitor into a rough and rowdy pursuit that held a special place in the hearts of the white southern working class.

During this post–World War II era, stock car racing was growing all over the country, in the North as well as the South. After four wartime years of no new cars, gasoline rationing, and little fun, America's historic passion for the automobile was on full boil. Millions of families took a Sunday drive every week. The stock cars that raced at local quarter-mile tracks looked like the automobiles many of the spectators had driven on the streets. Most were Ford coupes, with mechanical modifications to make them more speedway-friendly. They appealed to fans who couldn't identify with sophisticated open-wheeled race cars, such as the costly, custom-built, single-seat machines that raced in the Indianapolis 500. Everyday motorists had a hard time imagining how it might feel to drive such an odd vehicle. Stock car buffs loved the slam-bam violence of the races. Anyone who'd driven home from work in heavy traffic understood how pleasurable it would be to knock the other guy out of the way.

Although stock car racing flourished in many places, the sport's roots grew especially deep and wide below the Mason-Dixon Line. Much of the postwar South remained rural, hundreds of small towns connected only by country roads. Southerners needed cars to go just about anywhere. A typical blue-collar or farm family had less money than those in urbanized areas, so more men knew how to work on their own cars. A man with skills as a mechanic enjoyed some prestige even if he had a low-status job and not much education.

In these years, the South had an entertainment shortage: few big-league sports, millions of people in towns with just one movie theater. The unique red-clay soil of the Piedmont plateau, which covers large areas of Georgia, the Carolinas, and Virginia, made a perfect natural surface for racetracks. A farmer with a bulldozer and couple of spare acres could become a racetrack proprietor in a few days. Some of South's earliest stock car races took place when moonshine runners got together on those tracks to see who really had the fastest whiskey car.

The sport drew a hard-edged crowd, both on the track and in the bleachers — people who weren't from the upper levels of southern society. Author

Jerry Bledsoe captured the scene succinctly: "'Respectable' people didn't think much of stock car racing at the time. Stock car racers were looked down on much as motorcycle gang members are today. Roughnecks. A wild bunch banging around on those dirt tracks, drinking, gambling, fighting — always fighting . . . A lot of people loved it. The wilder the better. That was why they came to races. They wanted drivers to be hard-charging and hard-living. Wild. Somebody they could swap stories about."

In 1948, a new organization called NASCAR began trying to organize the sport into a more business-like operation, but rival sanctioning bodies still had their own fiefdoms, and it would take NASCAR years to achieve dominance over the South's much-beloved sport.

During Scott's first race at the Danville Fairgrounds, some of the spectators booed him; a few threw things. "But they all came out to watch me run," Scott said. "Right from the first, I loved driving that car in that race." He wasn't there, he would always say, to make a stand against segregation. "The racial issue didn't have anything to do with it. I'd been a fast driver all my life, and I wanted to do it without paying tickets."

Hoping to run his first NASCAR race, he repaired the Ford the next day and towed it to Winston-Salem, North Carolina. Some of southern stock car racing's best drivers competed there on Saturday nights at Bowman Gray Stadium. NASCAR's dynamic founder, Bill France Sr., ran the program with a partner, J. Alvin Hawkins. "They were equal partners financially, but I think Hawkins accepted France as the boss," said Hank Schoolfield, who covered racing at Bowman Gray for the *Winston-Salem Journal* in the 1950s and worked as a publicist for the speedway in the 1960s.

Scott towed the Ford with a 1939 Cadillac limousine that had been used in funeral processions and was large enough for him to bring along several friends. At first, track officials didn't notice that the light-skinned Scott was black. They told him he'd have to put a safety belt in the Ford, and he bought one at the track's store. As Scott was installing the belt, with his darker friends gathered around him, the officials realized that he, too, was black. They said he'd have to leave. Someday, they added, the track might allow black drivers to race against one another in an all-black event. But until then, Scott said, they told him that "we can't let you run." While driving back to Danville, Scott recalled, "I had tears in my eyes. Every time I met a car on the road, the lights would almost blind me because of the tears."

A few days later, Scott phoned a NASCAR-sanctioned track in High Point, North Carolina. Without mentioning he was black, he asked if he could enter. "They told me okay. When I got down there," Scott said, "they just flat told me I couldn't race. They told me I could let a white boy drive my car. I told 'em weren't no damn white boy going to drive my car."

Quickly Scott began proving his talent. On June 1, he ran the Dixie Circuit's amateur races at the Camp Butner track in North Carolina and finished third in the feature race. (Drivers qualify for the feature race, the main attraction of the event, by finishing well in a preliminary heat race or in a last-chance race called a consolation.) But at another Dixie Circuit track in Eden, North Carolina, officials turned him away without giving him a reason. Either they hadn't gotten the word that the Dixie Circuit had accepted him, or they'd chosen to ignore it. The rejections didn't surprise him. "I expected all of that," he said. "It felt kind of bad sometimes. But during that time, everywhere you'd go, you'd see signs up at the water fountain and bathrooms — WHITE ONLY. White man back in those days, he let a colored man know when he was out of place."

Scott decided to stay away from NASCAR races for the time being and focus on the Dixie Circuit's tracks in Virginia. Twelve days into his racing career, he won for the first time, on June 4 at Lynchburg's Shrader Field speedway, a half-mile oval of red clay. It was just an obscure amateur heat race, only five miles from start to finish, but for Scott the victory was like the barb on a hook. At the age of thirty, he had found his calling.

# 6

## "He had to be tough-skinned."

For Scott, the racing life looked like the opposite of everything he'd hated about the regimentation of school, jobs, and soldiering. In the 1950s, before television began to dominate America's evenings, local speedways often ran races on weeknights. He began racing several times a week. Now that he'd experienced a win, every racing day felt rich with possibilities — at worst, a challenge, a rush of excitement; at best, the elation of coming in first.

To somebody with a passion for racing, even a small-time local speedway seems to glitter with an intoxicating energy as one drives toward it on a darkening summer evening. The roar of engines carries for miles over quiet farmland, proclaiming the track as the epicenter of excitement. The floodlights create a glowing canopy that seems to pulsate as exhaust fumes and dust rise up. The race cars look more vibrantly colored under the lights. Everyone is edgy with anticipation. Just towing his race car down the highway set Scott apart from other people on the road. They would turn their heads to watch him go by. Wide-eyed children pressed their noses against car windows, looking out from their ordinary world at an adventurer on a quest.

Mary Scott came to some races and rooted noisily for her husband. She shouted insults at drivers who drove dirty against him. The hostile glares she got from some white fans worried the Scott children, but their mother persisted in speaking her mind. "I'd look around the grandstand," Wendell Jr. said, "and I'd be amazed: 'These people actually ain't messing with my mom.'"

Wendell Jr. found the atmosphere particularly unsettling at the Danville Fairgrounds. The facility was physically cruder than the other speedways, the seats cut into a bank of earth, a creek flowing alongside the backstretch, floodlights tacked up on trees whose leaves cast big moving shadows. For a six-year-old, it felt as if he were in a scary movie — the eerie lighting, the angry bellow of engines, the rough and profane white men, the possibility that something bad could happen to his father at any time. The track was close to the Dan River, and occasionally on a warm summer night, a cool breeze off the water, and perhaps a touch of fear, would make the boy suddenly shiver.

Though the promoters had welcomed Scott into the Dixie Circuit, some drivers and crewmen didn't want him there and didn't mind saying so. "He had to be tough-skinned to take the guff that everybody give him, 'cause everybody called him nigger and all that stuff," driver Brice Stultz III said. "They didn't care back in them days. In the 1950s, a nigger had his place, and that was it. But no matter what they said, or how they cussed him, or what they did to him, he just took it on the chin and went right on. He had what it took to hang in. Next race they had, he was there." Eddie Allgood, the Dixie Circuit's president, said that during Scott's early weeks on the circuit, he had to call in a few drivers who kept knocking Scott off the track. "I had to say, 'Listen, either Wendell races, or you don't race.' That's how he kept on racing."

Mostly, though, Scott won acceptance because of the way he handled himself, other drivers said. It didn't take the racers long to see that Scott was much like them, another blue-collar guy swept up in the adrenaline rush of racing, a mechanic with talent in his hands, not somebody trying to make a racial point. They'd watch Scott put hot motor oil or gear lube on his tongue, looking for the burned taste or metal particles that warned of trouble. If time was short and Scott had to know if a cylinder was getting spark, he'd touch the plug wire and take the shock.

In the infield dirt, he'd slide under his car after a transmission failure, a flashlight sticking out of his mouth, the replacement transmission balanced on his chest, and he'd have the car ready for the feature race in half an hour. "He was a racer — you could look at somebody and tell whether they were a racer or not," driver Rodney Ligon said. "Didn't nobody send him down there to represent his race — he come down because he wanted to drive a damn race car." Scott brought large quantities of spare parts to the races, much more than he needed for himself, and he was quick to loan them out. Those who borrowed parts, he figured, were less likely to give him trouble.

Sometimes when Wendell Jr. and his younger brother, Frank, would ride home with their father after a race, he'd put his arm around them and pull them close and talk about the things they needed to know. A man needs to have something that's his own, he'd say. If you've got something of your own, something you worked hard to get — your skill, your business — then you've always got the right to it; the white man can't take it away. The race car rolled along behind on its tow bar, their father's name lettered over the driver's door. The boys would snuggle close, absorbing the words that they'd just seen Scott put into action.

But while the Scott children admired their father's courage and thrived under their mother's warmth, their family life was not a simple idyll. Their parents' marriage was going through a hard period, and sometimes there were bitter arguments, with Scott shouting insults, Wendell Jr. said. In the 1950s, many parents disciplined children physically. Wendell Jr. said he got most of the physical punishment in his family, especially when he'd take his mother's side in a dispute. "The whippings I got from my daddy when I was young, it made me think he hated me. My mind told me he hated me. But there were other times he was so endearing."

The children learned that expressions of self-doubt would not get a sympathetic hearing. Their father's blue-gray eyes would narrow and, to the children, appear to darken with anger. He wouldn't allow them to say *can't* or *never,* Frank Scott said. One night at dinner, he recalled, one of the children said, "I can't do that." Their father's "eyes started changing and he said, 'Get up and come back when your attitude is right.'"

At Lynchburg, announcers sometimes introduced Scott as "the world's only nigger race car driver." That was far from true — black drivers had raced elsewhere in the country since before World War I. An all-black stock car series had been running in Georgia and Tennessee since the 1940s. Promoters, though, love superlatives and controversy. They want drivers whom fans can see as sympathetic figures or villains, and with Scott they got both. Some white fans at Lynchburg rooted for him fiercely. Others "would holler *nigger* at him, and in a humble way he just continued to labor, and he'd never say anything," said Carl Simpson, a white fan who became a lifelong friend of Scott's.

Scott bought a faster car, an odd hybrid he called the Duke's Mixture, borrowing the name from a brand of tobacco for roll-your-own cigarettes. The DeSoto coupe had a Hudson Commander straight-eight engine with a Chrysler transmission and rear axle. Some people laughed at it, Scott said, but "that car wouldn't do nothing but fly."

He ran the Duke's Mixture at Lynchburg on July 24, 1952, a night that, for Scott, veered from elation to wrenching distress. He began by scoring his first feature win. He dominated the amateur field, finishing two laps ahead of the second-place car. He asked promoter Allgood if he could run with the faster cars in the sportsman-class feature. Allgood let the crowd vote on the question. More than half of the twenty-five hundred spectators stood up in support of Scott.

Starting last, he worked his way up to fourth place by the sixteenth lap. Then he hit a bump, and his right-rear axle broke. The wheel and hub flew up into the poorly protected grandstand and bounced from row to row, hitting spectators. Pete Peters, a mechanic who'd just swapped a Lincoln V-12 engine into one of the Ford coupes in the race, was standing up in his seat, watching his driver's progress, when the wheel slammed into his stomach, knocking the breath out of him, the hot rubber smearing his white shirt. Then the wheel walloped Raymond Riley, fracturing several ribs and his collarbone, knocking him unconscious as the broken axle's sharp stub slashed a long, deep gash into his head.

The race was red-flagged to a halt. Scott climbed out of his car and threw his helmet down on the track. Riley, Peters, and three other bloody victims were rushed to Lynchburg General Hospital in ambulances. A photographer snapped Scott's picture for the *Lynchburg News* as he leaned against his race car, looking stunned.

Carl Simpson remembered some of the hecklers "really abusing him. They were hollering, 'Nigger, you didn't have no business being out there.'

"As always, he didn't say anything about it."

Scott, his face still grimy with racetrack dirt, drove to the hospital and came upon Frances Dalton, a twenty-one-year-old white fan who had voted for him to race in the sportsman feature. The wheel had struck her in the face and arm, knocking her out. Blood had been pouring from her mouth, and the workers who carried her stretcher to the ambulance feared she had internal injuries.

"His tears was streaming down his face," she recalled. "He came up to me, and the first thing he said was, 'Honey, are you all right?'

"And I said, 'Well, yes, I think I'm all right, Wendell.'" Her bleeding had been from a cut tongue, not internal injuries.

"He said, 'Well, glory be for that.'"

Scott stayed at the hospital for two hours, she said, talking to other victims. "His tears was just flowing. The only clean place on his face was the streaks his tears had made."

Riley, a farmworker whom everyone knew as Mutt, had the worst injuries; his head wound required about thirty stitches. Riley remained unconscious when Scott went home that night. Another victim, an eight-year-old boy, was admitted for observation. Dalton and two others were treated for cuts and bruises and sent home.

The next day's *Lynchburg News* ran two prominent stories describing the incident and emphasizing that Scott was a Negro. Scott went back to the hospital several times to visit Riley. One day he brought along six-year-old Wendell Jr.

On the drive up from Danville, both father and son were apprehensive. Wendell Sr. feared that the wheel mishap and the bad publicity might hurt his racing career, perhaps even end it. "I thought Daddy was going crazy," Wendell Jr. recalled. "He was cursing the tire, questioning himself — 'Why did it have to be me?'"

His son was frightened of walking into a white hospital. Already the boy had learned the many taboos dictating where Negroes weren't allowed to go. White bathrooms, white schools, the white seats at the movies — terrible things could happen if you broke those rules. He expected Riley to be hostile. As they walked to the hospital door, he grabbed the leg of his father's trousers. He didn't want his daddy to know he was scared. He dug his fingers into the cloth and held on tight.

All of the Scotts' worries, however, turned out to be unnecessary. Riley greeted them from his bed with a big smile, his head wrapped in bandages, and talked with them cordially. The nurses joked with Wendell Sr. about his frequent visits, telling him Riley would probably heal even if Scott didn't come so frequently. (Riley spent several weeks in the hospital and recovered completely.) "They all treated Daddy like royalty, just like he was a white man." And Scott's racing career wasn't hurt by the wheel incident. Instead, it continued to improve.

After Scott showed he could win races, he soon crossed another racial barrier. He began driving some races for white car owners. One of the first was Bob Neal of Gretna, Virginia. Scott went into the arrangement warily. In some ways, Neal had the look and manner of a redneck. A stocky, uneducated man who almost always wore bib overalls, Neal dealt in moonshine, hiding his supply in his smokehouse's basement. He drank a lot of moonshine himself, and his cars weren't always reliable. He spent a lot of money on them, though, and when they ran right, they were often fast. At first, Scott expected that when something went wrong at the racetrack, Neal would show prejudice. But over their long and friendly relationship, nothing like that ever happened.

Sometimes Neal tried driving himself. His attempts to race frightened his family and friends. After a particularly shaky performance in an amateur heat race at Lynchburg, Neal's wife begged Scott to take over the car for the amateur feature. Since Scott had been promoted to the sportsman class, he was no longer allowed to drive in amateur races. But as a prank, he started the race in last place, pretending to be Neal. Scott passed several cars on each lap, took the lead, and pulled away from the field. He saw the flagman peering intently into the car every time he went by. In the grandstand, Wendell Jr. and Frank, who were in on the joke, jumped up and down gleefully. By the time Scott won the race, the officials had figured out who was driving.

"Wen-*dell,* what you doin' in that car? You get on out of there," announcer Eddie Allgood ordered, laughing. Amid much hilarity, Scott was disqualified.

After the races, Scott took Wendell Jr. out for his first ride in the race car. As they circled the track under the lights, the engine's growl echoing in the gutted-out interior, his father sitting happy and assured behind the wheel, the boy got a stronger sense of the passion at the center of his father's life. This was a moment he would always remember: his realization that he, too, could drive a race car someday. "The desire to race hit me right away," Wendell Scott Jr. recalled.

In the small world of Danville in the early 1950s, his daddy seemed unlike any other black person that Wendell Jr. knew. He could walk without fear into segregated places, deal with the white people who ran things, turn rusty old cars into exciting chariots, and beat white drivers in front of cheering crowds. He thought his father could be one of the most remarkable black men anywhere. For the boy who was his namesake, that brought a good deal of pride and, sometimes, a feeling of burdensome responsibility. He was realizing that he had a lot to live up to.

## 7

### "I said, 'Well, I won the steaks.'"

Searching for more non-NASCAR speedways that would allow him to race, Scott began traveling outside of the Dixie Circuit to tracks in the Shenandoah Valley and elsewhere in northern Virginia. He became a determined presence at Staunton, Waynesboro, Zion Crossroads, Craigsville, Natural Bridge, Winchester, and Pulaski. He persevered through the same cycle of hostility and acceptance as in Danville and Lynchburg.

At first, some drivers would try to knock him off the track. Cal Johnson, one of the Shenandoah Valley's top drivers at the time, said: "You'd hear, 'We're gonna get a hunk of that nigger — he ain't gonna finish a race.' But they got over it. When Wendell breaks an axle, and he gets out, takes a bumper jack, jacks his car up by himself, puts a Coca-Cola crate under there, puts a flashlight in his mouth, and crawls under there and works on the car, you got to respect him. Everybody finally got so they did."

Some racers discovered another reason to accept Scott. After the races, he'd discreetly sell jars of high-quality moonshine from the stash he kept hidden in his truck. One man, whose father was a driver and an occasional customer, remembered how Scott would size up a new acquaintance: talk a little, feel him out, see if he drank, then offer to sell him some whiskey. The drivers who enjoyed moonshine liked to see Scott arrive.

Sometimes, Johnson said, new drivers would show up, notice Scott, and make angry threats. "They'd say, 'Who's that nigger out there? I'm gonna get him.' The regulars, Johnson said, would reply, "Wait a minute — that's our nigger. Don't you mess with him or you got to mess with us."

Scott began winning races and building a following among fans and drivers who saw his talent. He began the 1953 season on the northern Virginia circuit, for example, by winning the Staunton feature on May 10. He tied the Waynesboro qualifying record on May 16. Then he won the feature at Waynesboro on May 23, after placing first in his heat race and setting a new qualifying record. The *Waynesboro News Virginian* reported that Scott had become "recognized as one of the most popular drivers to appear here." The *Staunton News Leader* said he "has been among the top drivers in every race here."

At the speedways, Scott carefully maintained the subdued, nonaggressive manner that the times and his situation demanded. But in his garage at home, he talked expansively to his black friends about the future he saw for himself as an accomplished racer and as a racial pioneer whose prominence would rival Jackie Robinson's. "They'll make a movie about me," he would say. "They'll write books about me. I'm going to be the most famous person you ever met."

Often, though, his daily experiences made such predictions seem quite unlikely. For one of his wins at Staunton, the prizes included steak dinners at two local restaurants. This was, of course, long before southern restaurants began serving black customers. That night Scott and a friend went to one of the restaurants, still grimy from the race.

"The lady got all excited. She said, 'We just don't serve colored here.'

"I said, 'Well, I won the steaks.'"

The woman finally agreed to seat them. But their presence made her so jittery, Scott said, that his steak fell to the floor while she was bringing it to the table. She took it back to the kitchen, then quickly returned and served him a steak that looked exactly like the one she'd just dropped.

At the second restaurant, they didn't even make it through the door: The manager wouldn't let them in. As compensation, he paid Scott $1.75. Those are "some damn cheap steaks," Scott replied. At the speedways, though, Scott continued to make new white friends. After a Waynesboro race, a white spectator, Buck Drummond, came up to Scott in the pits and complimented Scott's driving. He'd be proud to give Scott a few dollars, he said, to give his young sons a ride around the track. Scott gave Donnie and Skeeter a ride, and Drummond began coming to all of Scott's races in the area to root for him.

Scott towed his race car with a '48 Ford panel truck, which gave him a place to sleep on his travels around northern Virginia. One night Drummond invited Scott to sleep at his house. Scott felt uncomfortable, he recalled, at the idea of being a white family's houseguest. "I never had mingled with many white people, so I told him no," Scott said. "So the next morning about six o'clock, he was out there with hot coffee, sandwiches, and all. Every week when I'd race up there, I'd sleep in my truck, and he's out there the next morning."

They became good friends. At a time when few black and white families socialized, the Drummonds began coming to Danville for dinner at the Scotts' house. "My daddy was brought up so he wasn't prejudiced or nothing," Donnie Drummond said. "Hell, we sat right there at the table and ate with them. They got to be like family."

After a racing day ended, the Scott boys and Drummond's sons would roll tires around the track, racing each other. One day Donnie and Skeeter were at the Scott's house playing with Wendell Jr. and Frank in the cars that Scott kept in his back lot. Danville police officers stopped at the house and questioned Mary Scott — why were black and white children playing together in her yard? "We was probably the only two white kids in that neighborhood," Donnie Drummond said. "It really made Mary Scott mad. She jumped in the car, and down to the *po*-lice station she went to tell them off."

In these early years, the stock car scene often included violence. Drivers frequently fought after a race if one felt the other had used dirty tactics. Sometimes their fistfights expanded into brawls involving both pit crews. Sometimes fans got drunk and obstreperous. When promoter Eddie Allgood had to call off a race at Lynchburg because the track got too dusty, an angry crowd surrounded him in the flag stand and, he said, shook the structure so hard he tumbled out and fell several feet to the ground. "Skinned me all to hell."

As the only black man in this roughneck atmosphere, Scott felt he had to avoid doing anything, on the track or off, that could provoke a fight. In the era's culture of segregation, it would have been unthinkable for a Negro to strike a white man for any reason. He had to keep his driving scrupulously sportsman-like, even when others didn't. The understated personality that Scott brought to the racetrack also put him at a disadvantage in any disputes with promoters. Often these were aggressive men with the gift of gab, accustomed to winning arguments and being belligerent authority figures. Scott's place in the racial hierarchy gave him some discomfort about confronting that sort of white man. "They intimidated him," recalled one of Scott's black friends, Leonard Miller.

Two of Scott's white friends, Buck Drummond and Lynchburg racer Earl Brooks, played a vital role for Scott in these early years of his driving career. Both were large, tough men who didn't mind arguing or throwing a punch. Sometimes they served as Scott's bodyguards and advocates, protecting him from fights and taking his side in wrangles with officials. "I'd have had to fight my way out of some of the places where I raced because the drivers didn't accept me if it hadn't been for Earl Brooks . . . He took care of a lot of business for me," said Scott. At Zion Crossroads, officials told Scott before an event that his carburetor didn't conform to the track's rules. He put on a different carburetor, and they approved him to compete, Carl Simpson recalled. After Scott won the feature race, however, the promoter claimed his carburetor was still illegal and refused to pay him any prize money.

Drummond tore off his shirt and confronted the promoter. A brawny roofer and building contractor, Drummond stood over six feet tall and weighed more than two hundred pounds. He told the promoter, Scott said, that "'Y'all going to pay this boy. This boy here's a nigger, and you think you ain't going to pay him, but I'll die for him right here.' Man, he was ready to go to war." Quickly the promoter paid Scott, who never had any more trouble at Zion Crossroads. Later, Scott said, Drummond apologized to him for saying the word *nigger.* He said he'd just wanted to talk to the promoter in his own language. Scott told him not to worry. He never heard Drummond use the word again. Drummond was fiercely protective of the whole Scott family, Wendell Scott Jr. said. "He was real, real tough. People knew that if you messed with us, you had major trouble on your hands."

Another early white supporter was Howard Cook, a race car owner from Danville. Cook had a couple of fast, well-prepared cars and used various local drivers. A union electrician, Cook made good money at major construction jobs, sometimes hundreds of miles away. He was a fat man, single, with little social life. His life was focused on racing. Almost every weekend, Cook drove back to Danville to run his cars, spending much of his money rebuilding and improving them.

When Scott began racing, Rodney Ligon drove for Cook, but he found that Cook's finely tuned machines were often too fast for him. Scott watched Ligon struggling to handle Cook's cars. He thought about offering to drive for Cook, but he had some doubts about Cook's attitudes. For one thing, Cook's number eight car had lettering identifying it as the CONFEDER-8 and displayed the Confederate flag.

Nevertheless, Scott asked Cook one day if he could drive one of his race cars. Cook, Scott recalled, left him with the distinct impression that he didn't want a black man to drive for him. Two or three weeks passed. Ligon was still having a rough time with Cook's cars while Scott continued to win races, or place second or third, with his ramshackle machines. One Monday morning, Scott woke up to find both of Cook's cars sitting in his yard. Cook had left Scott a note. Run the cars anywhere you want, the note said, and do anything to them that needs to be done. Cook was working in Pittsburgh then, and every Friday he'd drive home for a weekend of racing. "That was his life, those race cars," Scott said. "He didn't care nothing about the money. Anything I needed, the motors, rear ends, tires, he bought them and paid cash, and he never took a dime of the prize money." Scott decided he'd been mistaken about Cook's attitudes. "After him and I went into business together, he never, never showed no kind of partiality, no kind of way," Scott said. He came to consider Cook a trusted friend.

One afternoon at Maryland's Hagerstown Speedway, Scott could have used someone with Buck Drummond's ability to intimidate a promoter. Scott phoned the track the day after he won a feature race in Harrisonburg, Virginia. He'd heard that the Hagerstown prize money was generous — at least two hundred dollars to win the sportsman feature, sometimes more. He told the promoter about his Harrisonburg victory and asked if he could run that night. The promoter, Scott said, predicted a big crowd and an especially generous purse and told him, "Come on up — glad to have you."

Scott didn't mention that he was black. He drove up to the speedway by himself.

A few hours before the race, Scott walked two laps around the track, first on the inside, then the outside, thinking about gear ratios. Another driver, Dick "Pappy" Hansberger, and his young son, P.C., walked the half-mile dirt oval with Scott. "Wendell says, 'I think I got it figured out,'" P.C. Hansberger recalled. "Dad said, 'Hope you do.'" The Hansbergers helped Scott put a different rear end into his car, an unimpressive-looking Ford two-door with the original black paint and white numbers that looked like they'd been hand-painted in a hurry.

The car was quick, though, and Scott won his heat. Back in the pits, he overheard two men whom he didn't know talking about him. They were discussing a five-dollar bet they'd made on whether he was white or black. "They walked up close to me, and then one of them said, 'Hell, I knowed all along he was a nigger.'" Scott didn't confront the men. Instead, he turned his anger to his driving in the feature. "I have to admit I overdrove myself that day and took a lot of chances I wouldn't normally take," he said. "I went right through the holes [in the traffic] whether there was a hole or not."

For P.C. Hansberger, this was a memorable day. First, his father won the amateur feature. Then the boy watched admiringly as Scott bulled his way through traffic in the sportsman feature, the main event of the day. "I think he started twelfth out of about twenty-two cars, and he come up on through there and won it," Hansberger said. "He really drove. Them boys there said they never seen anybody drive like that on dirt. There wasn't no way they was going to catch him. He had 'em by about fifteen car lengths at the end."

Scott lined up with the other drivers at the pay window. When it was his turn, the promoter asked, "What do you want?" Scott said he'd won the feature race. The promoter handed him a check for thirty-six dollars, then paid Pappy Hansberger sixty-five dollars for winning the less prestigious amateur feature.

"The guy told Wendell, 'Take your money and be on your way,'" P.C. Hansberger said. "Wendell told Daddy, 'Man, they did me dirty.'"

To make an aggravating day worse, Scott's tow truck had sprung a small radiator leak. Driver Bill Nalley, one of the local stars, felt sorry for Scott. Nalley couldn't be sure that the prize-money incident was racially motivated, he recalled, but he felt it wasn't right. He told Scott to follow him home to Brunswick, Maryland. He and his wife had a picnic dinner with Scott in their backyard. After dinner, Nalley soldered the leaky radiator and gave Scott some gas money to get back to Danville.

Just as Scott had anticipated, the racing world had plenty of prejudiced roughnecks and slippery promoters. More quickly than he'd expected, though, he was making white friends and winning their respect.

# 8

## "You're going to be knocked around."

After winning some recognition in Virginia racing circles, Scott decided he'd try again to somehow get past the color barrier and gain admission to NASCAR. To rise in the sport, he knew he had to become a NASCAR driver.

By the early 1950s, NASCAR had become the fastest-growing organization in American racing. The centerpiece of its program was a national-level series for late-model sedans, the Grand National circuit, which would evolve into today's Sprint Cup series. Already NASCAR ran two of stock car racing's biggest events, the Southern 500 at South Carolina's Darlington Raceway and the February races on the beach-and-road course at Daytona Beach. Although the Indianapolis 500 and its star drivers still commanded far more prestige, NASCAR was pushing aggressively to become a national presence.

In some sports, the authority over big decisions is divided among various power centers — commissioners, team owners, player unions, and so on. That's never been the case with NASCAR. From its incorporation in 1948, one family has controlled the organization — that of NASCAR's founder and first president, an energetic, visionary promoter named William Henry Getty France.

Born in 1909, the man whose talents launched one of the major success stories in American sports grew up in modest circumstances in Washington, DC. France's father, a bank clerk, and his mother, an immigrant from Northern Ireland, had three children. His parents gave him the extra middle name of Getty in hopes that he'd become a forceful executive like the oil mogul J. Paul Getty. In high school, he excelled at basketball, but cars and fast driving were his major preoccupations. As a young man, he worked as a bank clerk for a couple of years, then became a mechanic and drove in local auto races near Washington.

In 1934, the twenty-five-year-old France set out for Florida in his Hupmobile with his wife, Anne, and their infant son, seeking his fortune

— and warmer weather. They settled in Daytona Beach. He established his own auto-repair shop and drove stock cars in city-sanctioned races on a unique course that used part of the ocean beach and a nearby highway. France was six foot five, handsome and gregarious, a natural leader. His shop became the unofficial headquarters for local racers, and in 1938 he became the official promoter of the beach events. World War II shut down auto racing across the United States. France spent the war years as a civilian executive in a Daytona Beach boatyard that built navy antisubmarine craft.

By 1946, he was promoting the beach races again and working on two new ideas that eventually would make him rich. Over the years, France and fellow drivers had been cheated repeatedly by unscrupulous promoters. Some promoters paid them only a fraction of the prize money they'd promised. Others just absconded with all of the gate receipts. Such scams weren't uncommon in the anarchic business world of stock car racing during the 1930s and '40s. France saw the need for a national organization to regulate and promote the sport.

He also wanted to create a new national racing circuit he believed would draw a much larger audience: a series for new, unaltered family sedans, identical to those in millions of American driveways. Those cars, France believed, would have far wider appeal than the cut-down, souped-up 1930s coupes that dominated local stock car racing. Although racing buffs loved those cars, France said, they looked to many people like low-class jalopies. "Plain, ordinary working people have to be able to associate with the cars," he said. "Standard street stock cars are what we should be running."

During 1947 and 1948, France orchestrated the creation of NASCAR, the National Association for Stock Car Auto Racing. He put the group together with considerable help from other promoters and various sidekicks, but he quickly became its dominant figure. The organization had two central goals: promoting races at local tracks for the older, jalopy-style cars and advancing France's national aspirations for the sport. In 1949, NASCAR launched the new circuit he had envisioned for modern sedans, the Grand National series. As France expected, the new cars attracted many new fans.

The schedules included some Northeast and Midwest tracks, but most Grand National races took place in the South. In these early years, NASCAR had to joust with several competing sanctioning bodies just for dominance on its home turf, and for decades NASCAR racing would remain a mostly Dixie-centered sport.

In NASCAR, France was known to everyone as Big Bill. When he strode into a room, he captured the focus of attention without seeming to try. He had the assured presence of a wealthy, powerful entrepreneur long before he actually became one. He was confident and persuasive, sometimes an autocrat, sometimes an adept manipulator. He had the aggressive toughness to handle the prickly egos, short fuses, and rough edges of his racers, and he could switch in an instant to the smooth geniality that charmed those corporate executives and politicians whose goodwill could benefit NASCAR. His personal politics were strongly conservative. *Stock Car Racing* magazine called him "a force of nature with an iron will." His favorite song was "My Way."

Nevertheless, the decision to allow a black driver into NASCAR — no small matter for a southern-based sport in the 1950s — apparently took place without France's knowledge or consent. After gaining some experience and respect as a racer, Scott resolved to try again to get into NASCAR. He had never met France, and he didn't talk to anybody near the top of NASCAR's chain of command. Instead he found a way, essentially, to slip into NASCAR through a side door. He decided just to show up again at a local-level NASCAR event and see if the officials would let him run.

Scott towed his race car to the old Richmond Speedway in Virginia, a quarter-mile dirt oval, and told the NASCAR official on duty, Maurice Poston, that he wanted to apply for a racing license. Poston, known to everyone as Mike, was NASCAR's chief steward for the region. In those early years, that title didn't mean he was a powerful figure in the organization's hierarchy. In fact, Poston was a part-timer: He worked for NASCAR at racing events and held a day job at the post office. But he did have the authority to issue NASCAR licenses.

Poston asked Scott if he knew what he was getting into. "I told him we've never had any black drivers, and you're going to be knocked around,"

Poston said. "He said, 'I can take it.'" Poston gave him a license, and Scott became the first black driver to compete in a NASCAR-sanctioned race.

Later, Poston confided to Scott that officials at NASCAR's Daytona Beach headquarters hadn't been pleased with his decision. "He told me that when they found out at Daytona Beach that he had signed me up, they raised hell with him," Scott said.

Poston's daughter, Barbara Tennant, recalled that as far as her father was concerned, Wendell was a good man and a good driver, and that was all that should matter. Poston always backed his drivers, Tennant said, and never regretted approving Scott's license. Poston and Scott maintained a friendly relationship until Poston died in 1983.

Scott's experience in breaking NASCAR's color barrier could hardly have been more different from that of Jackie Robinson, who had become the twentieth century's first black major-league baseball player in 1947. Robinson joined the Brooklyn Dodgers under a strategy carefully worked out by two of his sport's most powerful figures. The Dodgers' owner, Branch Rickey, decided the time had come to integrate, and he chose Robinson after screening many candidates. Baseball commissioner Albert "Happy" Chandler, the sport's closest counterpart to Bill France, agreed with Rickey's decision and supported Robinson when the inevitable incidents of bigotry began to occur. In contrast, Scott made his unobtrusive entry into NASCAR without the backing of any influential white patron. He had no idea what support, if any, he could expect from the sport's management.

Although Scott's crossing of NASCAR's color barrier was a notable milestone in American sports history, it got no public attention. Clearly, the arrival of a black competitor in this all-white southern sport wasn't regarded by NASCAR as a development to celebrate, promote, or even talk about publicly. There was no announcement and, consequently, no press coverage. The national news media largely ignored NASCAR during these early years, and even in many southern newspapers coverage was spotty. As things turned out, NASCAR's evident disinterest in any publicity about its integration served to rob Scott during his lifetime of the distinction he had earned as the group's first black driver.

Throughout the twentieth century, other black athletic pioneers were able to enjoy the acclaim and satisfaction of being properly recognized as the first African American in the history of their sports. Besides Robinson, such pioneers have included Charles Follis, the first black professional football player (1902); Mabel Fairbanks, the first black figure skater to tour professionally (1947); Althea Gibson, the first black tennis player admitted to the US Nationals (1950); and Charlie Sifford, the first black golfer allowed on the PGA tour (1961). But that sort of recognition didn't happen for Scott. Instead, throughout Scott's racing career and his retirement years, newspaper stories, magazine articles, and books repeatedly identified a different early black racer, Joie Ray, as the first African American to drive in a NASCAR race.

Joie Ray, who lived in Louisville, Kentucky, began racing soon after World War II. A racial pioneer in his own right, Ray competed around the Midwest in several racing organizations, mostly driving open-wheeled cars, not stock cars. He became the first black driver ever licensed by the American Automobile Association, which had previously banned African American competitors. Even now, news stories, documentaries, and Internet sites often credit Joie Ray with being NASCAR's first black driver, reporting that he achieved that distinction by driving in a NASCAR Grand National race at Daytona Beach on February 10, 1952.

In fact, although a driver using the name Joie Ray did compete in that Daytona Beach race, he was a white man. The black Joie Ray told the author in an interview that he had never driven in that race or any other NASCAR event. His account is confirmed by the work of a professional film crew that documented the 1952 Daytona race. That film includes a pre-race interview with the Joie Ray who did compete that day. The film shows unmistakably that he was white and bore no resemblance to the black Joie Ray.

Pressed on this point, a NASCAR spokesman acknowledged that Wendell Scott, not Joie Ray, deserves to be recognized as NASCAR's first black driver. Early NASCAR records do not document the exact date when Scott ran his first NASCAR race at Richmond, the spokesman said. (Scott himself wasn't sure when it happened.) One authority on Richmond racing history, veteran radio broadcaster Joe Kelly, believes it took place in 1952, the same year that Scott first began racing on the non-NASCAR Dixie Circuit. The earliest public record of Scott as a licensed NASCAR competitor shows him driving in the annual sportsman-class race at Daytona Beach on February 19, 1954. At that point, Scott already would have gotten his NASCAR license at Richmond during a prior season. NASCAR's archives suggest that probably happened in 1953, the spokesman said. That scenario matches Scott's own recollection: that he raced in non-NASCAR events for a substantial period before he found a NASCAR track that would allow him to run.

Scott drove Bob Neal's '38 Ford in his first race at the famous Daytona Beach course in February 1954. This 4.1-mile track, unlike anything before or since in motorsports, featured huge starting fields and frequent multicar pileups. First the drivers sped north up a two-mile straightaway along the hard-packed sand near the water's edge. (The races could be run only at low tide.) Squinting through sand-coated windshields, they could often barely see the first turn as they approached it at over a hundred miles an hour. Most first-time competitors, like Scott, arrived with no experience on any track longer than half a mile.

In the north turn, they skidded through sand that quickly became rutted and mushy. Dodging overturned cars, they emerged onto the backstretch — the narrow Route AlA — and ran south through violent dips and rises for another two miles. Sometimes spectators crossed the unfenced road in front of the cars. Around the outside of the sandy south turn lay a steep embankment. When drivers misjudged that turn, their cars tumbled down the slope. After a race, the pile of wrecked cars at the bottom looked like a heap of broken toys in a giant sandbox.

Sixty-nine sportsman cars took the green flag for Scott's race, run during a light rain to beat the arrival of high tide. When the checkered flag waved, 123 miles later, NASCAR scored Scott as finishing thirty-third. He strongly believed he'd done better and thought the scorers had cheated him. The money he got at the pay window, twenty-five dollars, seemed paltry for such a major event and such a long haul. But at least he'd been allowed to run one of NASCAR's most prestigious races. He kept quiet about his suspicions.

Two months later, though, a promoter treated Scott with blatant prejudice, and Scott felt he had to do something. He had towed his race car to a NASCAR event in Raleigh, North Carolina, but the races were rained out. Promoter Enoch Staley, a tall, lean, hawk-faced man who called himself "just a simple ol' mountain boy," told the drivers he'd pay them the customary "tow money" to help cover their expenses — in this case, fifteen dollars for gas.

"When he got to me, old Enoch Staley, he say, 'What you win, you get, but we're not going to give you any tow money.' So they didn't pay me," Scott recalled. Arguing with the hard, taciturn Staley in front of a group seemed a bad idea, so Scott just left.

The next day, April 17, 1954, Scott went to a NASCAR race at Lynchburg. This was the season's opening night at the track, a significant evening for Bill France. NASCAR had just added this former Dixie Circuit venue to its expanding sphere of influence, and France showed up to make sure things went smoothly. In many ways, France was an archetype of the white authority figures that Scott would think twice about confronting. France towered over Scott, as he did over almost everybody. He was loquacious, assertive, and used to getting his way. Still, Staley's treatment had rankled Scott. He waited until nobody else was nearby, walked up to France, and told him what had happened in Raleigh.

To France, Staley wasn't just another promoter with a routine streak of prejudice. Staley was among France's trusted business associates and confidants. They were like brothers, promoter Paul Sawyer said. They were partners in the speedway at Hillsborough, North Carolina, and Staley would go on to hold executive positions in France's organization.

Nevertheless, France immediately pulled some money out of his pocket and went out of his way to put Scott at ease. "He let me know my color didn't have anything to do with anything," Scott said. "He said, 'You're a NASCAR member, and as of now you will always be treated as a NASCAR member.' And instead of giving me fifteen dollars, he reached in his pocket and gave me thirty dollars."

Not long afterward, a clash with a hostile white driver would reinforce Scott's positive impression of France. One night at Lynchburg, Scott won a race after a tight battle with Ward McDonald. After the checkered flag fell, McDonald angrily slammed his car into the rear of Scott's several times. Then he pushed Scott's car into the infield. McDonald "just hated to get beat by a black man — that's what it was all about," Donnie Drummond said. Both cars came to a stop. McDonald began scrambling out of his car, apparently about to go after Scott.

Earl Brooks, Scott's friend and occasional protector, had been sitting on the hood of a car in the infield, watching the race. He jumped up and ran toward McDonald. As the angry driver was climbing out of his car's window, Brooks yanked McDonald out of the car and, said Drummond, "gave him a good whupping."

Brooks's intervention averted a potentially disastrous situation. Scott had a cousin with him that day, a man who enjoyed trouble. Once, Scott had pointed a shotgun at this cousin after catching him stealing from a family member. The cousin walked up to Scott coolly, took the gun by the barrel, and pulled it out of Scott's hands. "I guess I'll just take this, too," his cousin said, and walked away.

When McDonald began ramming Scott's car, the cousin, who had been drinking heavily, pulled out a large knife. Before the race, he'd visited Buck Drummond, who had entertained him generously with the moonshine hidden under the smokehouse. The cousin — according to Scott's friend Carl Simpson — "was starting after McDonald with the knife. It would have been real bad for Wendell if this had happened." Scott had no doubt that his cousin would have slashed McDonald if Brooks hadn't gotten to him first. "I'm glad he didn't get to that boy," Scott said. "He'd have cut him all to pieces."

A week after the McDonald incident, France sent out a letter to drivers warning that anyone who deliberately wrecked Scott would be suspended. France's action won Scott's loyalty. (France could not be interviewed for this book. He died in 1992 at age eighty-two after a long bout with Alzheimer's disease.)

A race at Danville provided another reason for Scott's optimism about his future in NASCAR. Two of NASCAR's top stars came to Scott's hometown to run against the local drivers. They were brothers, Billy and Bobby Myers.

Each had won dozens of features in sportsman and modified cars. Both had scored season championships at Bowman Gray Stadium in Winston-Salem, North Carolina, against some of the South's strongest competition. In the previous season's national sportsman-class points, Billy had placed second and Bobby was third.

At the Danville Fairgrounds, Scott drove one of Howard Cook's cars against the Myers brothers on June 13, 1954, a fiercely hot day. He dueled with Billy Myers for the lead throughout the feature race, each passing the other several times. "I had worn tires and he had good tires," Scott said. "He could beat me off the corners up to the flagman's stand. I was passing him after we went by the flag stand, about halfway down the track. That's how close the race was. It went like that the whole race." At the finish, as both cars passed the flagging stand, Billy Myers edged out Scott by roughly half a car length. Bobby Myers finished third. For the rest of his life, Scott would wish he'd had better tires that day. Still, the race gave him deep pride. Now he knew that he could race wheel-to-wheel with two of NASCAR's best.

For Scott, it had been an eventful couple of years since he'd sat in the fairgrounds grandstand watching other men race. He'd broken the color barrier in the all-white world of southern stock car racing. He'd driven successfully for white car owners. He'd shown he could win features and run with the Myers brothers. Most important, the man who controlled NASCAR had promised him that he'd be treated like any other driver, and Scott thought Bill France seemed like a man of his word.

## 9

### "The more you do it, the more you like to do it."

With a NASCAR license in his pocket at last, Scott began testing his skills against tougher competition. Quickly he was able to show that his performance against the Myers brothers hadn't been a fluke. He ran competitively against other top NASCAR drivers, sometimes even when they drove much more powerful cars.

Under sportsman-class rules, Scott's Fords had to run the original type of engine that came from the factory, the so-called flathead V-8. The primitive design of the flatheads severely restricted their ability to breathe and make power. The costlier cars in the next class up, called modified stock cars, could use modern overhead-valve engines and other power-boosting technology such as fuel injection. Some tracks combined both classes in their races, and the modifieds usually dominated.

But not always. At the Cockade City Speedway in Petersburg, Virginia, the region's fastest modified drivers competed weekly in their fuel-injected machines. They included drivers still well known to enthusiasts two generations later: Ray Hendrick, Banjo Matthews, Runt Harris, Eddie Crouse, Cotton Owens, Emanuel Zervakis. Scott ran a sportsman car against this formidable crowd with striking results. He placed second in two preliminary races on the dirt oval on June 24, 1954, and outran every modified driver in the feature except for Hendrick, whom NASCAR now ranks among its fifty greatest drivers.

Petersburg's newspaper, the *Progress-Index,* gave Scott's driving a rave review: "Fans who witnessed last week's races will recall seeing one of the top sportsman drivers in this section and the leading colored driver in the nation in Wendell Scott, the top money winner for the night . . . Scott's performance led many to believe that he was driving a modified race car, but his car was a sportsman, powered by a Ford strictly stock motor that was so hot at times that it appeared to be in a blaze of fire." In newspaper ads, the speedway began listing Scott among its star drivers, identifying him as "Wendell Scott (colored)."

That Fourth of July weekend, Scott got more favorable attention for his driving in a two-hundred-mile all-star race for modified and sportsman cars at Raleigh, North Carolina. This high-banked, one-mile oval was the fastest paved speedway he'd ever run. The forty-six-car field included most of the top guns at Petersburg and other NASCAR aces such as Curtis Turner, Glen Wood, and Glenn "Fireball" Roberts. For the first half of the race, Scott kept his flathead sportsman car among the leaders until a botched refueling stop dropped him back to midfield.

The rest of the season brought more recognition. He became a regular winner in heat races and consolations, the last-chance races to determine final qualifiers for the feature. He regularly finished in the top five in features at several tracks, including Petersburg. Just a week after the Raleigh race, Scott beat twenty-one cars to win the feature at Waynesboro, also winning his heat.

During the 1950s, the region's newspapers were strongly segregationist. They stridently condemned the Supreme Court's 1954 ruling in favor of school integration. They ran separate real estate ads for whites and blacks. Even their news space was segregated, with features called "Colored News" or "Activities of Colored People."

Nevertheless, Scott's racing successes got a good deal of positive coverage. The integration of sports was a less inflammatory issue than putting black children into white schools. The *Norfolk Virginian-Pilot,* for instance, ran Scott's photo with a story quoting local promoter and driver Joe Weatherly as describing Scott as "one of the best drivers he has ever seen."

"It seems Scott convinced last week's sellout crowd that this was true to a great extent," the story continued. "After he had damaged a front wheel running high on a turn, Scott pulled off the track, lost at least one lap and then came back to place fourth in the 25-lap race." The next week the paper praised his "startling brand of driving."

Under the headline "Scott Ranked High as Driver," the *Danville Commercial Appeal* reported that he was "fast becoming one of the area's most well-known and popular drivers." In a feature story, the Petersburg newspaper highlighted his close battle against Emanuel Zervakis, one of the country's top drivers of modified-class stock cars: "Wendell Scott, popular colored driver of Danville, after starting from 14th position in a field of 18 cars, pushed Zervakis all the way to finish in the second position." The *Waynesboro News Virginian* reported that Scott "has been winning statewide acclaim lately." In NASCAR's national point standings for the sportsman class in 1954, Scott placed 19th of 1,935 drivers across the country.

At Lawrenceville, Virginia, the next season, Scott won his heat and battled Cal Johnson for the lead in the thirty-five-lap feature race, whose field included some of the region's big names — Ray Hendrick, Ted Hatfield, Eddie Crouse. Johnson, a frequent winner and one of the stars of the Shenandoah Valley area, drove with bandages on both arms. This was his first race since fire had engulfed his car five weeks ago, burning him badly. Scott started on the pole and led for thirty-four laps.

The fire had scared Johnson profoundly. He worried that perhaps he'd lost the courage to race. On the last lap, Johnson was still behind Scott. He figured Scott had the race won. But then Scott hit a big hole in the track between the first and second turns that both drivers had managed to avoid until then. Scott bounced wide, and Johnson took the lead. Scott finished second. Afterward, he approached Johnson and, in a wry voice, complained, "Cal, that was my chance to win the race, and you got away from me."

Johnson's duel with Scott had freed him from his anxiety about racing — he knew now that he still had his nerve. He held out his arms to Scott. "I said, 'Scotty, look at me — I just got out of the hospital from being burnt. I needed that win more than you did.'

"He says, 'Yeah, you're right. You did.'"

Simpson went with Scott to collect his prize money. "The promoter was standing there, big cigar in his mouth. He said, 'Wendell, a man who run like you did here tonight, he don't lose no money at my racetrack.' And he paid him first-place money, the same as Cal."

Although more drivers and fans were coming to regard Scott with affection, he often received pointed reminders that some drivers still resented his presence, particularly when he did well. Again and again, some drivers would go beyond the customary bumping and rubbing of short-track stock car racing to deliberately wreck him. France's warning of suspensions had helped Scott at Lynchburg but not elsewhere.

A typical incident took place in 1955 at the fast half-mile dirt track at Morehead City, North Carolina. Scott had won his heat race and was leading the feature. He began lapping the slower cars, passing them on the outside. One driver looked over, recognized Scott, and shoved his car into the fence, knocking him out of the race.

Stock cars had little safety equipment back then, so crashes were much more dangerous. A typical car had only a lap belt and a crude, single-hoop roll bar, sometimes just the flimsy headboard hoop from a cast-iron bed. Helmet rules were lax. There were no shoulder belts, roll cages, window nets, fuel cells, or fire suits. Many drivers died or suffered bad burns in crashes that would cause no injuries in a modern stock car.

As the only black driver, Scott knew he could not follow the common practice of paying back competitors who wrecked him by wrecking them in the next race. Once other drivers understood that Scott felt he could neither fight them nor take revenge on the track, they realized they could simply knock him out of their way with impunity. As a result, some drivers "just hammered on Wendell," former chief NASCAR photographer T. Taylor Warren said. "They figured he wasn't going to retaliate."

When someone in his family was threatened or harmed, Scott was quick to show anger. At Fredericksburg, Virginia, somebody threw a lighted firecracker at Wendell Jr. as he walked past a spectator area. The firecracker exploded as it hit his hand, leaving a bloody wound. Instantly, his father charged across the track, shouting curses at all of the spectators nearby. But when Scott himself was wronged, he fell back on the code of behavior he felt circumstances had forced upon him. He maintained a stoic silence, not complaining to promoters or officials, not confronting the other driver. "Mostly I'd just leave them to their ignorance," he said.

Many years would pass before Scott began to speak publicly about the dirty driving he faced in his early racing years. He told *Stock Car Racing* magazine in 1968 that "I spent more time duckin' wrecks than I did racing . . . I got run off more tracks than I can remember." He told the Fredericksburg newspaper in 1977: "I remember every driver that ever drove dirty against me. There have been a lot of them."

For most of his career, Scott felt it best to lie when reporters brought up the subject, which wasn't often. "I don't think any white driver ever intentionally tried to wreck me," he told the *Danville Commercial Appeal* in 1958, apparently with a straight face. Sure, some were unfriendly at first, he acknowledged. "But everything is okay now, and I guess the best friends I have in the world are race drivers and race officials."

More and more, racing dominated the family's life. In a typical week, Scott would race on Tuesday in Richmond, Wednesday in Norfolk, Thursday in Petersburg, Friday in Raleigh, Saturday in Winston-Salem, and Sunday in Waynesboro. "When I look back, I don't know when my father slept because he was in the garage all the time working on the race cars," Frank Scott said. "He would go in and get two or three hours sleep and go back out to the garage." Racing had become Scott's primary occupation. It was only in the winter that he had time to repair passenger cars for customers. Sometimes Scott joked about how racing would crowd other concerns from his mind. The *Commercial Appeal* reported that Scott "tells the story of how his wife was in a family way for several months once before he knew about it because of his time being devoted to racing." When a reporter asked about his punishing schedule, Scott replied: "Only way to make any money in this business is to race." To be sure, the financial pressures of a big family were part of what drove Scott. Mary Scott was pregnant with their sixth child, Sybil; soon he'd have to build a larger house. When a race went poorly, he'd have his sons search the area for deposit soda bottles before they left the track.

But Scott's obsessive desire to race, like that of many drivers, came from a deeper impulse than just financial gain. By his own account, a central reason for the passion he brought to the sport was that the experience of driving in races was something he both loved and craved. Motor racing can put a driver into a mental zone where adrenaline combined with deep concentration brings about a profound altered state — a "racing high," as some drivers call it.

During a race, the mental background noise of ordinary life, the static that chatters along in the everyday consciousness, is muted, and the racer fuses with the car and the craft of driving, absorbed completely in the slow-motion passage of the seconds. Racing can offer a taste of the intense states experienced by meditators and mystics. The experience, some drivers say, can be highly addictive. Scott himself put it this way: "Racing cars gets to be about like being a drug addict or an alcoholic. The more you do it, the more you like to do it."

Former NASCAR driver Larry Frank, a friend of Scott's, described his own feelings about racing as "like an addiction . . . There was many, many years — and I'm sure Wendell was the same way — that you just didn't know anything existed outside this little racing circle. Your whole life was getting an old car fixed up and making it to the next racetrack and then doing it all over again. It just seemed like you had it in your mind that they couldn't run a race without you — you had to be there. After the race, win or lose, if you just run hard, you got out all of your frustration, and you just felt clean and good."

This was still a turbulent period in Scott's marriage. There were other women. This part of his life wasn't a secret in racing circles. His women friends sometimes accompanied him to races. Later his son Michael, his seventh child, would be born to one of those women.

On weekends when his father took him racing, Wendell Scott Jr., already imagining himself as a racing driver, soaked up the vivid details of his father's world — which drivers had faster cars than his daddy's, what made those cars faster, which competitors were racists, which were friendly. But while he was admiring his father's driving, his mechanical skills, and his courage in a daunting environment, Wendell Jr. was troubled over the conflicts in his parents' marriage and over the way his father would punish him.

"I think he wanted so much from me that he tried to beat me into perfection," Wendell Scott Jr. said. Sometimes, he added, the punishment left welts. "Time came for him to correct me, he did it in absolutely the wrong way." He was forming the view of his father that would be a powerful force in his life for many years — intense admiration, bordering on awe, entwined with strong threads of anger and fear.

Scott still supplemented his racing income by making occasional late-night runs with loads of moonshine whiskey. He and Mary also sold moonshine by the drink at their house — twenty-five cents for a small shot, fifty cents for a big shot, seventy-five cents for a good-sized glass. When Scott was away, Wendell Jr. said, "the drunks respected Mommy, and she would sell it till three and four o'clock in the morning." The police suspected that Scott hadn't quit the moonshine trade, so the Scotts kept the Mason jars of whiskey hidden inside the chimney, dangling from cords. Customers used a special knock on the door.

The chimney had a removable plate in the bedroom where Wendell Jr. and Frank slept. During the night, their mother or father would come in occasionally to pull up another jar, like a fisherman with a hand line. Sometimes, of course, the boys would haul up a jar themselves and sample the potent brew. They'd reel in the jar slowly and carefully, avoiding any clinking sounds that might alert a parent. "You'd drink it, and you'd catch your breath, and you'd say, 'Huuuuh!'" Wendell Scott Jr. said. "And then you'd get drunk instantly. And then you'd say, 'Give me another one!'"

## 10

### "He knew just how to hit me."

During the second half of the 1950s, Scott found himself thinking about how to move up in the hierarchy of his sport, perhaps to the national level. NASCAR's Daytona Beach event in February 1955 encouraged his ambitions.

The beach races, an unofficial all-star competition of that era, drew the elite of stock car drivers from all over the South, along with some stars from other circuits. Scott ran his sportsman-class '37 Ford against several dozen other drivers in a combined race for sportsman and modified cars. He placed ninth in his class, finishing ahead of some front-runners from NASCAR's top series, the Grand National circuit. By itself, one race didn't prove much, but it offered another promising sign that he could run respectably against the best in his sport.

Around the country, social change began to stir. The mutilation and murder of a fourteen-year-old black boy, Emmett Till, in August 1955, for allegedly whistling at a white woman in Mississippi helped to bring thousands of new supporters into the fledgling civil rights movement. The movement gained more momentum when black women in Montgomery, Alabama, began refusing in 1955 to give up their seats on buses to white people. First Claudette Colvin said no, then Mary Louise Smith, then Rosa Parks. For months, black riders boycotted the city bus system. Their lawsuit brought a historic victory a year later when the Supreme Court declared segregated buses unconstitutional.

Gradually, the old system's foundations were cracking. By now the nation's armed forces were mostly integrated. Professional baseball, football, and basketball had many black athletes, unlike NASCAR. For many black people, this was a time when the chance for a life not defined solely by race began to appear less improbable.

For Scott, though, sometimes it seemed that his color would never stop being an obstacle. Looking for experience and exposure outside his home state, he decided to try to race at one of the Deep South's most daunting tracks, Lakewood Park in Atlanta. About a week before the event (which was not NASCAR-sanctioned), Scott called the promoter to find out if a Negro would be allowed to compete. He didn't want to tow all the way to Georgia only to be turned away. The speedway was part of a city park, and at that time Atlanta had segregated parks. No problem, said the promoter, come on down — he'd get the Atlanta City Council to approve his participation. The council's minutes, however, give no indication that ever happened, and when Scott arrived on April 24, 1955, things didn't go as smoothly as promised.

The promoter "said, 'Man, I had a hell of a time getting permission to let Wen-*dell* run down here today.' He kept running his mouth, and I didn't say nothing, just let him talk.

"He said, 'By the way, which one of them is Wen-*dell*?'

"I said, 'You're talking to him.'"

The promoter took a closer look at the light-skinned Scott, then pointed toward a remote corner of the pit area. "He said, 'Well, I'll tell you what you do — you park way up there by yourself. You know, just don't mingle with these guys, and I believe everything will be all right.'"

Scott's problem, however, turned out not to be the other racers but the officials running the event. Just before practice began, they said they could not let him onto the track. The speedway's ambulance, they explained, was for white people only. If Scott was injured, there would be no way to take him to the hospital. The track would try to find a Negro ambulance, they said — maybe later that day, maybe some other time.

Hiding his anger behind the poker face he always brought to the racetrack, Scott decided to hang around and see what happened. Lakewood was fast and dangerous, banked at one end, flat at the other, particularly tough to master. At least a dozen drivers had died there. "A murderer," the *Atlanta Journal* called it, "one oval mile of sullen, vicious, ill-tempered red clay." For the next several hours, while the other drivers practiced and ran preliminary races, Scott stood on the sidelines. Without an opportunity to learn the track, he'd have little chance to do well in the feature race if he got to run. He wondered if the officials had cooked up the ambulance problem for just that reason.

As drivers were lining up for the feature, a second ambulance showed up, and Scott was allowed to start. A few minutes later, Alabama driver Roy Boddie, also new to Lakewood, lost control of his Cadillac-powered '38 Chevy while trying to pass two cars on the outside. He rolled over three times and came to rest upside down, unconscious, his skull fractured. Officials stopped the race so Boddie could be rushed to the hospital.

The white ambulance, however, wouldn't start. Its driver had overheated the engine and run down the battery by idling the vehicle with the air conditioner blasting. So Boddie had to be taken away in the black ambulance. For many years, Scott recalled, "I often wondered if I had of got hurt, and the black ambulance hadn't started, would they have taken me in the white ambulance? They probably would've let me lay there and die, back in them days."

This wasn't a good year for aspiring black drivers in Georgia, even those who were children. A few weeks later, two black boys tried to enter Augusta's Soap Box Derby. A "states' rights" group opposed their entries, the event's sponsors announced, and "a large percentage" of the white parents "indicated they did not care to have their sons participate" if the black boys raced. The derby was canceled.

Scott began keeping a close eye on the Grand National series, particularly Billy Myers's results. During Myers's first Grand National season in 1956, he ran up front often, finishing sixth in points with two wins. Scott remembered how well he'd raced against Myers at the Danville Fairgrounds. Perhaps he, too, could run competitively in Grand National. Scott's own statistics were encouraging — after a solid 1956 season, he placed sixth in NASCAR's sportsman standings for Virginia and fourteenth in nationwide points.

He began racing during the mid-1950s at Winston-Salem's Bowman Gray Stadium, the NASCAR track that had turned him away in 1952 because he was black. True to Bill France's promise, he was admitted without any problems. When he drove onto the track, the announcer introduced him as the Negro driver who'd been burning up the tracks in the Dixie Circuit, and the spectators applauded.

Bowman Gray drew much bigger crowds than Dixie Circuit tracks; some Grand National drivers raced there when they had a Saturday night free. A win there would have been especially satisfying. But Scott's cars lacked the power of the top competitors' machines, and passing on the narrow, flat, quarter-mile oval was particularly hard for a driver who felt that he couldn't risk bumping other cars out of the way. Generally Scott qualified and finished in midfield.

On June 30, 1957, however, Scott got a lucky break at Bowman Gray. The drivers drew for starting spots that night, and Scott got the pole position: the inside spot on the front row of the starting lineup. He would start inside of Tom Webster, who was leading in points with four feature wins. With ten thousand fans watching, Scott was determined to take advantage of his good luck.

Webster approached him before the race, Scott said, expecting Scott to defer to him. "He said, 'When they drop the green, just drop down a little bit, and I'll shoot right on by you.' I said, 'Okay.'" But Scott didn't mean it. When the starter waved the flag, he floored the gas and pulled away from Webster and everybody else. Over the next several laps Scott opened up a fifty-yard lead, "driving better and faster than we have ever seen him," as one motorsports writer would report. But his hopes for recognition at one of NASCAR's most popular tracks didn't last long. As he began lapping slower cars, one of them spun, colliding with Scott and allowing many cars to get by. Webster won; Scott finished twelfth. "It hurt me to my heart," he said.

Scott became a regular top-three finisher in 1957 at Roanoke, Virginia's, Starkey Speedway and at 501 Speedway in Brookneal, Virginia. He had strong finishes, too, at Norfolk and Martinsville, Virginia. On August 10, he battled for the feature win at Starkey against Bob McGinnis, who'd helped him to learn the Danville Fairgrounds track at his first race five years earlier.

Scott felt confident at Starkey — he'd placed second in the feature just a week before. He took the lead from McGinnis at the start. He held him off for ten laps. Both drivers were running as hard as they could, aware that Raymond Carter was behind them with the fastest car in the field. A car that was running a few laps off the leaders' pace slowed Scott down. McGinnis squeezed past him and led the next fourteen laps, with Scott close behind. They charged into the final turn on the last lap, and this time, it was Scott's turn to give the driving lesson. McGinnis slid wide, and Scott dove under him to win the race.

At Brookneal on September 22, Scott again ran right behind the leader as the feature came down to the final laps, and the leader was holding him up. One firm tap on his rear bumper and Scott could get the win. The problem was that the leader was Gordon Mangum, a burly, 265-pound truck driver with an explosive temper.

Five years earlier at Lynchburg, the diminutive Runt Harris had made the mistake of knocking Mangum out of his way. Mangum got out of his car and threw a big log from the infield onto the track; the flagman waved his red flag to stop the race. Then Mangum climbed into the 135-pound Harris's car and punched him in the face. When officials restarted the race, Mangum rammed Harris, wrecking both cars. The state police had to be called in "to settle the fracas and calm the crowd," the *Lynchburg News* reported.

While chasing Mangum, Scott considered his choices. "I could have won, but Gordon was mean, man," Scott said. "Only way I could get by him, I'd have to spin him. Gordon Mangum wasn't nobody to play with. You spin him out, you going to get your ass whipped; that's all there was to it. There ain't going to be no fight — you going to get your ass whipped. So I run second, and he won the race. He come over and thanked me for driving clean against him."

With six children and an unpredictable income, Scott sometimes found himself flat broke. One afternoon at the Charlotte Fairgrounds dirt track, he blew an engine and finished out of the money. Eleven-year-old Frank was with him, and they'd run out of food. Scott had only a few dollars in his pocket. His truck was low on fuel. They were getting hungry. He'd counted on prize money to buy gas and something to eat on the trip home. Scott went to the promoter, O. Bruton Smith, and asked, he said, for some "tow money" cash — the kind of payment, typically about fifteen dollars, that promoters often gave to racers who'd had a hard-luck day. "He wouldn't give it to me. I said, 'Well, just give me three dollars, just enough for gas to get home.'" Smith refused to give him anything, Scott said.

At a filling station near the track, Scott bought $1.80 worth of gas. And with the last money in his pocket, he bought a chicken-salad sandwich from a machine and gave it to Frank. The boy tried to give half of it back to his father. Scott, who had eaten little all day, insisted that Frank eat the whole sandwich. On the way home, his father held him close and told him not to worry. "He was telling me that one day things were going to be all right, that people were going to change, not everybody's like that — that type of thing," Frank Scott said. "Really almost apologizing for the man and what he'd done."

They ran out of gas several miles south of Danville that night in a gusting rainstorm. Scott got out with a length of rubber tubing to siphon some gas from the race car. From inside the truck, Frank watched through the water-streaked window as his father worked in the dark, the passing traffic soaking him in clouds of spray. Eventually, Scott got enough gas out of the race car to restart the truck, and he drove back to Danville in his soggy coveralls. Talking about that day years later, Frank Scott suddenly found his eyes filled with tears. The story had begun as just an anecdote, but as he spoke, it became for him a metaphor about his father's life.

Wendell Scott described Smith as "a real reb" — a term he used to describe white southerners of the old school — and said he still got angry every time he recalled the incident. "They didn't really want no blacks in racing then."

In today's business world of stock car racing, Smith, still a domineering presence in his eighties, has become the most powerful mogul of anyone outside the France family. His extensive holdings include a company that owns seven major speedways. Those tracks host twelve of the thirty-six races on NASCAR's Sprint Cup circuit. Asked about the Scott's account, Smith said, "I never remember him approaching me to borrow any money." He said he'd always treated Scott well.

Scott, like his father, had developed a strong appetite for gambling, particularly poker. After out-of-town races, sometimes he'd spend much of the night in a poker game. It wasn't unusual for Wendell Jr. and Frank to sit with their father at the poker table, to run out to get burgers and coffee for him. "We were confused by this," Wendell Jr. said. "Why is it that Daddy had maybe won a race and made a whole hundred dollars, a lot of money back then, so why aren't we going home and telling Mommy? Why's Daddy sitting there with the money, and usually losing?" After one race in Richmond, Scott lost his prize money trying to win a watch on a wheel of fortune, and driver Runt Harris had to loan him fifteen dollars so that he and Frank could get to the next race.

Scott also gambled, on occasion, with his reputation as a driver. Sometimes he chose to run less competitively, hoping to end the day with more prize money and an undamaged car, Wendell Jr. recalled. At some events, Scott would deliberately hang back in his heat race so that he'd be bumped into the consolation race; then he'd qualify for the feature by driving as hard as he could in the consolation. That way he could collect prize money in both preliminary races, though he'd start the feature behind the drivers who'd done well in the heats. Some tracks paid twenty dollars to win the consolation and only fifteen to win a heat. Scott's goal would be to win twenty-five dollars in the heat race and consolation before starting the feature. He'd go home with some extra money for household bills, but at the cost of somewhat compromising his stature as a driver.

To be sure, many racers chose to run conservatively at times, particularly when they realized that their car just couldn't keep up with the front-runners. As NASCAR's only black competitor, however, Scott was competing against racial stereotypes as well as for money. Consolation races, as the name suggests, carry some stigma of being a competition for also-rans. Inevitably, Scott was taking a bigger gamble than a white driver of being labeled a "stroker" — a mediocrity lacking the desire or courage to make an all-out effort.

Even with some sandbagging for financial reasons, Scott's overall results continued to improve. For the 1957 season, he placed third in NASCAR's sportsman points for Virginia, behind Ned Jarrett and Ray Hendrick — three positions higher than the previous year. At Norfolk Speedway, Scott also finished third in season points, with Jarrett and Hendrick in the first two spots.

Jarrett, who would go on to win two Grand National championships, was impressed by Scott's driving and the low-key way he handled himself. Scott's driving style on dirt, broadsliding his car into the turns, reminded Jarrett of the celebrated Curtis Turner and Junior Johnson. "If he'd had a big ego or been a publicity hound back then, I think it would have come back to haunt him," Jarrett said. "But the way he handled it, he just went about it quietly and didn't make any waves, and I think that worked to his advantage as to how he was perceived by the drivers and fans."

The 1958 season brought more good results. On April 20, Scott won the 501 Speedway feature, with his friend Earl Brooks placing second. It was a profitable weekend for Scott: The night before, he'd finished third in the Roanoke feature. In August, a new track called 58 Speedway opened outside Danville, and Scott invited all his friends to come and root for him.

"Wendell Scott, who once said he would rather win a feature race for the local fans than to eat when he was hungry, got his wish," the *Danville Commercial Appeal* reported. "Wendell with his new sportsman car outran the field of 19 sportsman cars to win the feature event and put $100 in his pocket." Later on in the event, Scott got the chance to return a favor to Brooks, who had protected him from fights in his early racing years. Brooks was entered in the amateur class, the event's final race. But the amateur field was too small, so the promoter opened the field to sportsman cars as well. Scott ran the race and could easily have won again, he said, but he hung back in second place and let Brooks take the victory.

One day the Scotts' friend Carl Simpson stopped by for a casual visit and found the family in emotional turmoil. "Frankie told me, 'Man, things are bad around here. Mom and Dad may be about to separate.'" Scott had finally revealed to his wife that he had fathered a son, Michael, by another woman. Recently the boy's mother had been murdered, leaving Michael a ward of the state. Scott had left for North Carolina to take custody of the boy and bring him back to Danville.

Before Scott drove away, he "went to Mary and told her all about it. She didn't know anything about this lady or the baby. And he said, 'I got to go get him,'" Simpson recalled.

"It wasn't long after I got there that day that Wendell came home with him. Little bitty joker, about three years old. Looked just like Wendell.

"Wendell told me, 'I just can't throw him away.' He accepted responsibility at the risk of losing his wife."

To Scott's good fortune, neither his infidelities nor his consuming preoccupation with racing would destroy his marriage. Mary Scott remained loyal and loving, the bond between them intense. She drew strength from her religious faith. They were a couple whose affinity was obvious to casual acquaintances. They could complete each other's sentences and communicate an involved train of thought with the lift of an eyebrow. Mary Scott accepted Michael, and he became part of the family.

Mary agreed that Michael could live down the street with Scott's mother, in the second family house that Scott had built next to his garage. Mary Scott's nature, Simpson said, was "more forgiving than most of us." Many years later, after Scott's death, Simpson recalled her making one of her rare comments about Scott's infidelity: "She said, 'Wendell was a real man, but he had a weakness, and it was women.'"

While the Scotts were a close family, they went through more episodes of turmoil as Wendell Jr. grew into a rebellious adolescence. Often, his emotions gave him a thrashing. He'd be happy and mischievous, and then abruptly a dark mood or wounded feeling would hit him like a punch. He wondered if his father loved racing more than he loved him.

Sometimes, he said, he ran away from home for short periods after clashes with his father. "I'd rebel. If it got to be a bit too much, I would leave. I learned to hustle pool as a kid as a result of leaving home because he was so furious sometimes. He wasn't as stern with Frankie. I was the oldest son, I was the namesake, and I was reticent. There were certain parts of me that he couldn't figure out, which bothered him, because he always wondered what I was thinking about him, about his lifestyle."

Although Scott had made many white friends during his racing career, he still had to wonder at every race if some prejudiced driver would try to wreck him. Two of the most blatant examples of deliberate dirty driving against Scott took place at Bowman Gray Stadium — both involving the same driver. The stadium's racing program was run by promoters Bill France and his partner Alvin Hawkins. In neither incident, however, did Scott get any support from France or other NASCAR officials.

The driver who wrecked Scott both times was Shorty York, well known on the circuit for his hostility toward black people. York ran a gas station in Mocksville, North Carolina. "He didn't like colored people at all," Scott said. "He wouldn't even sell colored people gas. They'd pull up there, he'd tell 'em, keep on going."

Twice, York intentionally slammed his front bumper into the rear of Scott's car and rolled him over, Scott said, first in 1958, then again in an identical incident a year later. "He'd catch me just right when I was in a turn and flip me over." One of the rollovers tore the front axle and both front wheels off Scott's car.

Several years earlier, France had written his letter warning drivers they would be suspended for such conduct. This time, no such warnings were issued. Scott never found out why. He stuck to his usual practice of keeping quiet about his problems and never spoke to France about the crashes. He didn't confront York.

"He was a hell of a driver," Scott recalled sarcastically. "I ain't gonna take that away from him. He knew just how to hit me."

## 11

### "If he had the power, he'd come on at you."

Scott's successes at Virginia tracks got the attention of a well-to-do car owner, Monroe Shook of Keysville, some seventy miles from Danville. Shook wanted to win NASCAR's sportsman-class championship for the state of Virginia, and he hired Scott as his driver for the 1959 season.

Unlike Scott's rough-edged race cars, the Shook team's Ford coupe had a flawless body, painted a lustrous ivory. Monroe's cousin, Shorty Shook, worked as the team's meticulous mechanic. Every time he used a wrench, Shorty would wipe off every smudge and put it away in exactly the same place. "I loved to touch that car — it seemed to glow," Wendell Jr. said. "When you raised the hood, even the nuts and bolts were perfectly clean. The floor in their shop, you could eat breakfast on it. It was a new experience for us, culture shock."

Scott regularly finished in the top five in features at several tracks, though Shook's car wasn't quite as fast as he'd hoped. A trucking company owner, Shook was a no-nonsense executive, more aloof and less friendly than the white car owners Scott had driven for in the past. Shorty, though, was always cheerful and supportive. He'd stop work to joke with Scott's sons, greeting them with an affectionate rub on their heads. The Scotts never saw any reluctance by Shorty to take suggestions from a black driver about how to set up the car. The team seemed to be working well. After several races, Monroe Shook raised Scott's share of the prize money from 40 percent to 50. Scott hoped his relationship with Shook would take him to NASCAR's top level. For the following season, 1960, Shook planned to campaign a Grand National car. He wanted to win races, and he'd hired racer Rex White, a star on the Grand National circuit, to build a highly competitive race car. White already had his own Grand National car, and no driver had been named for the new car White was building for Shook. Scott thought he would get the nod.

A feature race at Virginia's South Boston Speedway that summer would seal Shook's decision. Early in the race, Scott put Shook's car right on the back bumper of the race leader, Gip Gibson. Lap after lap, Scott dogged Gibson as their cars pulled away from the rest of the field. But Scott couldn't get past him. South Boston was a high-banked dirt track then, and Gibson's flamboyant, broadsliding style blocked the racing line in every turn.

Wendell Scott Jr. watched with admiration as the two men slid their cars around the fast turns inches apart, like skaters in a synchronized routine. He saw that Gibson was holding his father up. If Scott would just nudge Gibson's car out of the way, he could win his first feature of the year. Wendell Jr. wondered if his father, pursuing a state championship and a Grand National ride, would put aside his long-standing practice of avoiding deliberate contact.

For Wendell Scott Sr., the situation had several complications. There was the perennial racial question — how aggressively could NASCAR's only black racer afford to drive? Besides that, there was the fact that Scott liked Gibson, who'd shown that he understood and sympathized with Scott's unique problems in this white man's sport.

Early in Scott's career, a driver at Zion Crossroads had bragged that he'd intimidated Scott with an aggressive pass. Gibson, often a winner at the track, gave the man a scornful rebuke. "He told him, 'Wendell Scott let you outrun him, but not because he was scared of you — he was scared about his career,'" Wendell Scott Jr. recalled.

Would Scott now drive against Gibson the way Shorty York had driven against Scott? Was a little nudge to the rear bumper different from deliberately wrecking someone? The outcome could be the same. If a black driver did the nudging and the crowd got ugly, who would take his side?

Scott was also coping with another distraction: Unlike other cars he'd driven, Shook's had a hand pump for the engine's fuel pressure. While chasing Gibson, Scott had to watch a pressure gauge and work the pump whenever the needle began to drop. With only a few laps to go, Gibson suddenly lost traction, spun in a full circle, and came to a stop on the track. At the same time, Scott abruptly slowed and stopped beside Gibson. For a few moments, both cars sat motionless while everyone stared in astonishment. Then they began moving again, Gibson still just ahead of Scott, and they finished the race that way — Gibson first, Scott second.

Monroe Shook was furious. "He's cussing Daddy out — 'Why in hell did Wendell let him go? I can't afford to invest in him,'" said Wendell Jr. "Gip told Daddy after the race, 'I thought you had me.'

"I believe Daddy let him go. When Daddy came in, he said, 'I couldn't get him.'

"I told him, 'I thought you could.'

"Daddy said, 'The damn fuel pressure kept dropping.'" The engine had died, his father claimed, and he couldn't restart it in time to beat Gibson.

"I was a guy that didn't spin out nobody," Scott said years later, "and I was so busy trying to run fair, I let my pressure run out." Then the engine wouldn't fire until Gibson already was rolling. "They thought I sat there and waited on him, and they got angry with me."

Shorty Shook tried to persuade Monroe that Scott deserved the benefit of the doubt. "Shorty was arguing — he was pro-Daddy," Wendell Scott Jr. said. "He was saying, 'Man, the guy did all he could.'"

That wasn't the prevailing opinion, though. "The general consensus," Wendell Scott Jr. said, "was that Daddy let him go."

The incident cost Scott the confidence of Monroe Shook. He fired Scott as his driver. "Daddy was insulted and hurt," Wendell Scott Jr. said. "He said to hell with Shook."

For his new driver, Shook brought in a top name in Virginia racing circles, Eddie Crouse of Richmond, often a winner in NASCAR's modified division, the class for the fastest, most sophisticated cars in regional-level racing. Crouse would go on to win two national NASCAR championships in such cars. When he drove Shook's car, however, Crouse said he could never get it to perform any better than Scott had. "It wasn't a feature winner," Crouse said. "It was a first-five finisher, and that's what Wendell done with it. Wendell was a good, fast driver. If he had the power, he'd come on at you."

Scott went back to driving his own sportsman car. He continued finishing up front in feature races and winning in heats. At Richmond's Southside Speedway, Scott was particularly successful, often placing well in features. Southside was a short, flat track that rewarded a sensitive driving touch. Scott's sons, sensing that he might have a chance at the track's championship, kept urging him to be consistent, to make sure he finished every race, to keep on collecting points.

Later in the season, after Crouse had done all he could with Shook's car, Shook invited Scott to come back and drive for him again, and they had some strong finishes. But the team's chemistry wasn't the same, and the possibility of Scott's driving Shook's new Grand National car the following year wasn't mentioned.

At the end of the 1959 season, Scott's consistent finishes near the front of the field paid off. He won both the NASCAR sportsman championship for the state of Virginia and the season championship in the sportsman class at Southside Speedway. "I never won a feature that whole year," Scott recalled. In auto racing, however, a driver with a steady record of up-front finishes often collects more points for the season than a competitor who scores brilliant wins but sometimes fails to finish. "I always finished so good, my points counted up." As a state champion, Scott won a guaranteed starting spot and expense money for NASCAR's 250-mile race for modified and sportsman cars on February 13, 1960, at an enormous racing facility that Bill France had opened a year earlier: Daytona International Speedway, the Mount Everest of the stock car world. Scott's race would be a preliminary event to the next day's Daytona 500 for NASCAR's top circuit, the Grand National series.

For years, France had aspired to create the country's fastest, most exciting speedway — ideally, one that would outclass the historic Indianapolis Motor Speedway. France had been rudely ejected from that track in 1954, one day before the Indy 500. A security guard told him that "the front office" had revoked his admission pass to the speedway. The facility's owner, Tony Hulman, later apologized, but the reason for the insulting treatment of France was never explained. France knew that many insiders in the Indy establishment considered NASCAR an inferior, low-class form of racing, and the humiliating incident left him determined to build a speedway at least as prestigious as Indianapolis.

As the colossus of France's expanding business of NASCAR racing, the

Daytona track represented the biggest reward yet of his gift for realizing his ambitions, and of his growing political savvy. France's flag-waving politics helped him to get along comfortably with leading southern politicians of the time, who equated liberals with forced racial change and wasteful social spending. "Bill was a real conservative when it came to giveaway programs," said one friend, Alabama political operative Charles Snider. "He didn't like giveaway programs."

That didn't mean, however, that France opposed government subsidies for speedways. He had adroitly played the politicians of Daytona Beach against those of Palm Beach County in a competition over which municipality would give his project the most lucrative package of governmental benefits. He built the speedway under a tax-free, low-rent lease on 443 acres of public land.

His Daytona venture represented an early example of something that would become a recurring theme in France's career: his affinity for powerful political figures identified with extreme-right politics, racial prejudice, or both. By France's account, the crucial funding for his Daytona project came about because of his close personal relationship with the controversial Texas oil mogul Clint Murchison Jr. Over the years, the list of similar friendships France cultivated would include such polarizing figures as General Curtis LeMay, an ultra-hawk best known for advocating the aggressive American use of nuclear bombs, and some of the South's most harshly segregationist politicians, including Alabama governor George Wallace and South Carolina congressman L. Mendel Rivers.

Murchison was the second-generation tycoon of a business dynasty. The family business's alleged involvement with official corruption, far-right politics, and organized crime figured in various government investigations and public controversies during the 1950s and '60s. France's Daytona venture was strapped for money when Murchison's Lamar Life Insurance Co. put up six hundred thousand dollars in new financing. Without "Murchison's financial clout," France said, "we would never have accomplished the job of building Daytona Speedway as it is today."

The controversies surrounding Murchison included racial matters. A Murchison company closely related to the one that financed the Daytona track lost its federal license to run Mississippi's largest television station after a court battle over its racist practices. Lamar Life Broadcasting in Jackson refused to sell ads to black candidates, aired Ku Klux Klan programs, suppressed civil rights news, and routinely blanked out the images of black leaders such as Thurgood Marshall from network broadcasts.

Documents in the court proceedings include a chilling account from a local activist, Robert Smith, a black Methodist minister who owned a grocery store. He said that because he criticized the Murchison company, one of its executives, a white supremacist active in the local White Citizens' Council, walked him to the edge of the Pearl River, put his arm around him, and told him "my home and my place of business would likely be blown up and that my body would likely be found floating in the river."

Even for NASCAR's best drivers, their first sight of the immense Daytona speedway inspired awe and, some admitted, a touch of fear. The track is two and a half miles long with turns banked at thirty-one degrees, so steep a person can barely walk up them. "There wasn't a man there who wasn't scared to death of the place," said Lee Petty, Richard Petty's father and the winner of the first Daytona 500 in 1959. ". . . [W]e were all rookies going thirty to forty miles an hour faster than we had ever gone before."

Scott built a 1953 Ford especially for his first Daytona race. He took the green flag in a huge starting field of seventy-three cars dating from the 1930s, 1940s, and 1950s. Some became wickedly unstable as they headed into the turns flat-out in tight packs at up to 140 miles an hour. At the time nobody understood the aerodynamic forces acting on stock cars at such speeds. Drivers would fly into the turns and find their front end abruptly becoming light and the car plowing toward the wall. Some of the 1930s vehicles would suddenly jump a full lane sideways as their clamshell fenders caught the air, lifting the front wheels.

On the first lap of Scott's race, a driver's spin in turn four touched off a chain reaction of crashes and flips that turned into one of the biggest pileups in motorsports history. Suddenly cars were going backward, sideways, and flying through the air. Scott dodged several crashes, then tried to avoid another by swerving left down the steep banking. His car rolled over

— he wasn't sure how many times — and came to rest on its wheels in the infield. Scott was uninjured, but his car was badly battered, the windshield smashed. He was among the more fortunate. Scattered around him when NASCAR stopped the race were thirty-six other wrecked cars, twelve of them completely demolished. All of the drivers survived, but eight had to be rushed to the hospital.

Scott's sons assumed that their father, with a damaged car and no spare windshield, would call it a day. But Scott climbed out of his car already planning how to get back in competition. With half of the field involved in the wreck, NASCAR waived the usual ban on repairing cars during a red-flag time-out. The boys scrambled to help Scott, wondering what he would do about the missing windshield. At a tense time like this, they knew it was best not to ask questions. A few minutes before the restart, they got their answer. Scott popped out the car's rear window glass and wired it into place as a makeshift windshield. It wasn't a perfect fit, but it would deflect enough air to make the car drivable.

The pits at Daytona were full of men who were strangers to the Scotts, many from racing teams backed by serious money. There were top-flight modified teams from all over the East Coast. Some of the Grand National circuit's racers, who would run tomorrow's Daytona 500, were watching, too. Wendell Jr. thought he saw quite a few looks of surprise and respect as his father rolled down the pit lane to restart the race in his wounded Ford, only thirty-nine minutes after he'd rolled over at more than a hundred miles an hour. The engine blew before the race was over, but to Wendell Jr., that hardly mattered. They'd been to Daytona, the sport's largest and fastest speedway, and they'd shown the elite of NASCAR that they were serious racers. "They were looking at us like we were *somebody* — somebody they might have to deal with," he said.

The respect the Scotts had earned at Daytona, of course, didn't affect the way they were treated during their travels through the South of the early 1960s. In 1960, civil rights activists began conducting sit-ins and going to jail to protest segregation at southern lunch counters. Change came slowly, however, and for years Scott had to assume he should stay out of white restaurants. Some would sell take-out meals to blacks if they went around back to the kitchen door. But everyone knew that kitchen workers sometimes spit in those meals.

On road trips, Scott's white racing friends, such as Carl Simpson, had to go in and get the food while Scott and his black friends or family members waited in the truck, trying to stay out of sight. Simpson had a deep affection and respect for the Scotts, and this experience always left him angry and sad. In the racing world, Scott had become a state champion, but out on the highways, he still had to make sure his dinner didn't include a white man's saliva.

# 12

## "We're movin' up."

At thirty-nine, Scott had reached a point where he needed to think hard about what to do next with his career. He spent 1960 racing in NASCAR's modified division. The cost of fielding a competitive car in this fast-growing class was rising dramatically. As in the previous season, Scott's cars were fast enough to finish well in features, not quite fast enough to win.

His performances at South Boston in Virginia were typical. At that track Scott drove for Bob Neal, one of the white car owners who'd helped him early in his career. Neal had a Plymouth coupe with a 361 Chrysler hemi engine and two four-barrel carburetors. Scott could finish features in the top five and win occasional heat races and consolations, but the feature winners such as Eddie Crouse and Ray Hendrick had fuel-injected engines in cars with a mechanical superiority that Neal simply couldn't afford.

The track championship Scott had won at Richmond earned him an invitation to a prestigious annual race of champions at the 1.5-mile speedway in Trenton, New Jersey. The Scotts found the Trenton weekend both discouraging and enlightening. Modified racing in the Northeast had become especially popular and sophisticated. They saw sleek, low, showpiece modifieds that looked almost as exotic as Indianapolis cars. Scott, uncompetitive in the race, was proud just to get one of the trophies awarded to everyone who qualified, on a day when other aspirants failed even to make the field.

"We had no business being there," Wendell Scott Jr. said. "We were absolutely, totally outclassed."

Monroe Shook, meanwhile, had chosen Emanuel Zervakis instead of Scott to drive his Grand National car. Rex White, who would win the 1960 Grand National championship, had built Shook's Chevrolet as an identical sister car to his own factory-backed Chevy. "Everything on Monroe's car was identical to mine," White said.

Zervakis ran a limited Grand National schedule with Shook in 1960, concentrating on the larger speedways. He placed tenth in the Daytona 500. He had top-ten finishes in nine of the eleven other Grand Nationals he started. His best was a fourth in NASCAR's second most prestigious race, the Southern 500 at South Carolina's Darlington Raceway.

For Scott, Zervakis's Grand National successes were somewhat painful to follow. He'd dueled closely with Zervakis in modified and sportsman races in Virginia. Now Zervakis was making a national reputation in a car that Scott thought he should be driving. Scott's decision not to bump Gip Gibson out of his way at South Boston evidently had cost him one of the more competitive rides in NASCAR's top series. "Whether Wendell would have showed as much as Emanuel did, I don't know," Rex White said. "But he would have been in a good piece of equipment and had the potential to run up front."

When Zervakis's Grand National schedule allowed, he also drove modifieds at South Boston. Scott's best feature finish there was a second place on July 9 — right behind Zervakis. "I sat on his bumper from flag to flag," Scott said. "We left the field, but I couldn't outrun him. Emanuel was a hell of a driver, man, but we was right there on him."

Scott had been racing sportsman and modified cars for nine seasons. Since he'd won his first heat race in 1952, he'd been keeping a mental count of his wins — heats, consolations, and features — and he was proud of the total: 128. Thanks to consistency, and to running a large number of races, Scott finished the 1960 season ranked sixth in NASCAR's national points for the modified division, one spot ahead of the renowned Ray Hendrick, often a dominant competitor in the class.

Without costly new cars, however, he'd be unlikely to do that well again. At Trenton, those expensive, alcohol-burning, state-of-the-art modifieds had looked, sounded, and even smelled much fiercer than any car Scott could reasonably expect to acquire. If he stayed in the modified division, he'd likely be just an easy snack for this new breed of predators. Also, stock car racing was evolving toward newer-model cars, so even if he could somehow make a respectable showing in modifieds, that no longer seemed to be a sure path to wider recognition.

Scott kept his plans to himself, but Wendell Jr. understood what his father was thinking. "He's saying to himself, 'Okay, where I'm at financially, this is all I can do — I can win locally at certain tracks; I can finish second and third at certain tracks. I ain't gonna spend no more money trying to get better at doing the same thing.'"

Scott drove down to Charlotte to see Buck Baker, a Grand National driver with a used Chevrolet race car for sale. An accomplished veteran, Baker was a stocky, swaggering man who reminded some admirers of a Wild West gunslinger. Like Scott, he'd been a whiskey runner before taking up racing. He carried pistols and blackjacks, and he had a formidable mean streak. By his own account, Baker once blackjacked a driver who'd tangled with him on a track in Ona, West Virginia. Then, as the man crawled around in a daze, Baker said he just barely restrained himself from shooting him with a .44 magnum. It was very hard, Baker said, to get his finger to relax its pressure on the trigger. Another time, annoyed by a newspaper story, Baker sought out the reporter and slugged him.

For Scott, Baker wasn't necessarily the best choice for a used-car deal. "Buck didn't like Wendell," Rex White said. "In fact, Buck was the most open about not liking Wendell of any of the drivers." White recalled Baker frequently using the word *nigger* and other slurs when speaking of black people.

For all of Baker's barbed edges, however, it was reasonable to think that one of his former cars might well be competitive. He'd won two Grand National championships. In the past season, he'd won twice, finished fifteen times in the top five, and placed fourth in points. Scott bought the Chevy, not one of Baker's top cars, for two thousand dollars.

Margaret Baker, Buck's wife at the time, said Scott told them the money came from moonshine profits. "Buck asked if he wanted a receipt," she said. "Wendell said, 'Hell, no. The government don't know I even got this money.'"

Scott towed his new race car back to Danville. The family came out to look it over, and to consider what it meant. Without Scott saying a word, they knew when they saw the big Chevy that they were going Grand National racing, and that their lives would become quite different.

As a move for his career and family, Scott's decision to go into Grand National was a gambler's choice. He was doing this without any encouragement from NASCAR's leadership, hoping that Bill France's handshake promise of six years ago — that he would be treated like any other NASCAR driver — still carried some weight. He'd be the only black driver in a series that ran many of its races deep in the segregated South, in places where prejudice ran far stronger than in Virginia.

That was just one of the large obstacles the Scotts would face. Without a sponsor or professional crew, they'd be competing on a circuit where financial backing from an auto manufacturer was vital to success. They would be taking on competitors with big reputations and strong teams, drivers such as Baker, Lee Petty, Ned Jarrett, and Junior Johnson. They'd be attempting this with a used car that might or might not be competitive.

Standing in the driveway that day, Scott's family could see that the Chevy looked somewhat worn. Baker had raced the car during the late '50s in two NASCAR divisions, one for Grand National sedans, the other for convertibles. He would cut off the top for a convertible race, weld it back on for a Grand National, then cut it off again for the next convertible race. The car had endured much; as Rex White said, "It was pretty well used up by the time Wendell got it."

"We're movin' up," Scott told his family.

They looked at Scott and his Chevy, both of them no longer young, and they smiled to hide their doubts.

# 13

## "They didn't want to use the word *Wendell*."

When Jackie Robinson joined major-league baseball in 1947, top officials of the sport made it clear to the public that they welcomed him and wanted him treated fairly. But when Wendell Scott drove in his first Grand National race on March 4, 1961, the officials in charge didn't even want the crowd to know he was there.

Scott's debut in NASCAR's major league took place in South Carolina, at the half-mile dirt track in Spartanburg. The promoter, Joe Littlejohn, a close friend of Bill France, decided the spectators shouldn't be told that a black driver was competing, and NASCAR went along with his wishes. "Joe was worried because this was the first time that many people in the Carolinas had ever seen a black driver," said a former NASCAR official who helped to run the event and would discuss the matter only anonymously.

As a landmark for NASCAR, Scott's arrival as the first black driver to become a regular Grand National competitor echoed Robinson's historic first game as a Brooklyn Dodger. Clearly, this was a newsworthy development, and some publicity might have helped Scott. The integration of baseball took place under extensive media coverage, which helped to hold the sport's leaders accountable for how Robinson was treated. For Scott, however, a news blackout preceded his first race on NASCAR's premier circuit. During the week before the event, Spartanburg's two newspapers interviewed Littlejohn and published four stories previewing the race and discussing who had entered. There was no mention of a black driver joining the circuit, and Scott's name wasn't included.

Scott left his family at home for the Spartanburg event. He traveled with just one friend, the burly Earl Brooks, who had helped to protect him from trouble during his early racing years. During practice, Scott found the big Chevy a handful to drive, much clumsier than his lightweight sportsman cars. Grand National cars had no power steering then. "I thought I had a freight train on my hands," he said. Still, he managed to qualify ninth out of eighteen cars.

In the racial atmosphere of early-1960s South Carolina, Scott's qualifying performance, though undistinguished, still had the potential to anger some of the six thousand fans at the Piedmont Interstate Fairgrounds. Some would not have been pleased that a Negro — even worse, a Negro rookie — had outperformed nine white men. Littlejohn told the track announcer to blur Scott's identity when he broadcast the drivers' names before the race, the former NASCAR official said.

Among knowledgeable stock car fans, "Wendell Scott was fairly well known — people knew of Wendell," the former official said. "So they introduced him as W.D. Scott. They didn't want to use the word *Wendell* because that might have given it away."

Any concerns about trouble from the crowd if Scott ran well in the race were put to rest early. A piston failed in his Chevy, and Scott finished seventeenth, second to last. The next day's newspaper coverage didn't mention that a black driver had competed, though Scott's real name did appear in tiny agate type in the standings.

Littlejohn, a prosperous local businessman, had been friends for many years with Bill France. In the late 1930s, France helped Littlejohn promote his first race at Spartanburg. A decade later, Littlejohn was among the promoters who worked with France to organize NASCAR.

After France opened Daytona International Speedway in 1959, he and Littlejohn began planning a major business venture, one that made good public relations in South Carolina particularly important. They wanted to build the country's largest superspeedway, a track even longer and faster than Daytona, in the Spartanburg area. Driver Rex White, who had his racing shop in Spartanburg, recalled Littlejohn talking about the proposed new track not long after Daytona opened. "Joe was good buddies with Bill France, and I remember him talking about it way back in the early '60s," White said. "Joe had his eye on a piece of property, maybe owned some part of it."

By this time, the Grand National series had begun its transition from the dirt tracks of its early years to the superspeedways of the modern era.

At superspeedways (the racing industry's term for paved ovals at least one mile long) the cars went much faster, crowds were much bigger, and promoters didn't have to worry about dust, the unpredictable curse of operating a dirt track. At Scott's first Grand National, the dust coated many spectators so heavily that they looked "like wooden Indians," the *Spartanburg Herald* reported. Only the most ardent of fans would regularly pay money to undergo this experience.

For France, an ownership stake in another superspeedway became a central priority in the 1960s, the next big step he envisioned for the growth of his business. Already the eight Grand National races held at four such tracks — Darlington, Daytona, Charlotte, and Atlanta — had become the top events on NASCAR's calendar. As matters stood now, however, six of those races took place at superspeedways owned by other people. France wanted a larger slice of this pie.

As he'd learned at Daytona, a new superspeedway venture requires many millions of dollars' worth of highway construction, tax breaks, and other favorable government decisions. The politically savvy France cultivated the goodwill of two of South Carolina's most influential politicians, who were also among the South's most prominent and adamant segregationists. US senator Strom Thurmond, formerly the state's governor, and Charleston congressman L. Mendel Rivers, who was becoming one of Capitol Hill's most powerful lawmakers, were often showcased in high-visibility roles as honorary officials at NASCAR's biggest races, waving to crowds from pace cars and parade floats, their photos featured prominently in the programs.

Even among southern politicians of the time, Thurmond and Rivers stood out for their hard-line racism. "There's not enough troops in the Army to force the southern people to break down segregation and admit the nigger race into our theaters, into our swimming pools, into our homes, and into our churches," Thurmond shouted to thunderous applause while running for president in 1948 as a third-party segregationist candidate. (At that time, Thurmond's own biracial daughter was twenty-two. He had fathered her in 1925, when he was twenty-two, with a sixteen-year-old black maid in his parents' home. He successfully concealed their relationship throughout his long career as a revered figure among white supremacists.)

Rivers regularly delivered the most inflammatory rhetoric of all the regular speakers at meetings of Charleston's White Citizens' Councils, a militant pro-segregation organization that operated in several southern states as a white-collar alternative to the Klan. In impassioned speeches, Rivers would tell council members that the Supreme Court and the NAACP were in "an unholy alliance to destroy white civilization and the orderly way of life as it is known in the South." He called the NAACP a communist group seeking "mongrelization" of the races. His son, L. Mendel Rivers Jr., a lawyer and former family court judge, wrote in a book of family reminiscences that his father "was a racist by any definition . . . He made no pretense of his beliefs, shared by most white Southerners, that the Negro was not a member of the human race . . . He used the word 'niggah' as part of his daily vocabulary and saw no shame in it."

France's success in courting such politicians as Thurmond and Rivers illustrated his mastery at developing political connections that could help NASCAR to grow, Rex White said. "He knew how to get things done, and it's good to know people like that. When you're wanting to build a racetrack, you got to have a little help from the politicians to get it cleared so you can build. He always went to work on that high up — way up at the top."

Scott would remember another South Carolina race as part of his rookie education in Grand National. As he sped down the backstretch of the half-mile dirt track in Columbia on April 20, 1961, his Chevrolet suddenly broke into two parts. Both rails of the frame snapped, right behind the rear axle. Everything connected to those frame rails — the trunk, the gas tank, the rest of the rear bodywork — abruptly tore itself away from the rest of the car.

His sons looked on from the pits, astounded, as the detached rear portion of the Chevy bounced down the track a few yards behind the rest of the car. For a moment, Scott didn't understand what was happening, either. Briefly, the car kept on rolling, the engine still ran, and for a few seconds the broken-off rear parts tagged along behind, pulled along by the fuel line. Then the fuel line broke, the engine died, and the Chevy came to a stop.

Scott climbed out and began to look over the car that had seemed, back in Buck Baker's shop, to be a good deal for the money. Now, examining the broken frame, noticing that the damage didn't look entirely fresh, Scott had to conclude that maybe he'd been taken. "It was a pile of junk," he said.

He'd expected Grand National to be more cutthroat than the local speedways of Virginia, but even so, this was a tough welcome to the series. Of course, any used racing car can have some unnoticed flaw. But in this situation, Scott had been the victim of a deception.

When Baker still owned the car, somebody had discovered that the frame had begun to crack and, instead of welding up the cracks, concealed them with body filler. Baker claimed that a crewman, whom he wouldn't identify, had done this without his knowledge. "I had a guy that I had just hired not too long before," Baker said, "and the frame had a crack in it, and this guy had put Bondo over this crack and ground it down and took a can of flat black and painted it." He offered no explanation for why a crewman would do that.

In any case, Scott followed his usual practice of sidestepping controversy and did not talk to Baker about the incident; the question of what Baker knew about the frame never came up between them. Scott missed the next two races while he tore down and repaired the Chevy.

The civil rights movement gained momentum in the spring of 1961, inflaming prejudices, sometimes sparking violence. White mobs in Alabama attacked Trailways buses carrying Freedom Riders, who were civil rights activists, both black and white, trying to integrate bus travel. Near Anniston, a mob burned a bus; the riders were lucky to escape alive. In Birmingham, the police gave the mob fifteen minutes to assault the riders before intervening. The attack left one rider paralyzed for life.

On May 21, with Freedom Rider stories on front pages across the country, Scott arrived with Wendell Jr. at Charlotte Motor Speedway, where he hoped to qualify for his first Grand National race on a superspeedway. As they approached the gate to the pits, towing the race car, a portly man in a NASCAR uniform, Norris Friel, hurried up to intercept them, wheezing as he jogged. He ordered them to stop.

Friel, NASCAR's chief of technical inspections, had a blunt instrument of a personality. A gruff, abrupt man, he liked to announce that he'd just taken some extra "mean pills." He came across, Frank Scott said, as "one of the toughest old iron-head guys you ever seen." Friel's style was to bark out an order, turn his back, and walk away, and that's how he handled Scott's presence at Charlotte.

"I didn't get no further than the front gate," Scott said. "He told me, 'Take that pile of junk back up the road.' Wouldn't even let me in the track." The Scotts saw that there would be no arguing with Friel, who offered no explanation. They knew they couldn't get his decision overruled. Friel and Bill France were old, close friends.

The experience seemed like a troubling replay of the first time Scott had ever tried to race in NASCAR, nine years before, when officials turned him away at the races France was promoting at Bowman Gray Stadium. The Scotts wondered if Friel thought their Chevy looked too scruffy. NASCAR put more emphasis on car appearance at major superspeedway events. But Scott and his son saw other low-budget drivers getting ready for qualifying whose cars looked no better than theirs.

Some drivers had told Scott that Friel was fair-minded, but from what he had done today, or been told to do, Scott could reach only one conclusion: "It was a racial issue." They left the speedway and drove back to Danville.

## 14

### "A standoffish position."

Scott decided to skip the next superspeedway race, the July 4 event at Daytona. That was too long a haul to risk being turned away again. For now, he'd stick to the smaller events. He scored his first top-ten finishes in June — three in a row: tenth at Norwood, Massachusetts; ninth at Hartsville, South Carolina; eighth at Roanoke.

He raced at Bristol, Tennessee, in July, bringing along his sons and one of their uncles as his crew. As often happened, they'd gone to Bristol without knowing where they would sleep. "Normally we'd find out where we could stay from black people we met at the track, people doing custodial work and so on," Wendell Jr. said. "But that day, we did not see one black person."

The night before the race, they wound up sleeping in an open field near the speedway. During the night, Wendell Jr.'s uncle shook him awake. "He said, 'Brother, look, don't get scared, but I've got something to tell you.'

"I said, 'What is it?'

"He said, 'It's a bear, not far from us.'

"I turned over and saw that humongous bear, and all I remember is the wind hitting me in the face, I ran so fast."

For their subsequent Bristol races they stayed at a black honky-tonk hotel next to the railroad tracks, grateful that the only things waking them up were the passing trains and the raucous chatter of prostitutes and their customers.

As Labor Day approached, Scott sent in his entry form for the Southern 500 at Darlington Raceway. This race was one of NASCAR's most popular and prestigious events. Fans loved the Southern 500 both as a uniquely difficult, exciting race and as an unapologetic celebration of the redneck, Confederate-flag-waving, hard-partying side of southern life.

Darlington had played an important role in NASCAR's success since 1950, when local businessmen opened the track among the cotton and tobacco fields of central South Carolina. Mrs. Strom Thurmond had cut the opening-day ribbon. They'd built the facility with nine thousand seats, but about twenty thousand people showed up for NASCAR's first superspeedway race.

For drivers, Darlington was by far the Grand National circuit's most treacherous speedway. The track, a mile and three-eighths long, had narrow, high-banked turns where passing was tricky. The cars often brushed the outside guardrails while exiting the turns, leaving scrapes along the right side. This "Darlington stripe" became a mark of valor, stock car racing's version of the dueling scar.

The Klan was active around Darlington, which racing writer Hank Schoolfield described as "a part of the country where prejudice against Negroes was extremely rampant." The speedway's president, Bob Colvin, was a Confederacy buff and a resolute segregationist. Stocky, bald, and dynamic, quick with barbed jokes, Colvin promoted the Southern 500 as a defiant tribute to the Old South. Confederate soldier reenactors entertained the crowds. Rebel battle flags flew everywhere. Darlington was NASCAR's only track to use a Confederate flag, instead of a green flag, to start its races. Colvin "was just dead set against a black man running in the race," said Tom Kirkland, Darlington's official photographer at the time. Colvin told Kirkland that if a black man ever won the Southern 500, that driver would "never make it to victory lane. He was just a complete racist."

The Darlington infield, where fans camped overnight and country bands played until the wee hours, was the circuit's most notorious place for boozy carousing and, some racers recall, the easy availability of prostitutes. "True story — this guy had an ambulance, and he had two gals in the back of that thing," driver Tim Flock said. "He'd drive through the infield and pick up a couple of guys. They'd get in the back and get with it, and then he'd drop them off and pick up two more. He done this all night, with two whores in the back."

A few days before the race, Scott said, Colvin sent his entry form back in the mail, rejected without explanation. At NASCAR headquarters, officials knew perfectly well why this had happened, according to former NASCAR chief scorer Joe Epton. "Colvin was a good South Carolina boy, and a lot of folks in South Carolina, they believed blacks were supposed to ride in the back of the bus," Epton said. "He lived by that virtue, that Wendell had no place on the racetrack."

For this Southern 500, NASCAR had chosen Strom Thurmond as an honorary judge. Despite France's promise that Scott would be treated like any other driver, NASCAR took a hands-off position on Darlington's exclusion of Scott, former NASCAR officials said. The fine print on NASCAR's entry forms gave both NASCAR and the management of a host speedway the right to refuse a driver entry. "The entry blank was an invitation to race that he [Colvin] had control over," former NASCAR vice president Bill Gazaway said. "It was like a birthday party — if they don't want you, they don't send you no invitation."

Veteran Charlotte promoter Humpy Wheeler said it would have been "fairly unrealistic" at the time to expect Bill France to pressure Colvin on Scott's behalf. In the NASCAR world, Colvin was a power in his own right, the cocky visionary who had created the Southern 500, refuting skeptics who said "no one would come to the little burg in the heart of the Bible Belt," as the *Charlotte Observer* put it. Now the southern press liked to describe Colvin's race as the Kentucky Derby of stock car racing; its prestige rivaled that of the Daytona 500.

Long before the question of Scott came up, France and Colvin already had a contentious relationship, Wheeler said. "I think that France didn't take a hard stand on it [Scott's exclusion] because he and Colvin were butting heads on major items all the time, and he probably didn't regard this as anything. Not like you would today, when you'd have the federal court down your throat."

A friend and admirer of France, racing author William Neely, who traveled the circuit in the 1960s as public relations chief for Goodyear's racing program, said France evidently chose "a standoffish position" instead of pressuring Colvin. "He probably didn't try, because Bill France didn't fail many times. He ruled with an iron hand . . . Bill France was realistic, and he knew what most of his fan base was." Racer Junior Johnson, referring to France and the Darlington issue, observed drily: "He knew when to do something and when not to."

For NASCAR, the language of the entry form seems to have provided the kind of loophole that organizations often use when faced with choices that threaten their self-interest. It was a legalistic excuse to do nothing. Scott did not make an issue of his exclusion, choosing to wait to see what the next season brought. The press didn't pick up on the story, sparing NASCAR the discomfort of a discrimination controversy fourteen years after major-league baseball had admitted Jackie Robinson.

October brought two encouraging developments for Scott. At Charlotte, where Norris Friel had turned him away in May, he was allowed to race with no problems. At South Carolina's Greenville-Pickens Speedway, Scott turned in his best qualifying effort of the season. He qualified second out of eighteen cars — faster than such front-runners as Junior Johnson, Joe Weatherly, Fireball Roberts, and Ned Jarrett — and he finished eighth.

In all, for a rookie in a third-rate car, Scott had put together a respectable season. He'd run twenty-three races, finished five times in the top ten, and qualified once on the front row. The end of the season presented France with the decision of whom he should select for the series' Rookie of the Year award. If France had based his decision on finishing positions and points scored, some drivers and racing historians say, Scott would have been the obvious choice. "Wendell deserved it," said Marvin Panch, who won the Daytona 500 that year. Journalist Gene Granger, known as an expert on NASCAR history and statistics, said: "Wendell Scott won it hands-down."

Today, the rookie with the most points automatically gets the award. Back then, however, the choice was discretionary. NASCAR considered not only a driver's results on the track but also such subjective matters as sportsmanship, poise, future potential, and the opinions of NASCAR officials who traveled the circuit.

If France had chosen Scott, the decision could have attracted considerable attention. It would have brought some prestige and publicity for Scott, perhaps opened a door to sponsorship, and it would have signaled to the public, as baseball had done with Robinson, that the leadership of an all-white sport was welcoming a black driver at its highest level. For NASCAR, however, there were potential disadvantages. The choice of

Scott could have drawn attention to the fact that he had been banned from Darlington. And the same issue could come up the next season, if Colvin didn't change his mind and France didn't challenge him. And certainly a NASCAR honor for a black driver would have been noticed disapprovingly by politicians such as Thurmond and Rivers, whose favor France had been courting as potential supporters of his plans for a new superspeedway.

France selected Woodrow "Woodie" Wilson of Mobile, Alabama, for the Rookie of the Year award and its fifteen hundred dollars in prize money. Driving a car considerably faster than Scott's, Wilson ran only five races that year, all on superspeedways. He scored one top-ten finish, a ninth at Atlanta. Scott's five top-tens included a best finish of seventh, though on a smaller track. Wilson's best qualifying effort was fifteenth. His 3,580 points put him forty-first in the season standings. Scott, with 4,726 points, was thirty-second in the standings, nine places ahead of Wilson.

France's announcement said Wilson was chosen "after an extensive poll of the men who conduct races" in Grand National. Wilson "gave plenty of evidence," the statement said, "that he would be a top-rated driver in seasons to come." That didn't happen; Wilson started three Grand Nationals in 1962 and then never returned to the circuit.

Granger said he believed France decided against giving Scott the award because of the racial climate. "If you want to talk about where Wendell really got screwed, he should have been Rookie of the Year," Granger said. "He really got screwed out of that. There's no doubt in my mind there was a conspiracy . . . They did not want a black man to get it." Another stock car historian and statistics expert, Greg Fielden, author of several books about NASCAR's early years, said: "It was a screwy decision. But back then, there were no rules governing rookies."

One reason Wilson got the honor, France's statement said, was that he always conducted himself as a gentleman. Wilson, who became a shrimper in Alabama after he quit racing, said he'd never heard anyone suggest that Scott should have won the award. "He was a nice old boy," Wilson said. "He stayed in his place. Back in them days you'd hardly ever see a nigger racing. But he stayed in his place, and everybody accepted him."

Scott refrained from commenting on the issue until after years after his racing career had ended. "They just brought him [Wilson] in to keep me from winning," he said. "I feel I lost it because I was a black man." As with his first Grand National race at Spartanburg, the sport seemed to prefer that his involvement attract as little attention as possible.

## 15

### "He hid the pain so well."

During Scott's second Grand National season, a significant change in the finances and politics of NASCAR racing was taking shape in the executive suites of the Big Three auto manufacturers. For the past few years, the carmakers had been secretly giving financial support to some top NASCAR teams while maintaining publicly that they had no involvement in motor racing. The sponsorship remained covert because back in 1957, Congress had pressured the companies into signing an agreement withdrawing from motorsports and disavowing the promotion of horsepower and speed as detrimental to public safety.

Horsepower and speed, however, were exactly what many of their customers wanted. Gasoline was cheap; oil crises and environmentalism were still years away. Even the ponderous family sedans of the era had whopping V-8 engines. For the manufacturers, an excellent way to show off their cars' performance was to win races in the Grand National series, which featured cars that looked just like those in the showrooms. Despite the earnest safety pronouncements of the anti-racing agreement, an industry slogan captured the business reality: "Win on Sunday, sell on Monday."

By the time Bill France opened Daytona International Speedway in 1959, boosting stock car racing to a new level of spectator and media interest, the companies had already begun cheating on the no-racing pact. For favored NASCAR teams, companies devised under-the-table channels for supplying cars, parts, technical assistance, and money. Ultrapowerful new engines would arrive at teams' shops in anonymous crates, flown in from Detroit on private planes. This clandestine industry support was one of NASCAR's more poorly kept secrets, but Congress's attention span was, as ever, short.

The whole undercover sponsorship system unraveled in 1962 when Ford Motor Co., which hadn't played the covert game as adroitly as Chevrolet and Pontiac, announced it was withdrawing from the industry agreement and would openly support racing. The Grand National series quickly became a marketing battleground contested publicly by Ford, Chrysler, and General Motors. The companies' spending soon escalated into the millions of dollars. More than ever before, the career prospects of country boys who drove in NASCAR would be decided by corporate suits in Detroit and Dearborn.

Grand National racing began in January or February and continued into November or December. Scott's only crewmen were a few loyal friends or, when school schedules allowed, his sons. Sometimes he'd have no crew. During pit stops in those races, he'd change his own tires and refuel his own car, losing many positions on the track.

Scott started the season by taking out a new mortgage on his house and buying a year-old Chevrolet from driver Ned Jarrett. This was a better car than his old one, though not as fast as those with auto-company backing. He spent most of the early races struggling for positions in the middle or rear of the pack. At Columbia, South Carolina, some spectators greeted Scott with a noisy chorus of jeers and racial slurs when he drove onto the speedway to qualify on April 13, racing journalist Dave Grayson recalled.

Grayson was ten years old that day, already a racing buff, soon to become a dedicated Wendell Scott fan. The spectators' shouting startled and disturbed the boy as he sat in the grandstand with his father, a career air force sergeant who had taught him to treat others with respect. His family's "sheltered life" on air force bases, he said, had insulated him from the realities of prejudice. "I remember thinking, *This is incredibly wrong.*"

Some fans, Grayson said, spent much of the event making loud, derisive comments about Scott. One spectator, he recalled, said, "'I wonder what the hell they gonna do if this boy ever wins a race?' referring to the white beauty queen kissing the winner in victory lane. It took me awhile to figure that one out. The racial slurs, particularly the N-word, were just horrendous. Things like *Sambo* — all the racial epithets that were so predominant, sadly, in that part of the country during that time."

Late in the race, Scott skidded over an embankment, tore up the car's bodywork, and couldn't continue. When young Grayson went to the pit area afterward and asked for his autograph, he found Scott remarkably calm and gracious. Scott signed the boy's program, turned to his father, and asked: "Mister, would it be all right if I picked the boy up and let him sit in the car?" His father agreed. Awed and excited, Grayson, who'd never been in a race car before, spent several minutes immersed in the experience. But for decades he would also remember the sneering slurs from passersby who resented seeing a white boy in Scott's car.

As the season went on, Scott began to show that he could run closer to the front, particularly on half-mile dirt tracks. At those speedways, with their short straightaways and slippery surfaces, the superior power of the factory-sponsored cars didn't give their drivers the overwhelming advantage they enjoyed on longer, paved speedways. At South Carolina's Greenville-Pickens Speedway on April 19, Scott was the fastest of the unsponsored "independents," as the owner-drivers were called. He qualified sixth of nineteen cars and finished fourth behind three of the circuit's stars: Jarrett, Jim Paschal, and Joe Weatherly. Two days later at Myrtle Beach, Scott again qualified sixth. He was running in the top five when his front suspension broke.

On May 6 at Bruton Smith's Concord Speedway in North Carolina, Scott scored his best Grand National finish so far. The dirt track was in abysmal condition, and for two hours the drivers struggled with blinding, billowing dust and potholes. Scott came in third behind Weatherly and Cotton Owens. He finished a lap ahead of fourth-place Jack Smith, in a factory-sponsored Pontiac.

Scott said he was faster than Weatherly and Owens that day and could have beaten them if dirt hadn't coated his windshield. Weatherly and Owens had covered their windshields with cellophane that could be ripped off quickly during a pit stop. Scott lost several laps getting his windshield cleaned by hand. Just as he was about to pull out of the pits, a well-meaning helper threw a bucket of water on the glass. The water dislodged dirt from the windshield frame, which coated the glass again, costing Scott several more laps in the pits. At Greenville-Pickens on July 14, Scott again ran up front, finishing third behind Richard Petty and Jack Smith.

At Georgia's Savannah Speedway, Scott broke one of the unwritten rules of his acceptance on the circuit. After qualifying sessions on the hot, sticky night of July 20, the announcement that came over the loudspeakers angered some of his competitors. Wendell Scott, the announcer declared, had not only set the fastest qualifying time — he'd also set a new track record on the slick clay oval.

Even many drivers and crewmen who'd often been friendly and helpful to the Scotts took the news badly, his sons recalled. Frank and Wendell Jr. had expected congratulations as they walked through the pits. Instead, they got hostile glares and a background muttering of "people calling us nigger this, nigger that," Wendell Scott Jr. said. "It was so hushed I could even hear the popcorn popping at the concession stand. It was like Daddy had forsaken a trust — 'It's okay if you do fairly well sometimes, but don't do this to us.'"

Art Mitchell, an official at the event, added: "A lot of them liked Wendell as a person, but it was the idea of a black outdoing them that got them disturbed." The statuesque race queen Linda Vaughan, who often chatted with the Scotts at races, heard some of the angry remarks. "There were some dear friends," she said sarcastically, "who said, 'Well, I guess you'd rather hang out with them niggers than with us.'"

During the pre-race drivers' meeting with NASCAR officials, driver Bob Welborn found a somewhat odd way to work a racial slur into the discussion. Welborn had qualified second and would start alongside Scott.

Another driver, former Grand National champion Lee Petty, asked the group, perhaps mischievously: "Who's got the pole tonight?"

"Two niggers on the pole," replied Welborn.

NASCAR starter Johnny Bruner, who was running the meeting, told the drivers they'd be penalized if they tried to wreck Scott, Mitchell recalled. "Johnny told them if they so much as bumped Wendell Scott's automobile on the start, they'd be put to the tail end of the field, and if it was done again, they would be disqualified.

"Johnny said, 'The man earned the pole fair and square. It's up to y'all to catch him.'"

Scott hadn't heard Welborn's remark about niggers on the pole. Earl Brooks told him about it, and after the meeting Scott went looking for Welborn.

A three-time champion in NASCAR's convertible division, Welborn was a formidable driver who'd won twenty track records. He had a flattop crew cut and, usually, a cigar jutting from the corner of his mouth. Welborn, journalist Hank Schoolfield recalled, was known as "a dyed-in-the-wool southern racist."

Scott walked over to Welborn. "I said, 'Bob, you called me a nigger?'" Scott recalled.

"He said, 'I called both of us niggers.'

"I said, 'I knew you were lowdown, but a nigger is a lowdown thing, and I didn't know you were that low,' and I put my finger in his face.

"He said, 'Take your finger out of my face.' And I didn't take nothing out of his face."

One of Scott's volunteer crewmen, Henry Holland, stepped up close behind Wendell Scott Jr. and pushed a metal object into his hand. For a moment Wendell Jr. thought it was a pistol; it was a pipe wrench. "We thought we were going to have to fight," Wendell Jr. said.

Bruner, the NASCAR starter, intervened, telling everyone to calm down. Nevertheless, driver Jack Smith, a burly, aggressive man, confronted Scott with a threat. A former whiskey bootlegger from Georgia, Smith was one of the Grand National circuit's top racers. Smokey Yunick, the renowned and blunt-spoken race car builder, considered Smith one of NASCAR's the most prejudiced drivers. "He certainly didn't care for Negroes. I'm afraid people like Jack thought all colored people are niggers, second-class humans . . . When somebody like Scott came around, they thought he was a joke, and they gave him a rough time."

Smith, who had qualified fifth, told Scott he planned to wreck him. Thanks to his generous sponsorship from Pontiac, Smith added, he didn't care if his own car got wrecked along with Scott's. "I got five of these Pontiacs, all alike, and when they drop the green flag, I'm going to stick this one clean up your ass."

"Jack, if you pass me, pass me on the outside," Scott said.

His calm reply took the voltage out of the confrontation. Wendell Jr. put the pipe wrench away. After the green flag, Scott led for several laps until an engine problem dropped him to eighth at the finish. Smith's car broke down — the wreck he'd threatened didn't occur.

After the race, the winner, Joe Weatherly, walked over to speak with the Scotts. "Wendell, I just came over to apologize for the rest of these stupid sons of bitches," he said.

For Scott's sons, working as his crew could be exhausting, and sometimes Wendell Jr., sixteen years old, felt unappreciated and resentful. At Nashville's Fairgrounds Speedway on August 5, his father had a violent crash, one that could easily have killed him. A front-wheel hub broke and put him into a fence. The Chevy tore out twenty wooden fence posts, mangling the chassis and body. A gasoline fire flared briefly.

Scott phoned his wife in Danville and told her to have the boys bring his old Buck Baker car to Nashville. This was an order, not a request. He was determined to make the next race in Huntsville, Alabama, three days later. Wendell Jr. and Frank towed the car, which had no engine, to Nashville, about a four-hundred-mile trip. They helped their father work on the two cars in an alley. Crumpled bodywork and crushed suspension parts had trapped the engine in the wrecked car, turning the job into a mechanic's nightmare. They struggled for many hours to transplant the engine into the older car.

Scott and his sons made it to Huntsville in time for the race. But he qualified last in the field and dropped out early with bad brakes. The prize money didn't come close to covering their extra expenses. The whole ordeal had produced less than nothing. Worse than the fatigue and futility, Wendell Scott Jr. said, was the hurt of hearing his father tell a group of people in the pits the long story about all of the problems he'd overcome to make it to the Alabama race — never mentioning any help from his sons.

"Every word he used in describing how it was done was *I*," Wendell Jr. said. That wasn't an isolated oversight, he added — it happened often during those years. The memory still stung many years later. "I love my daddy, and I think he was one of the best mechanics that ever lived, probably one of the most phenomenal thinkers, without being educated, that you will ever see. He had instinct and wisdom and a lot of integrity.

"But my father's career was his own, and my brother and I, as integral as we were in it, you wouldn't know it from Wendell Scott."

In an example, perhaps, of how racism can taint the thinking of victims as well as perpetrators, Scott occasionally got annoyed at his sons and referred to them, in front of white people, as niggers, according to several people in racing at the time. Journalist Hank Schoolfield recalled Scott complaining about his sons as "them niggers in my pit crew."

During a race at Martinsville, Virginia, Scott made a refueling stop and found that his sons weren't in his pit, a racing official said. "Where did them niggers go?" Scott asked a white onlooker, according to the official. The onlooker replied that they'd gone to the food stand, and Scott, disgusted, refueled the car himself.

Sometimes Scott would refer to a darker-skinned person as a nigger in front of Wendell Jr., who would wonder if his father, at some level, was giving him a lesson on the workings of racist thought. "It was almost like he was sharing with us what the white man was really like," Wendell Scott Jr. said. "I don't think I ever heard nobody say *nigger* with more definition than my daddy."

Black people who traveled the South in those years had more to worry about than segregated restaurants and bathrooms. The apprehensions included the possibility of a run-in with the Ku Klux Klan. One morning, driving alone, Scott was approaching the Rockingham, North Carolina, speedway when he came upon a group of Klansmen running a roadblock. "They was out on the road, stopping cars. I wasn't towing the race car; it was already at the track. They had those white sheets all over 'em and those pointed things on their heads. I was about ready to run over them. I wasn't going to stop. But they waved me on through. I reckon because I was light-skinned, they didn't know I was black."

Although Scott managed to hide it from almost everybody in racing, his ulcers often caused him intense pain and exhaustion during his early Grand National years. During the 1960s, the problem became severely punishing. Almost every day brought gut-wrenching attacks of cramps and vomiting, both at home and on the road. For those who traveled with Scott on his long hauls to and from races, these episodes became part of the regular routine. Scott would swerve onto the shoulder of the highway, stop the truck, and run to a ditch or a wooded area. He'd double over with pain and roll on the ground, groaning, retching, and holding his stomach.

If family members were with him, Scott would have them rub his stomach until the pain loosened its grip.

Scott never missed a race because of ulcers, however. He didn't want anyone but family and close friends to know about them — particularly not anyone from the auto companies. People in racing remained unaware of his condition, Frank Scott said, "because once he got in the race car, you wouldn't know it. He hid the pain so well. Once he got in the car he could go all day."

In those years, under the rigid social etiquette of segregation, whites addressed blacks only by their first names. The roll call at a NASCAR drivers meeting would honor this convention:

"Baker?"

"Here."

"Jarrett?"

"Here."

"Petty?"

"Yo."

"Wen-*dell*?"

"Yep."

Blacks were expected to address whites as "Mr." or "Mrs." In speaking with white men in NASCAR, particularly those in authority, Scott often observed this convention, several drivers said. "Everything was 'mister' and your first name — Mr. John, Mr. Ralph, Mr. Fred," driver Fred Lorenzen said. "He was a very polite person."

According to Charlotte promoter Humpy Wheeler, Scott really had no choice in those years. "It was the only way he could have survived," Wheeler said. "He couldn't have done it any other way. It was just part of the culture at that time, the only way to get along. Even though he might have been fuming inside, he did that." Referring to Scott's ulcers, Wanda Lund Early, the widow of driver Tiny Lund, said: "I'm sure a lot of it came from suppressing his feelings."

For a long time, Scott dealt with the ulcers through a combination of home remedies, a tough-it-out attitude, and stubborn denial about his need for surgery. He always traveled with a bag stuffed with drugstore medications and homebrew concoctions recommended by acquaintances, which contained everything from Jell-O to goat's milk. For every trip, Mary Scott restocked the bag.

As for surgery, she said, "He just kept putting it off, thinking he would get better."

Scott's friend and volunteer crewman Ray Arnold said Jack Smith's hostility and dirty driving caused problems for Scott several times in the 1962 season. "Jack was one of the guys who felt that blacks shouldn't have been there," Arnold said. "He would be wrecking Scott, spinning him out, crowding him out."

While leading a race at Bowman Gray Stadium, Smith came up behind Scott and knocked him out of the way, Scott said. Then Smith waited for Scott to circle the track once more and rammed him again. "He just got mad and wrecked me," Scott said.

Asked about the incident, Smith said Scott should have gotten out of his way sooner. He ridiculed Scott's driving: "He needed somebody to grab him by the hand and lead him around. That's what the man needed."

As Scott prepared for a race at Valdosta, Georgia, he thought about how tired he'd gotten of repairing crash damage caused by Smith. Scott said he rigged up a holster in his race car to hold his pistol. During the pace laps, Smith "was going around the track, before they dropped the green, pointing at me," Scott said. "He was letting me know he was going to get me.

"I had fixed a place on the side of my seat where I had my pistol." Scott said he drew the gun and pointed it at Smith. "He's pointing his finger at me, and I'm pointing my pistol right back at him." Was it loaded? "Damn right it was loaded, and I had my finger on the damn trigger. That's how mad I was with him."

Smith said: "If he ever pointed a gun at me, I never seen it." Scott's sons, however, said they saw Smith hit his brakes and fall back at the exact moment their father pointed the pistol at him. Luckily for Scott, NASCAR officials didn't see him threaten Smith with the pistol. If they had, Scott could have faced penalties, perhaps even been banned from the circuit. In any case, Scott said he spoke privately to Smith and made the threat explicit the next time they met, at Hickory Speedway in North Carolina, five months after the incident at Bowman Gray Stadium. "I said, 'Jack, let me tell you something — if you can outrun me fair and square, you do it. But if you ever hit my car again intentionally, I'm going to kill you.'" From then on, Scott said, "I never had no more trouble out of him."

Occasionally Scott thought about how senior officials in baseball had gone out of their way to intervene for Jackie Robinson when other players or officials treated him with prejudice, and how different things were in NASCAR. Although Robinson experienced death threats and many racial slurs, Scott felt his situation involved greater dangers. "Jackie Robinson probably had a lot of bad things said to him from white folks in the grandstand, but every time I got into a race car my life was involved," Scott said. "I ran against drivers who had their plans before the race ever began: 'Don't let the nigger by.'"

Again, Darlington Raceway refused to accept Scott's entries. At the 1962 Southern 500, Congressman L. Mendel Rivers, serving as honorary judge for the event, helped to welcome the Labor Day weekend crowd to the speedway and socialized with Bill France and speedway president Bob Colvin. "My dad was a big friend of Colvin," said the congressman's son, Mendel Rivers Jr., who accompanied his father to many NASCAR events. France and his father, the younger Rivers said, also "genuinely liked each other — they had a lot of similarities . . .

"I got the feeling about France that he was one of those successful men who like to collect politicians. Some men collect young wives; his trophies were notable politicians — George Wallace, Mendel Rivers, and so forth, men whom he liked. My father was kind of fun for him to have around, and France had kind of earned that."

NASCAR's chief scorer, Joe Epton, said he didn't believe that NASCAR made any attempt to pressure Darlington into accepting Scott. "I don't think so," Epton said, "because the entry blanks stipulated for a long, long time that the promoter has the right to refuse any entry. That was Colvin's right, and he didn't accept Wendell's entry."

NASCAR is, of course, a family-owned business that makes its own rules, and if the problem were merely the language of the entry form, NASCAR could simply have changed the form. Darlington had been refusing for a year now to let Scott compete, and NASCAR had left the form unchanged. Even a small fig leaf is more useful than none.

Scott dealt with the problem in the same way that he'd handled many of his racial troubles over the past eleven seasons — keep quiet, keep coming back, keep showing you're a racer and not a troublemaker, keep remembering that times are getting better. He regarded Colvin as a hardened racist who would never change, but he still considered France a decent man who probably would do the right thing when he felt he could. Going public with any complaint, Scott believed, could only backfire.

Wendell Scott Jr., quicker to anger, born into a generation more impatient about racial problems, sometimes felt a bitter frustration over his father's silence. All over the South now, black people were speaking out, demonstrating, fighting prejudice head-on. He questioned his father's approach. Part of his disappointment was that his father emphatically did not want to hear his thoughts on the subject. He had little hope that France would help his father. "Bill France didn't dare to violate that white sanctuary of Darlington, the mystique of it. The whole thing about Darlington was that it was a festive event, where a lot of the festivities went on at night in the infield, the prostitution, the drinking, the dancing, the partying. If a black man went into that infield, something was going to happen," Wendell Scott Jr. said.

As he saw it, France "didn't like Wendell Scott that much, and anything Bill France did for Wendell Scott was so people could see that Bill France always treated Wendell Scott right. It wasn't out of a feeling of empathy. It was a business arrangement, and he got away with it."

Scott's friend Carl Simpson said France remained in Scott's good favor partly because Scott simply was slow to develop a grudge in most situations. Another reason, Simpson said, was that France sometimes helped Scott when he ran short of money. Scott could call France and get occasional advances from the point money he was accruing for the season. When Scott's children began college, Simpson said, this line of credit became especially important. "For a long time, Wendell felt France was good to him." Since Scott would have gotten this money anyway at the season's end, the favor didn't cost France anything.

On September 13 at Augusta, Scott again was the top finisher among the unsponsored independents, coming in fifth behind Lorenzen, Petty, Weatherly, and Jarrett. This was his fourth top-five finish in a season that turned out significantly better than the previous year's. He ran forty-one races, finished nineteen times in the top ten, and placed twenty-second in points, ten spots higher than in his rookie season. And he'd handled his problem with Jack Smith.

To win a factory ride, though, Scott knew he'd need more than some respectable runs on short dirt tracks. The superspeedway races were the circuit's prestige events, and no factory team would want a driver who couldn't race in Darlington's Rebel 300 or Southern 500. What had worked with a bully like Smith wouldn't help Scott overcome that problem. He couldn't point a pistol at the executives of Darlington Raceway or of NASCAR.

## 16

### "Man, I come a long way."

Despite his Darlington troubles, Scott began the 1963 season with a newer car and an optimistic prediction. He'd bought a 1962 Chevrolet, one of Ned Jarrett's cars from the previous season. The car was "by far the best machine that I have had," Scott said as he left Danville on the longest trip he'd ever made to a racetrack: a cross-country tow to Riverside International Raceway, a road-racing course near Los Angeles. "I will outrun Jarrett with it." In fact, however, the Riverside event would set the tone for a season marked by more racial incidents, problems with NASCAR, and results that repeatedly fell short of his hopes.

The more that the auto companies spent on their front-running teams, the tougher it became for an independent to squeak into the top five. The factory-backed teams fielded cars with the most powerful engines, the best-handling suspensions, and the slickest rule-bending aerodynamic tricks that money — and, sometimes, insider influence with NASCAR — could buy. They had salaried crews to build engines, change transmissions and rear-axle gears, repair crash damage, and handle all the other work of keeping a stock car on the track.

Ford Motor Co., which would become the most successful manufacturer on the circuit in 1963 with twenty-three wins, now spent more than twenty million dollars a year on racing, insiders estimated, with perhaps 30 to 40 percent of that going into NASCAR. That meant there were several hundred thousand dollars — 1963 dollars — in annual Ford spending behind each of the six to nine factory-team Fords and Mercurys that took the green flag at major Grand National races. On superspeedways, those drivers could run fifteen to twenty miles an hour faster than low-budget racers like Scott.

At Riverside, the magnitude of Scott's disadvantage became painfully apparent, and one of NASCAR's top officials made a bad day worse, Scott said, by reneging on an agreement about money. Before Scott agreed to make the long haul to California, NASCAR's executive manager, Pat Purcell, promised him $150 in what racers call, he said, deal money — a payment for a driver's participation in a race beyond whatever the driver wins in prize money. The trip was wearying. Late one night in the desert, about thirty miles from Las Cruces, New Mexico, an axle bearing burned out in Scott's tow car and touched off a stubborn brake-fluid fire. He had to throw sand on the fire repeatedly before he extinguished it. Scott was stranded for a whole day, hitching rides and scrounging for parts.

In the race on January 20, Scott finished eighteenth out of forty-four cars. He came in sixteen laps behind the winner, Dan Gurney, in one of the factory-team Fords. Jarrett, also driving a factory Ford, lapped Scott twelve times on his way to fifth place.

"I won $175," Scott said, "and I went to Pat Purcell to get my $150, my deal money."

"He said, 'Hey, boy, you did all right — you made $175.'

"I said, 'Man, I come a long way, and I got to go now. How about letting me have my deal money?'

"He said, 'Oh no — I told you if you didn't make $150, I'd see that you got $150. But you done made $175.'

"And he didn't give me a dime . . . They robbed me."

The Chevy's engine failed during Scott's first try at the Daytona 500 on February 24, where Ford factory teams swept the first five places. At the next race, however, on Spartanburg's half-mile dirt oval, Scott was the fastest of the owner-drivers. He started ninth and came in fifth behind Richard Petty, Ned Jarrett, Jim Paschal, and Joe Weatherly.

Driver Larry Frank, who had won the previous season's Southern 500, said Scott's driving ability was obvious in his early Grand National years, especially on dirt. "At the time when he moved into Grand National, if somebody would have put him in a front-running car, I don't have the slightest doubt that he'd have been capable of running up front." But at this point in Scott's career, Frank added, his opportunity window for sponsorship wouldn't stay open much longer.

Scott was forty-one in early 1963, racing in an era when many top drivers retired in their thirties. The heavy Grand National sedans of the 1960s punished even the most physically fit drivers. "With those cars we had, it took all your muscles to get those big hulks around the track — no time for finesse," said driver James Hylton. "Think about driving 500 laps on skinny tires, no power steering and no aerodynamics. I was exhausted after one of those races."

Unless Scott got a big break soon, as Larry Frank saw it, people would begin to consider him "a little bit over the hill," especially since the life of an owner-driver was so exhausting. "When you had to stay up all night building engines," Frank said, "then get up early and try to make it to the race track, sometimes stay up two and three days at a time to make a race — back then, when you got to be forty years old, you were an *old* forty years old."

During 1963, the country's deepening and sometimes bloody conflicts over integration dominated the news. George Wallace took office as Alabama's governor, promising segregation forever. His administration took a hard line against protest. In May, police clubbed nonviolent black marchers in Birmingham, unleashing attack dogs against the demonstrators and tumbling them down the street with water from fire hoses at pressure that could rip bark from trees. In June, Wallace made his symbolic stand in the schoolhouse door, vowing that the University of Alabama would never be integrated. That same month, civil rights leader Medgar Evers was shot dead outside his home in Jackson, Mississippi. In August, more than a quarter million civil rights advocates marched in Washington, DC, and heard Martin Luther King's "I Have a Dream" speech.

As racial tensions grew, sometimes racetrack spectators seemed more hostile than when Scott had begun racing more than a decade ago. After a race on March 10, Scott and some friends and relatives were trying to leave Orange Speedway in Hillsborough, North Carolina, when a crowd of angry white spectators surrounded them, shouting and shaking their fists, some of them obviously drunk.

Scott had endured a frustrating day. He had broken an axle and finished last in the race. Now he was creeping along in a traffic jam from the infield on the way to the highway, he and his sons in his truck, his friends and relatives in a car right behind them.

The car, owned by Scott's friend Wooster Adams, was particularly conspicuous, a gleaming black 1956 Lincoln convertible with the top down. In this elegant car, the agitated fans believed, they saw a white man in the backseat sitting close to his girlfriend — an attractive, dark-skinned black woman. The spectators surged around Scott's truck and the Lincoln, yelling threats and racial slurs. They were mistaken about what they saw, but they were past the point where explanations would have made any difference.

"You ought to have seen that bunch of drunks and fools . . . ," Scott said. "Man, they really got rough. I happen to have a cousin with real light skin, and they thought he was white, and they were callin' him 'nigger lover,' and boy, they were just going to kill him."

Furious, Scott jumped out of his truck, shouting and cursing, warning the spectators to get away from his friends and family. The fracas could have turned deadly; both Scott and Adams had loaded pistols within easy reach. Luckily, policemen directing traffic ran over and broke up the confrontation. They let the Scott group cut into a line of cars and leave the track. For quite a while, Scott and Adams watched their rearview mirrors on their way home.

Darlington Raceway again refused to accept Scott's entry for its spring race on May 11, the Rebel 300, and NASCAR continued its hands-off policy on the matter. When Scott tried to sign up for the June 9 race at Birmingham, that entry form, too, came back rejected. The photos of police dogs attacking black marchers a few weeks earlier in Birmingham had been on front pages across the country. Scott called the promoter, who said that he didn't want any trouble and that Scott should stay away.

But Scott decided to go anyway. The Birmingham speedway was just a minor local track, a half-mile dirt oval, nowhere near as prestigious or influential as Darlington, and it didn't promote itself as a showcase of Confederate heritage. Often such smaller tracks were happy to have another car in the field; perhaps the racial issue would be tacitly ignored.

For most of the event, it appeared that Scott had been right. The first person he met at the track was the facility's black janitor. "I got there that day, and the colored guy what kept up the race track, he told me, 'Man, they won't let you run here today.'

"I said, 'I'm going to run here today.' And sure enough, I did run." The promoter's order that he stay away wasn't mentioned. He started fifteenth and finished seventh.

Right after the race, however, the tone of the day changed abruptly. NASCAR field manager Johnny Bruner hurried over to Scott and told him to load up his race car immediately and leave. "They wouldn't tell me what was going on. They told me, 'Hurry up and get away from the track, quick.'" Scott did as he was told and drove back to Virginia overnight.

It wasn't until three weeks later that NASCAR gave Scott a brief explanation. "They didn't tell me till after I got away and got to the next race," Scott said, describing a conversation reminiscent of a grown-up telling a child just so much and nothing more. "Johnny Bruner told me a bunch of those rednecks had got together and was going to come in and turn my car over and burn it up." All of the questions raised by this information went unanswered. How did NASCAR know this? Who were the men? Was anything reported to law enforcement? Bruner didn't say, and Scott never found out.

On June 10, Danville had one of its first civil rights demonstrations. The police, who had just been issued new clubs, beat some of the demonstrators severely, including women. Others were blasted down the streets by fire hoses. Scott told his children to stay out of any protest activity — any perceived connection between him and the civil rights movement, he felt, could only hurt him in NASCAR. "The only way I can help those rights people and their cause is to just be a man and a good race driver," he told a reporter later. One of Scott's longtime black friends, Ray Arnold, who crewed for him at many races during the 1960s, said Scott didn't once talk about the civil rights struggle during all of the time they spent together. "Never mentioned it," Arnold said.

On June 30, Scott drove his first race at Atlanta International Raceway, a high-banked, 1.5-mile superspeedway. His qualifying speed, 128.4 miles an hour, was 12 miles an hour slower than that of the factory-sponsored Ford of top qualifier Marvin Panch. As in Birmingham, racial tensions ran high in Atlanta. No black driver had ever run at the Atlanta facility. The day before the race, one of the city's best-known segregationists,

Lester Maddox, the fried-chicken restaurant owner who would go on to become Georgia's governor, published one of his frequent, inflammatory, prominently displayed essay ads in the *Atlanta Journal*, warning of "race mixing," "mongrelization," and "the destruction of the white civilization." He claimed that "this week the Red Cross has had white girl teenagers holding colored men in Candler Park, teaching them to swim and float."

Scott drove the entire Dixie 400 on one set of tires — the factory teams used four or five sets — and finished twentieth. Afterward, some fans became disorderly when they learned that Scott had been in the race. "When they found out I was black, them fans just went crazy in the infield," he said. A crowd of whites cornered a small group of blacks. Track superintendent Alf Knight, a big man with flattop crew cut and a first sergeant's jaw, grabbed a two-by-four and his .38-caliber pistol. He shouldered his way into the crowd and broke up the confrontation before anyone got hurt.

"Alf went over there and just cleaned it out," driver Rex White recalled. "He was a tough customer who could put you down in a hurry, and he was a good guy." Two years earlier in the same infield, Knight had helped to break up a rock-throwing white mob that had beaten and injured two black spectators. Scott often remembered Knight as one of the white southerners whose support helped to offset the hostility of others. Often Jarrett and White gave him parts for his Chevrolet, he said. Once White invited him to his Spartanburg shop and filled up his truck with Chevy parts.

Scott's ulcers got worse. At Atlanta, Frank Scott recalled, his father felt so weak before the race that he had to be lifted into the car. Sometimes at superspeedway events such as the Atlanta race, where Scott had little chance of finishing well, he would settle his stomach by having a snack and a soda during pit stops for fuel or tires. Some onlookers noticed this and, unaware of his ulcers, made it a topic of sneering gossip. These snacks, according to the scuttlebutt, showed that Scott was childishly impulsive and lackadaisical about his racing. "If he was serious about his racing, he wouldn't have come in and got cookies," driver and car builder Banjo Matthews argued years later in an interview. Even when Scott had placed third in the blinding dust at Concord, North Carolina, the *Charlotte Observer*, calling him a "perennial also-ran," reported his finish with the contemptuous aside that "he sometimes makes pit stops for crackers and a soft drink."

One of the few people outside of Scott's immediate circle who knew about his ulcer troubles was Richard Petty, whose quick grin and cheerful demeanor masked his own painful ulcer problem. As a fellow sufferer, Petty knew that Scott sometimes needed food during pit stops "to settle down his stomach. He did that from necessity . . . He wasn't just out there running and said, 'Hey, I got plenty of time, I'll stop and get something to eat.' He didn't eat for the sake of eating — he ate for the sake of surviving."

The Pettys and the Scotts were developing a friendly relationship, though it hadn't gotten off to a good start. At Augusta, Scott said, Petty had deliberately run him into the guardrail, robbing him of a chance for a strong finish. "Man, I was rolling that night," Scott said. "He caught me when I went into the turn, about halfway in. He never backed off, and he just kept pushing, and I went right into the inside guardrail." Ray Arnold, crewing for Scott that day, said Petty "was leaning on him — it looked intentional." Petty said he didn't recall the incident. At the next race, Lee Petty apologized to Scott and assured him that Richard would never do that again, Scott said. From then on, Richard Petty always treated him respectfully.

After a race in Georgia, Scott's tow car broke down on a rural road, and he coasted into the driveway of a shabby crossroads truck stop. His sons and a volunteer crewman were with him. Some rough-looking white men, working in the shop, looked up when they noticed the race car. The truck stop had a WHITES ONLY sign.

"Daddy said, 'Y'all know what we gotta do,'" Wendell Scott Jr. recalled. Everybody in the car would have to pretend that Scott was their white boss. Scott put on a cap to conceal his hair and got out to talk with the mechanics.

They were looking Scott over, listening to him explain the car problem, when Scott's crewman began the routine, speaking in a servile falsetto: "Mistah Scott, can I have a soda pop?"

"Daddy says, 'Shut up, nigger. What I done told you already?'"

Wendell Scott Jr., playing his part, scolded the crewman: "I told you not to say nothin' to Mr. Scott!"

"Daddy says, 'Boy, you shut up, too.'

"The white guy says, 'You really know how to handle them niggers.'

"Daddy says, 'Yeah, I know.'

"And all the time he wanted to kill that son of a bitch."

The mechanics helped Scott fix the tow car and admired his race car. "They wouldn't even charge him anything," Frank Scott said. "We pulled away from that truck stop, and Daddy says, 'You know, I've been in some close calls, but that was one of the worst.' The sweat was coming off of him about the size of fifty-cent pieces."

At Columbia, South Carolina, on August 8, Scott got caught in a wreck. He drove toward the pits with a bent hood and caved-in grille, his damaged radiator spewing steam. Trying to anticipate what his father would want, Wendell Jr. ran to get their gear ready for the trip home.

Then he saw that Scott had driven to the concession stand and parked near the water spigot. "He had his wits about him to know that's where the running water was," Wendell Scott Jr. said. "I said, 'What's happening?' So he's screaming, he's getting mad, and that frightened me — you can't do everything right, and I wanted to help, but I didn't know what to do." It was the familiar mixture of admiration, fear, and resentment that stressful events with his father often brought about.

"Frankie hollered, 'Brother, he wants needle-nose pliers! Needle-nose!'

"I'm thinking, *How do you fix a crushed hood with needle-nose pliers?* And I'm thinking, *If I'm going to live through this, I've got to find them.*

"So I find them, and he grabs them and says, 'Get the hose hooked up to the faucet!' And I still didn't understand." In his anxious confusion, the lettering his father had put on the Chevy's front fenders — MECHANIC: ME — seemed like a personal rebuke.

Scott grabbed the crumpled grille and tore it loose from the car, cutting his hand, ignoring the blood. He stuck a flashlight into his mouth, as he often did while working on cars, and began probing the damaged, steaming radiator with his pliers. A small crowd gathered to watch. Some of them laughed at how peculiar Scott looked with the light protruding from his mouth.

Suddenly Wendell Jr. understood his father's plan. Scott was finding each of the radiator's leaking tubes, then pinching each broken end to stop the leak. "He's finding these tubes and pinching them all over the radiator, and all of a sudden you heard this hush — it stopped steaming and water stopped spewing. We filled it up, and by then I'm feeling amazed and proud." The onlookers who had been joking about Scott began to cheer him when they realized how he'd fixed the radiator, Wendell Jr. said, and his father charged back onto the track to salvage a ninth-place finish.

At Darlington Raceway, as usual, Bob Colvin rejected Scott's entry for the Southern 500 on Labor Day. Senator Strom Thurmond and Congressman L. Mendel Rivers were the speedway's guests as honorary officials. Larry Frank, who was friendly with both Colvin and Scott, said the speedway's tight-knit board of directors clearly supported Colvin's position. The board included some of the area's leading businessmen and politicians. One director was the local state senator. Another was the chief criminal prosecutor.

"They all had money, the board of directors," Frank said. "These guys were old landowners, farmers, a bunch of them growing up together, years and years ago, and they cut up an old cotton field and made a racetrack out of it, and they all believed in it, and that whole group of guys was all the same." They were, he said, "a bunch of hardheads." For France, taking on not only Colvin but also the board of directors on Scott's behalf would have been challenging, Frank said, adding: "I don't feel like France was ever man enough to do it."

Racing journalist Hank Schoolfield said that France could have prevailed if he'd really wanted to help Scott. "France had a great knack for putting pressure on people." The renowned racer Junior Johnson agreed that NASCAR could have used its institutional clout to get Scott onto the track. "If they had stood up to Colvin, he would have let Wendell run," Johnson said. But there was no public controversy over the matter that might have pushed France to support Scott. The speedway's discrimination didn't become a publicly discussed issue. As before, the southern racing press, some of whose members also did promotional work for NASCAR, ignored the story of Scott's exclusion.

After a race at Randleman, North Carolina, Scott's sons and some white teenagers threw an impromptu party, playing music and dancing. A white spectator confronted Scott. He told Scott his boys shouldn't be dancing with white girls. "I said, 'I don't think you got nothing to do with that.' He swung at me. I ducked." Scott's friend Earl Brooks grabbed the man, who called Brooks a "nigger lover." Brooks beat him up.

Despite the repeated racial incidents, Scott felt encouraged by his progress. Even without any points from Darlington, he finished the 1963 season with one of the best records of the unsponsored owner-drivers. He placed fifteenth in points, seven places higher than in 1962. Mostly, he'd driven at a pace he knew his car would survive, counting on consistency and attrition for a decent finish. He nursed the same engine through all forty-seven races. He finished fifteen times in the top ten, though only once in the top five.

Although the season was officially over, Scott still had a few more races to run in 1963. In those years NASCAR ended its seasons for points-keeping purposes in October or November, and the last few races of the year counted as part of the next season. As he got his car ready for the Grand National on December 1 at Jacksonville, Florida, he was tired of racing conservatively. Jacksonville was his favorite type of track, a half-mile dirt oval, and Scott decided to run it as hard as he could. Maybe he'd run up front, maybe he'd impress somebody at Ford, maybe he'd wreck. In any case, he told folks at home, "This time I'm gonna go or blow."

## 17

### "They took all the kick out of it."

The day before the Jacksonville race, Scott pulled on his frayed coveralls and looked over the unpaid bills stacked up on his dresser. He'd been falling behind, and the pile had grown. His mortgage payment was overdue. The bank kept sending warnings. "I needed $1,000 so bad when I left home for that race, I didn't know what to do." Should he really push his car to the limit? Maybe he should just drive cautiously and make sure he finished. "I said to myself, if I can just finish good enough to make about $400 here, I'm going to pay everybody I owe a little something."

He worked on the race car for hours, the gravel in the driveway digging into his back, improvising repairs where he couldn't afford a new part. His crew for the race, two of Scott's Danville friends, Wild Horse Chaney and Brother Robinson, arrived late in the day. Like many of the volunteer crewmen who helped Scott occasionally, they knew little about race cars. But they were loyal companions who could share the nearly five hundred miles of driving, and for any black man traveling through the Deep South in those years, it was best not to travel alone.

It was eight days after the assassination of President John F. Kennedy, and eleven weeks after a bomb planted by the Ku Klux Klan killed four black schoolgirls as they studied the Bible at their Birmingham church. When Scott and his friends got to Florida, they drove through towns where the Klan had been protesting efforts to integrate lunch counters. The Klansmen had handed out thousands of little cards to white patrons. A NEGRO HAD THAT SPOON IN HIS MOUTH, the cards warned.

Doris Roberts, the wife of driver Glenn "Fireball" Roberts, had been thinking about Scott and the racial atmosphere not long before the Jacksonville race. She asked her husband something that others in Grand National had been asking one another.

"I asked Glenn, 'What will happen if someday Wendell Scott wins a race?'" she said.

"Glenn said, 'They won't let him do that. They'll find a way not to give it to him.'"

Scott felt weary from the long night on the road as they pulled into the pits at Jacksonville Speedway Park, shortly before qualifying sessions were to begin. His friends helped him unhook the race car from his faded pickup and get into the qualifying line.

The track's promoter, Julian Klein, had prospered in the rough-and-tumble jukebox industry. Apparently, he didn't spend much of the jukebox money on keeping the speedway in good condition. The track surface often broke up during a race day into a washboard of bumps and ruts.

During Scott's qualifying run, the track already had deteriorated. His Chevy handled badly, losing traction as it bounced over ruts and potholes. The qualifying results left him disappointed and annoyed. He would start deep in the field, fifteenth of twenty-two cars. And Jack Smith, the Georgia driver who had given him so much trouble last year, had qualified fastest and would start first.

Somehow, Scott realized, he needed make his car's suspension much softer. He decided to gamble on a drastic change: removing one of the two shock absorbers at each wheel. He finished the job just in time to make the starting grid.

The race started with a deafening outburst of sound, Smith leading, the field tightly bunched at first, a maelstrom of skidding, jockeying, bellowing sedans throwing dirt. Even the open exhausts of twenty-two V-8 engines, though, couldn't mask the clanging and banging of tortured suspensions as the cars bounced and slid through the rutted turns.

For Scott, the shock absorber change had worked even better than he'd hoped. He could sail through the bumps and get a good bite on the track, while the stiffer-sprung cars, bouncing around, spun their wheels, and lost speed. The rough track was canceling out the horsepower advantage of the factory-sponsored cars. On this bumpy surface, handling was the key to speed, and now Scott had probably the best-handling car in the field.

He could pass other cars on the inside or the outside. "My old car was just running and handling so pretty," he said.

One by one, competitors began dropping out. Jimmy Pardue broke an axle on the second lap. Crawfish Crider blew an engine. LeeRoy Yarbrough snapped an axle. Jimmy Lee Capps crashed. Larry Thomas broke a wheel and tumbled his Dodge into a screen protecting the grandstand. Luckily, the screen held.

Scott circled the track steadily, staying on the lead lap, picking up positions, watching more rivals struggle with problems. Joe Weatherly had to pit repeatedly. Roy Tyner broke an axle. Tiny Lund and Billy Wade broke differentials. Jack Smith tangled with Neil "Soapy" Castles and went off the track. Jarrett, dueling with Petty, grabbed the lead, then broke a wheel. Buck Baker, who had started second, was in and out of the pits with overheating and other troubles. Five times the yellow flag came out so that wrecks and debris could be cleared away.

Scott enjoyed giving Baker a quick wave each time he gained a lap on him. Later he'd recall giving Baker three of those half-mocking waves as he went by. Scott needed only one pit stop for gas. He made the stop while the yellow flag was out so he wouldn't lose a lap.

With twenty-five laps to go, Scott ran in second place, keeping pace with Richard Petty. Then Petty slowed with a damaged steering arm, and Scott took over the lead. On his next lap Scott looked over at the scoreboard, where NASCAR officials hung the numbers of the cars in the top positions. As soon as he'd taken the lead, however, the scoreboard had gone blank.

On what was supposed to be the last lap, Scott raced for the finish line, anticipating the beauty of a waving checkered flag. The NASCAR official in the flag stand watched him go by, but didn't move. Scott took another lap, wondering what was wrong, his suspicions growing. Again no flag appeared. He ran yet another lap, and again nothing happened. Then the checkered flag did begin waving — not for Scott, but for Buck Baker. The official flagged Smith for second place and Scott for third.

The only reporter at the track was Gene Granger, a twenty-eight-year-old sportswriter for the local newspaper. Tall, lanky, and intense, Granger had been jumpy with nervous energy all day, lighting up one Salem after another. New to the NASCAR beat, he'd covered only a few races, and he knew his story would go out over the Associated Press wire. He was concerned about getting everything right.

As Granger watched Baker get the checked flag as the winner, the routine anxiety of a reporter on deadline jumped up several notches. This wasn't just an ordinary sports story anymore, he realized — something else was going on. He'd been watching the race from the pits, and everybody around him, crewmen and drivers whose cars had broken, had been talking about the unusual fact that Scott was leading the race. "There didn't seem to be any doubt in their minds that he had won . . . ," Granger said. "I was sure, and so were all the people around me."

Driver Johnny Allen, who watched the race after his car overheated, recalled: "Toward the last part of the race, people thought that *Hey, Wendell's really doing good.* He was running real fast late in the race . . . There was a controversy in the pits about who was leading. It was the general consensus that Wendell was." Others agreed. "There's no way in the world that Wendell didn't win that race," driver Ed Livingston said. Smokey Yunick, a leading builder of cars for factory-sponsored teams, could see Scott's handling advantage. "He won the race — there was no question in my mind," Yunick said. "His car was so lightly sprung that he went through the goddamn holes and went on. He didn't have nothing in the way of power, but the chassis worked. He was working by far the best."

Those who watched from the pits included driver Eddie Crouse, the champion of NASCAR's modified division for the past two seasons. Everybody around him, Crouse said, knew that Scott had won. "It seemed like they was giving it to Baker knowing all the time that he couldn't have won . . . The way they went about it, it was just hanky-panky."

Baker stopped at the finish line on the front straightaway. Jack Smith pulled up behind Baker, climbed out, and began insisting loudly that he had won, not Baker. Scott drove to his pit and pulled himself out through the window. Granger was struck by how fired up and determined Scott looked — and how sure he was of his victory. He heard Scott tell his crew, "I know I won."

Scott walked over to where Baker had parked. "They had a little gathering, people around me," Baker said. "Wendell waited until some of the people got away and then walked up to me and said, 'Buck, you know something? I believe I won this race.'"

Granger watched them standing nose-to-nose, Baker brawny and aggressive, Scott wiry and intent, both of them dirty, edgy with adrenaline. Scott told Baker he didn't want to kiss any beauty queen. He had, after all, never kissed one at any race he'd won in the minor leagues. Conceding nothing, Baker told Scott curtly to talk to the NASCAR officials if he wanted to protest.

NASCAR's scoring crew had been working from the back of a flatbed truck. Scott walked up to NASCAR's gruff chief scorer, Joe Epton. As Epton recalled, Scott couched his protest in an Old South style of speaking.

"Wendell walked up to me and said, 'Mr. Joe, I might not have won this here race, but I swear I done outrun Buck,'" Epton recalled. "Those were his exact words." Epton told Scott he'd check the scoring records.

The infield crowd gathered around Baker and Smith. The two drivers were yelling at each other, each claiming that he had won and that Scott definitely hadn't. Some people were shouting the word *nigger,* Yunick and others said. "What you were hearing was that there ain't no way they were going to let a colored guy win the race . . . They were just running their mouth pretty bad," Yunick said. "What it all amounted to was, 'No nigger could beat us.'"

While Scott waited for a decision, NASCAR held the victory ceremony for Baker. Almost all of the spectators left the track, as did the beauty queen. Granger, anxious to file his story, kept pressing the NASCAR officials for a decision. "I kept saying, 'What's going on, folks — did he win it or didn't he?'"

By the time the NASCAR officials emerged from their closed meeting nearly two hours later, the sun had set, and only Scott, his crewmen, and a small group of others, including Baker and Smith, remained at the speedway. Scott had won the race, the officials acknowledged. There'd been a scoring error, they said: The correct results were Scott first, Baker second, Smith third. They didn't congratulate Scott. There was no new ceremony, no trophy, and nobody apologized. It was one of the quieter victory moments in NASCAR history.

Since that day, Epton and NASCAR have maintained that the organization simply made an honest mistake. Scoring disputes weren't unusual in those years, and officials said they really did believe at first that Baker won. Only when the records were reexamined, they added, did NASCAR realize that someone failed to credit Scott with two laps.

Others, however, said NASCAR knew all along that Baker hadn't won. Margaret Baker, Buck's wife at the time, had been the official NASCAR scorer for her husband. As soon as the race ended, she said, "I knew that Wendell had won it before they even checked the cards . . . And Joe [Epton] knew it, too . . . Everybody knew that Wendell had won, except Buck.

"When Wendell came up, I said, 'Joe, you know Wendell won that race.'

"And he said, 'Well, we'll check the cards.'"

Epton said he didn't remember any such conversation with Margaret Baker. "She never said anything like that to me that I recall."

Two spectators who stayed around for NASCAR's decision were a teenager, Mike Bell, who went on to become a well-known researcher of NASCAR history and an officer of the Georgia Automobile Racing Hall of Fame Association, and Bell's father, who was friendly with track promoter Julian Klein. Klein admitted to his father later, Bell said, that NASCAR officials announced what they knew were phony results.

"Klein told my daddy, 'I wasn't about to give that man the trophy and let him kiss the trophy queen,'" Bell noted. "He said, 'I'd probably have had a riot at the race track if I had.'"

Crouse, the NASCAR modified champion, said NASCAR's motive was obvious to racers at the event. "They just didn't want him to be presented with the trophy by the queen," he said. "That was the key thing."

After NASCAR finally declared Scott the winner, Baker kept on arguing furiously that Scott couldn't have won. Granger stopped to listen just as Jack Smith stepped up. "I was standing right there," Granger said. "Jack grabbed Buck by the arm and said, 'Come on, Buck — let the damn nigger have it.'" The remark seemed to calm Baker. He shrugged and stopped arguing. The onlookers drifted away. One of the most memorable days of Scott's racing career was finally over.

For the rest of his life, Baker would maintain that he never got any trophy at Jacksonville. Others, however, said they saw him get one. "Buck ran off with the trophy," Granger said. Sometimes Granger wondered if NASCAR would ever have acknowledged Scott's win if no reporter had been hanging around asking questions. "I was the only reporter there, and they knew I was there," he said. "If I hadn't been there, what would they have done?"

Scott towed his dirt-spattered Chevy back to Danville that same night. He stopped on the road to buy Wild Horse and Brother Robinson a bottle of good whiskey. As they rolled through the dark countryside, he was quiet, reflecting. He was bringing home a thousand dollars in prize money for his first Grand National win, and this should have been one of the best days of his life. It didn't feel that way, though. "They took all the kick out of it," he said.

He didn't believe the story about a scoring error. "Everybody in the place, the promoters, NASCAR and the fans knew I had won that race . . . But they wanted Buck Baker to kiss the beauty queen instead of me and everybody to get away from the track before they declared me the winner."

NASCAR's newsletter, which usually included a feature story about every Grand National describing how the winner got his victory, carried only a table of results for Jacksonville, in small type, with no article on the race. Granger's story, reporting that Scott had become "the first Negro in history to win a NASCAR Grand National," hadn't struck his editors as big news. They ran it on page thirty-two, where an account of a dog-racing meet called the Mutt Derby got much better display. Even though racial issues had become one of the country's biggest running stories during this era of civil rights conflict, Scott's unprecedented victory in an otherwise all-white southern sport didn't get any attention from the national media.

He wondered if he'd hear from anyone at Ford, but he didn't.

Sportswriter Dick Thompson of the *Roanoke Times,* however, interviewed Scott and wrote a long, laudatory column. "Scott has the driving ability to win . . . On a dirt track there are few who can match him . . . His equipment just isn't fast enough to beat the factory-backed cars," Thompson wrote. Scott told Thompson: "A dirt track, that's my best. You can take a piece [of junk] of a car and do real good on dirt. I can drive with any of them. I just need the car."

Somebody, Thompson wrote, "should be big-hearted enough" to give Scott a trophy. That night Thompson got a call from Martinsville Speedway's president, Clay Earles, an old friend and business partner of Bill France. Earles told Thompson he'd make sure Scott got a trophy. A few days later, Goodyear sent a $150 check for winning on its tires. That, finally, gave Scott something to chuckle over, a little scam to savor. His tires hadn't really been Goodyears; he couldn't afford them. He'd run on cheap recaps, old tires with new tread grafted on.

At NASCAR's next event, in Savannah, the race was postponed by rain after the drivers arrived. Scott left his Chevy with other race cars in the fenced yard of a warehouse, where racing officials assured him the cars would be safely locked in. He went home to work on a project he'd been putting off. He needed a new tow vehicle to replace his aged pickup. Danville's black funeral home, Cunningham & Hughes, had sold him an old limousine with a bad transmission. This break in his schedule gave him time to fix it.

He drove back to Savannah on December 29 in the limousine, picked up the Chevy at the warehouse, and towed it to the speedway. The drivers and mechanics working in the pits looked up when Scott and his sons pulled in. The limo was a black 1954 Cadillac, an extra-long, seven-passenger model. Several of the onlookers, Ned Jarrett recalled, made the same sort of derisive remark: "He wins the race, and just like a nigger, he gets a Cadillac."

The NASCAR officials summoned Scott to the scoring stand to get a trophy for the Jacksonville win. The presentation left Scott struggling to hide his anger. One official delivered what Scott considered a belittling account of his victory, talking at length about all of the cars that had broken down, emphasizing how attrition had helped Scott to win. Then he handed Scott the trophy.

It was a small block of wood, obviously inexpensive, the sort of trophy a child might get at a fourth-grade field day, quite different from the trophies Scott had seen other Grand National winners receive. "I will never forget the hurt on Daddy's face," Wendell Scott Jr. said. As they walked back to the pits, "Daddy was cussing, but he was so damn hurt, the cursing kept him from crying." The whole presentation, his son believed, "was staged to be very degrading."

Scott had to put new brake linings in the Chevy before the race. They jacked the car up, and Scott pulled off the right-front wheel, which bore much of the car's weight under hard cornering. Suddenly Frank Scott heard his father cry out in surprise: "Somebody cut my damn tire!"

Wendell Scott ran his fingernail around the inside sidewall, showing Frank what he'd found. Someone had made a cut around the whole inner sidewall, about an inch from the rim. The cut was just deep enough to sever many of the cords that gave the tire its strength, but not quite deep enough to make it go flat. It was a neat job, hard to detect. If he hadn't had to work on the brakes, he'd never have spotted it.

They looked around inside the fender well. There was no jagged metal that could have made the cut. Somebody had wanted Scott to crash. At that time, stock cars had only primitive safety equipment. Like most drivers then, Scott wore only a lap belt. In the Grand National racing of the early '60s, a blowout could cause a fatal wreck.

The Scotts didn't say much else as they finished the brake job. They were the only black people in the busy pits. All around them, white men were warming up unmuffled engines, shouting instructions and questions at one another, leaning over engines, slamming hoods. They'd known many of these men for years. Scott's sons had helped some of them during pit stops. Scott had loaned them parts, worked on their cars, shared jokes, disappointments, and baloney lunches. Many treated the Scotts as colleagues and companions. Sometimes it had been easy to forget that others would always consider them intruders.

Frank Scott wondered if his father would tell anybody about the tire. It seemed obvious that somebody from the Grand National circuit had cut it, somebody they knew. But Wendell Scott's face had gone blank and impassive, and Frank could tell he'd decided to say nothing.

Twelve years in this white man's world of racing, and they still couldn't be sure whom they could trust.

## 18

### "I just knew Ford was going to do something for me."

When he wasn't muscling competitors out of his way on racetracks, Ned Jarrett was courteous, soft-spoken, and serious, a NASCAR driver who didn't fit the rough-guy stereotype. Driving for Ford's racing organization, Jarrett achieved a stellar Grand National record for 1963: eight wins, thirty-two finishes in the top five, fourth in points. After the season, Ford hosted a luncheon in Dearborn, Michigan, at its corporate headquarters, known as the Glass House for its three thousand windows. Jarrett was a logical choice to sit next to the fast-rising superstar of auto executives, Lee Iacocca.

At thirty-eight, Iacocca already had become vice president of Ford Motor Co. and general manager of its Ford division. He and his boss, Henry Ford II, were spending millions on the most far-reaching motorsports program ever undertaken by an auto manufacturer. Ford was pouring money into teams competing in NASCAR, drag racing, the Le Mans twenty-four-hour race, the Indy 500, even European rallying. The ambitious and forceful Iacocca pressured his subordinates relentlessly to produce winning efforts in all of those venues.

As Jarrett and Iacocca chatted about racing, Jarrett said, he took the opportunity to recommend something new for Ford's program — that the company should put its support behind a Negro stock car driver named Wendell Scott and get him into a competitive car: "I told him I felt that any manufacturer was missing the boat by not helping Wendell Scott — that his performance on the race track could influence a bigger percentage of his race to buy cars than I could or any of the other white drivers."

Jarrett had begun to admire Scott's driving ability in 1957, when they'd raced each other in sportsman cars at Norfolk Speedway. Jarrett won the track championship, and Scott placed third in points. More recently, during Grand National races on dirt, Jarrett recalled, Scott had been able to put his less powerful car right on Jarrett's rear bumper and stay with him for many laps.

During his talk with Iacocca, Jarrett said, the auto executive asked questions and took notes. Jarrett told Iacocca that with good equipment, Scott "could run with anybody out there" and become a consistent winner. "He had the determination, and I think he had the talent."

Scott, meanwhile, prepared his 1962 Chevy for its third season, unaware of this conversation in the Glass House. Jarrett didn't tell Scott about his talk with Iacocca because "I honestly didn't expect anything to come from it."

Scott towed his Chevy to California's Riverside circuit in January 1964. For the second year in a row, he said, a problem with NASCAR turned the Riverside odyssey into a costly debacle. "I got there about two o'clock in the morning. I went to the same building where I signed in the year before, and I went to sleep." But the sign-in location, he said, had been changed. "I woke up the next morning, and there was a bunch of guys signing in at a trailer, down a ways."

Rainstorms disrupted qualifying, and NASCAR chose drivers for twenty-nine of forty-four starting positions according to when they had signed in. NASCAR officials told Scott and one other driver, Fresno independent Scotty Cain, that they'd registered too late to make the field. Scott said he drove onto the course for the pace lap anyway and tried to start the race, but officials flagged him off the track. "They wouldn't let me start that race, and they wouldn't give me one dime," Scott said. The round trip to California cost him about five hundred dollars.

Some of Scott's supporters believed that NASCAR wouldn't have banned drivers from influential teams under the same circumstances. Riverside was a 2.7-mile circuit, 0.2 mile longer than Daytona. At Daytona the starting field was forty-six cars. Why not let two more cars start the Riverside race? No explanation was given. NASCAR's decisions, according to driver Frank Warren, often "depended on who you were, back in those days." Referring to this Riverside incident, Danville radio station WBTM said in a 1965 editorial: "There's been plenty of evidence of discrimination against Scott over the years, some of it pretty raw stuff."

After two months of mechanical failures and midfield finishes in the old Chevrolet, Scott sent in his entry for the April 5 race at Atlanta's superspeedway. When word got around that a black driver was coming, track officials got many angry letters and phone calls, some including threats. The week before the race, an aide to promoter Nelson Weaver called Scott and asked him to consider staying home. "He said the Ku Klux Klan had been threatening to come and throw bottles and rocks onto the track if I raced there," Scott said. "He was afraid someone might get killed." With other drivers' safety at risk — and because the official had asked for his cooperation rather than ordering him to stay away — Scott felt he had to agree. "I didn't go, because he asked me so nice," Scott said. He listened to the race on the radio: "It really hurt."

Darlington Raceway followed its usual practice and refused Scott's entry for its spring race, the Rebel 300. The track's ban on Scott was going into its fourth season now. Although he had kept quiet about the matter, it was well known among racers, officials, and sportswriters who traveled the circuit, and this year the situation had an angle that made Scott's problem particularly newsworthy. In February, the House of Representatives had passed the proposed Civil Rights Act of 1964. An impassioned debate now raged in the Senate. Among other things, the bill would outlaw racial discrimination by businesses that served the public and engaged in interstate commerce — a definition that included Darlington Raceway and NASCAR. One of the Grand National series' established business practices, Scott's exclusion from Darlington, soon could become illegal.

Even so, the racing press still failed to pursue the story. The lapse reflected the cozy, sometimes compromised relationship that the press corps had with NASCAR at the time. France routinely paid travel and lodging expenses for some reporters who covered Daytona races, journalist Gene Granger said. One well-known racing writer moonlighted as a track announcer at Daytona and Darlington. Another reporter edited NASCAR programs and did publicity work for NASCAR races while covering NASCAR. Reporters wrote articles for NASCAR programs. France bailed one reporter out of a potential night in jail by paying a parking ticket the reporter couldn't afford.

There were free tickets for reporters' friends, free food and drink, expensive press parties where France or Colvin picked up the tab. "They were very good to the press — a lot of freebies," said Bob Greenberg, an advertising executive who was involved with NASCAR racing for Ford's ad agency, J. Walter Thompson. Journalists who were so inclined, sportswriter Tom Kelly said, could get free "hotel rooms, booze, meals, hookers, you name it."

Jim Foster, a former Spartanburg sports editor who became a senior NASCAR executive, said Colvin had a particularly effective press relations approach: "He'd put on a big party at a restaurant and invite the press. He'd have a lot of liquor and show dirty movies. That was the way to get the press to come out."

Driver Curtis Turner, whose talent and flamboyant spirit Scott admired, urged him to take Colvin to court for banning him from Darlington. Turner had a couple of reasons for advocating such a provocative move. For one, he liked Scott. For another, Turner was hardly averse to any idea that might cause problems for France, who had expelled him from NASCAR for trying to organize drivers into the Teamsters Union. He told Scott he could sue Colvin for harming his livelihood.

Scott went to France, he said, and brought up Turner's idea. "Bill France and them, they begged me not to," Scott said. "He said Darlington was the first superspeedway they'd ever run on, and Bob Colvin was one of his good friends. He said he would talk to Colvin and have it so I could run there by the next race."

In his efforts to obtain sponsorship, Scott said, he wrote to dozens of companies during his Grand National years. "I wrote the car companies, the beer companies. But it always came back with an 'if.' I tried to contact Pontiac. I got a letter back saying if I had so many thousand dollars . . ."

Scott also wrote to a successful black businessman in Philadelphia, Andrew Willis, who had a fleet of Ford trucks. Willis got in touch with Scott and said he'd try to help him win sponsorship from Ford. He assured Scott that he could get through to Henry Ford II, and he made good on that promise, Scott said. "He talked to Henry Ford. He called and called — Henry Ford was at the Waldorf-Astoria Hotel in New York when he located him." Ford "guaranteed him he'd help me some way," Scott said. "He didn't say how, just some way."

At the time, Bob Greenberg and his colleagues who handled the Ford Motor Co. account at the J. Walter Thompson advertising agency worked closely with the Ford executives who managed the company's racing program. Greenberg's job involved traveling with the Grand National circuit. The experience helped him to appreciate Scott's challenges in gaining acceptance.

One night Greenberg went out drinking in North Carolina with a group of racing people that included promoter Enoch Staley, whose refusal to pay Scott years earlier had prompted France's promise that Scott would always be treated like any other NASCAR driver. Staley was a principal in two North Carolina tracks that hosted Grand National events: He was president of North Wilkesboro Speedway and France's longtime partner in the Hillsborough speedway. He also served as one of NASCAR's chief stewards.

"At the end of the night, Staley says, 'You know, Greenberg, you ain't too bad a guy for a New York Jew.' That stayed with me for years. That sort of tells you what it was like in that group then."

Greenberg, a racing enthusiast who drove stock cars and midgets as a hobby at Long Island's Freeport Speedway, liked Scott and thought he might represent an opportunity for Ford. He invited Scott to visit the impressive Manhattan headquarters of J. Walter Thompson on the tenth floor of the Graybar Building on Lexington Avenue, next to Grand Central Station. Greenberg introduced Scott to the important people on the Ford account. "Everybody seemed to like him. He was shy, reserved, a friendly guy." Barney Clark, one of the executives who met with Scott, said he impressed the admen as "an extremely agreeable and intelligent man."

They took Scott to lunch at a restaurant in the Graybar Building — he was the only customer in a string tie — and Scott left New York feeling more optimistic than ever about getting a factory ride. "I was sure I was going to get some help from Ford then," Scott said. "I was really feeling good. I just knew Ford was going to do something for me."

With the support of his colleagues at J. Walter Thompson, Greenberg made a pitch to Ford's racing executives, suggesting that they give Scott a race car. His argument, Greenberg said, was that "he's a black guy, and lots of black people buy Fords." He said the Ford executives took the matter to Lee Iacocca.

"You can be pretty sure they ran it by Henry Ford II also," Greenberg said. "I'm sure, knowing Iacocca, and I did, that he probably said, 'Yeah, if this will sell cars, let's do it.' That was the objective. That's the reason they raced in the first place." However, Greenberg added, Ford executives were acutely aware that supporting a black driver could be unpopular among some people in NASCAR racing. "This was many years ago," he said. "The racial situation was considerably different. Considerably different." Some way had to be found to shield the company from controversy.

The phone rang at Scott's house about eleven o'clock one night in May 1964. Scott was taking a bath. He climbed out of the tub, wrapped a towel around his waist, and grabbed the receiver. The caller was Norris Friel, NASCAR's technical director, the official who had turned Scott away from the Charlotte Motor Speedway three years ago. He told Scott that a Ford stock car was waiting for him at the Holman-Moody racing shop in Charlotte.

Friel didn't have to explain Holman-Moody to Scott; every racer knew the company as a major player in American motor racing. Operating out of a complex of buildings at the Charlotte airport with more than two hundred employees, Holman-Moody served as Ford Motor Co.'s contractor for executing Henry Ford II's and Lee Iacocca's plans to dominate Grand National and win at Le Mans. Holman-Moody built state-of-the-art Ford racing cars and engines for its own Grand National team — whose driver, Fred Lorenzen, was the circuit's top money winner in 1963 — and for other factory-backed Ford teams in NASCAR. When Scott dreamed of getting a factory ride, essentially he was dreaming about a car from Holman-Moody.

Friel, Scott recalled, said he should talk to John Holman, who ran the business with his partner, Ralph Moody. "He said, 'Wendell, tell Holman

I sent you down there — they got a car for you. I don't know what it is or how good it is, but accept it, whatever it is.'" Scott was elated — this could be the most important phone call of his career. "I stood there dripping water all over the floor. I just knew it was all a dream, but my wife, Mary, yelled at me because I was getting the floor wet, and I knew it wasn't no dream."

A few days later, when Scott saw the car, his euphoria faded. It didn't look much like Fred Lorenzen's ride. "I went down there, and they had this old '63 Ford out in a field," Scott said. "Somebody stole the oil cooler off it. They had took a lot of stuff off it. So they gave it to me. I bought it for a dollar." Curtis Turner had driven the car on the United States Auto Club stock car circuit, which ran mostly in the Midwest.

NASCAR driver Bob Welborn, who was working for Ford at the time, had picked up the car in Indianapolis and towed it to Holman-Moody. To Welborn, the car looked worn out, ready for the scrap yard. "It was a pile of junk," Welborn said. "It was about a '60 model car but it had been updated, had new bodies put on it, for at least three years. It had the appearance of a '63 when I picked it up. I wouldn't have brought it home, really."

Nobody from Ford spoke to Scott about the car. He didn't know what it meant that NASCAR's Friel had been the intermediary, and he wasn't sure whether the company or John Holman had made the decision to give it to him. The transaction was vague, Greenberg said, because that's exactly how Ford wanted it. Concerned about racial controversy, he said, the company chose to keep its relationship with Scott very discreet, almost clandestine. "They didn't cover up the fact that the factory was supporting him, but they didn't bring it up, either."

The racial climate in the country and in NASCAR would have discouraged any auto manufacturer from fully supporting a black driver, said Barney Clark, Greenberg's colleague at J. Walter Thompson. He added: "The leaders of our great automotive companies are afraid of anything that's controversial."

Ford's approach to supporting Scott reflected the company's awareness that he was still banned from Darlington, Greenberg said, a situation that could potentially draw a sponsor into taking sides in a discrimination dispute. The company decided, he said, to help Scott a little but not a lot. "They wanted him in a Ford, but they didn't want to put him in the same Ford, the current model, as their hotshot drivers were driving. So they gave him a three-year-old car . . . They didn't want to get their hotshots all angry. Put him in a Ford — but it can't be what the other guys have."

## 19

### "How come way out here?"

Scott spent many hours tearing down and rebuilding the Ford. Perhaps Ford executives wanted to see some good results before supporting him openly. Although the well-used vehicle wasn't of factory-team quality, Scott's overhaul gave him a race car quicker than his old Chevrolet, and his results improved significantly.

He drove the Ford for the first time on May 15, 1964, at Virginia's Langley Field Speedway. Starting eleventh, he finished fourth, the best performance by an owner-driver. Only Jarrett, Marvin Panch, and Buddy Baker, Buck's son, could outrun him. On the circuit's short tracks, Scott's top-ten and top-five finishes became more frequent. In ten short-track races during May and June, he placed in the top ten eight times.

At two of those races, NASCAR scored him fourth, but Scott said he really finished third both times. NASCAR took away his third-place finishes at Valdosta and Spartanburg, according to Scott, after the drivers who came in fourth went to NASCAR officials and claimed they'd beaten him. The officials, Scott said, "ripped me off two races in a row." Consistently he finished among the fastest independents. In the World 600 at Charlotte, a crowd of sixty-eight thousand watched Scott set a NASCAR record for positions gained. He charged from his fortieth starting position to finish ninth. After the race, fans crowded around him for autographs.

At the Atlanta superspeedway, where Scott had skipped the April race because of warnings that bottles would be thrown onto the track if he were allowed to race, speedway officials accepted his entry for the June event. Apprehensive, the management hired about twenty extra security guards to watch the crowd. Nobody threw anything, and nothing was said publicly about the earlier threats.

Scott's engine blew during the first qualifying day at Atlanta. He went through the garage asking who could spare any engine parts. One of the

Ford-sponsored teams, the Wood brothers, gave him some used heads. Larry Frank also gave him used heads, along with an old crankshaft that might survive one more race. Frank watched Scott scrounging for handouts late that afternoon and thought about how different the racing life was for the factory drivers, who were getting ready to begin an evening of fun, confident of engines that were dynamometer-tested, "everything balanced, everything blueprinted, the best that money could buy."

Frank and another driver, Tiny Lund, went out for a night of partying. About four in the morning, driving down a remote country road, they passed a shabby, cement-block motel. Out in the dirt parking lot, somebody was working on an engine under a single lightbulb.

"Hey, that's Wendell," Frank exclaimed.

They turned around and went back. Scott was rebuilding his engine with the used parts he'd collected. He'd removed the valves from all of the old heads and assembled sixteen that weren't warped or burned. Despite the late hour, the engine was far from finished and, of course, still had to go back into the car.

"What are you doing out here?" Frank asked Scott.

"He said, 'Well, this is where I stay when we come to Atlanta.'

"I said, 'Why way out here?' I just really wasn't thinking.

"He said, 'Well, Larry, this is a black motel.'"

Frank said the scene brought home to him abruptly something he'd never fully realized: how much Scott remained an outsider in their world, and perhaps always would be. "We'd run together for years, and it had just never occurred to me that he couldn't stay with us or go eat with us or be part of us. But that was just the way that Wendell lived."

Scott qualified twenty-fourth of thirty-five cars at 135.7 miles per hour with the makeshift engine. That was ten miles an hour slower than the factory-team Ford of the top qualifier, Junior Johnson. Scott's engine lasted the whole race, and he finished twelfth.

With mediocre engines such as the parking-lot special, Scott was badly outclassed by the five-hundred-horsepower factory cars on the longer tracks. The mechanical problems typical of a low-budget operation knocked him out of several other races. But on shorter ovals, he continued to put together some respectable finishes. He was fourth at New Oxford, Pennsylvania; sixth at Manassas, Virginia; fourth at Hillsborough, North Carolina; fifth at Savannah.

With his solid performances in the Ford, along with last year's Jacksonville win and his pole position at Savannah, Scott felt he was showing that he could drive as well as anyone on the circuit. When driving jobs became available at Ford factory teams, however, other drivers got them. Bob Welborn and Cale Yarborough produced good results; Bobby Johns and Benny Parsons were less successful.

Scott's chances weren't helped by a false story that circulated around NASCAR and the Ford racing organization during this period. According to that rumor, Scott won at Jacksonville only because the other drivers secretly agreed to let him win. Advertising executive Bob Greenberg, who worked with Ford's racing program, said that the story was widely believed and that he believed it himself.

"A week after the race, that [story] was all over," Greenberg said. "Everybody knew that. That was not a well-kept secret . . . The story that I heard at the time was that they threw the race to him, because the good ol' boys thought it was a funny thing to do, to have a black driver win in a beat-up old car. That is, I'm sure, to some degree correct. A couple of the leading drivers got together and said, 'Gee, wouldn't it be funny if the nigger won the race.'"

That summer, Congress finally approved the Civil Rights Act of 1964, after many months of impassioned opposition from southern members. In July, President Lyndon Johnson signed the legislation. Now, for the first time, Scott's exclusion from Darlington would violate federal law. The track accepted his entry, and he began getting ready for his first Southern 500.

Bob Colvin planned the traditional sort of festivities for the Labor Day weekend event. A group called the Edisto Rifles, dressed as a Rebel infantry company, would be firing volleys and simulating battle charges with the Confederate flag. NASCAR's honorary chief steward, Senator Strom Thurmond, would fire one of the group's rifles to start the ceremonies. Congressman L. Mendel Rivers, soon to become House Armed Services Committee chairman, would take part in the festivities as an honorary

**After Wendell Scott broke southern stock car racing's color barrier in 1952, he won dozens of races in Virginia, his home state. He drove this Ford to victory in 1957 at Roanoke. Often the only black people at the speedways were Scott and his family. His mother (print dress) and wife are on the left. His daughter Ann (center) kept her fingers crossed.** (PHOTOS COURTESY OF THE SCOTT FAMILY.)

**Like many early NASCAR racers, Scott learned fast driving by outrunning police while transporting moonshine. The police seized some of his cars, including this modified Ford, but caught him only once. His arrest was front-page news in his hometown newspaper, the *Danville Register*.** (PHOTO COURTESY OF THE SCOTT FAMILY.)

# THE DANVILLE REGISTER

DANVILLE, VA., SUNDAY MORNING, MAY 1, 1949

## Whisky-Bearing Auto Smashes House In Chase

A whisky-laden automobile which had outdistanced police officers in a chase earlier went out of control and smashed into a house on White street last night

Scott as he was getting out, they said.

None of the jars in the luggage compartment were broken.

route one. Damages were $220.

Next came Bert Lofie Thomas, 39, of Durham, N. C., route four, who stopped for traffic while driving south on Main street and

## *It's Bootlegged Whisky, Police Charge*

Traffic Officers J. G. Samuels and H. F. Price arrested Wendell O. Scott, 27-year-old colored resident of King's Mill Road, as he started to slid from under the steering wheel of the car which, police said, was carrying 22 half-gallon fruit jars filled with bootlegged whisky.

Scott was charged with reckless driving by city police while federal agents accused him of transporting untaxed whisky.

According to police reports, the 1946 Packard sedan had outrun a police cruiser on Claiborne street earlier in the night, resulting in an alert to all cars.

—Register Staff Photo

Danville traffic officers who were chasing this automobile when it went out of control and smashed into a house on White Street early last night said that the 22 half-gallon fruit jars shown in the back of the car contain bootlegged whisky. Officers Garland Samuels and H. F. Price arrested Wendell O. Scott, colored, on a charge of reckless driving after the crash while alleged whisky violation case was turned over to federal authorities.

**In 1959 Scott drove the number 85 Ford coupe and won NASCAR's Virginia state championship for sportsman-class racers. Sometimes prejudiced white drivers deliberately wrecked him. Below, he climbs out of his car after one such incident at Bowman Gray Stadium in Winston-Salem, North Carolina.** (PHOTOS COURTESY OF THE SCOTT FAMILY.)

**As a racer with no sponsor, Scott did his own mechanical work, often helped by his sons. In center photo, Frank Scott and family friends try to fix crash damage and get Scott back into competition. Below, Scott welds another damaged race car in his backyard garage.** (PHOTOS OF WENDELL SCOTT WORKING ON ENGINE AND OF FRANK SCOTT COURTESY OF THE SCOTT FAMILY. PHOTO OF SCOTT WELDING TAKEN BY JACK COUSINS.)

**One of NASCAR's major events, the 1972 World 600 at Charlotte, included a bogus publicity campaign. The promoter attracted a record crowd after promising Scott would drive a highly competitive car built by legendary racer Junior Johnson (above, with Scott). In fact, the car was inferior, rented from a low-budget team, and it broke down in mid-race.** (PHOTOS COURTESY OF THE SCOTT FAMILY.)

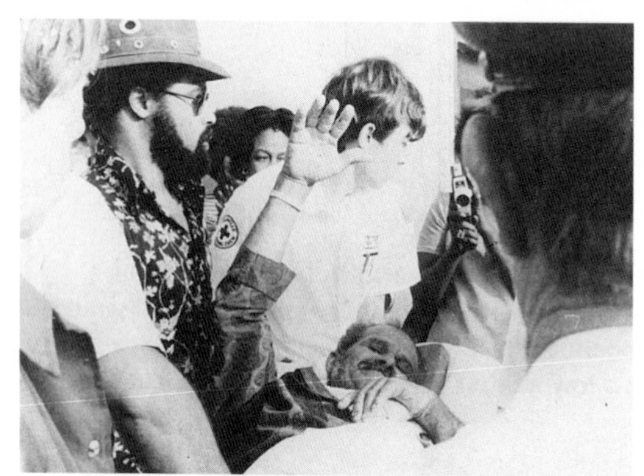

**Still hoping to prove his talent, Scott borrowed heavily in 1973 to buy this fast Mercury. But a twenty-one-car wreck at Talladega, Alabama, destroyed the car and his career, injuring him badly. In center photo, Scott, unable to speak, waves to fans from a gurney. His son Wendell Jr. is at left.** (PHOTOS COURTESY OF THE SCOTT FAMILY.)

NASCAR judge. Both had been among the most fervent opponents of the Civil Rights Act.

There were, of course, other ways to keep a driver out of a race besides refusing to accept his entry. One of Scott's loyal supporters, Bobby Fleming, who raced stock cars and ran an auto-body shop in Danville, worried that NASCAR might reject Scott's car as not appearing polished enough for a major race. "We brought it over to my shop, and we just stripped it all the way down to the roll cage and put everything on the car new — doors, fenders, hood, trunk — and painted it all over, solid red," Fleming said. "It looked like a brand-new car, right off the showroom. We took pictures of it before he left, so if they did say anything, we'd have proof of what it looked like."

At the track, however, NASCAR officials gave Scott so many problems that he wasn't able to get through tech inspection and run the race, according to Fleming and Scott. NASCAR officials, Scott said, made him tear down his engine before the inspection, then moved up a key deadline so that he didn't have time to get the motor back together. In the time allowed, Scott said, "there weren't no way I could do all that."

Later, Fleming wrote letters to NASCAR protesting the inspection and asking what specific problems had been found, but NASCAR, he said, responded only with generalities. "We wrote a couple of times, but they'd just write us these letters back, telling us that his car just wasn't legal, it was so cheated-up . . . wasn't safe for the racetrack, all of this junk. But there wasn't anything wrong with it. It was the same car he raced at Charlotte two or three weeks later, and it passed inspection there.

"They disqualified him because of him being black. NASCAR was that way — they got the people that they gonna put in; they got the people they don't want in. If a promoter tells them, 'Don't let this man in,' then that's the way it's gonna be."

The deadline that NASCAR moved up, Scott said, was the timing of his driving test as a rookie at Darlington, something required of all first-timers because of the speedway's unique difficulty. Drivers had to show they could run laps at more than 120 miles an hour. Since he didn't have time to reassemble his own engine, Scott borrowed an uncompetitive car from another owner-driver. He ran 116 miles an hour on his first lap, he said, and then the engine blew on the second lap. "So I didn't pass the test, and I had to go home." After the event, a racing newspaper, *Southern MotoRacing,* criticized Scott for having "grumbled that he didn't have a fair chance to qualify."

Bobby Fleming fired off an indignant letter to the editor: "In my opinion Scott had plenty of good reasons to do a little grumbling. He was handed the same old song and dance about his car not being in good shape. I do the body and fender work and painting on Scott's car, and I know the car was in perfect shape."

Four drivers, Fleming continued, "did not qualify at 120 mph but started the race. Scott ran 116 and was disqualified. Roy Tyner qualified at 111 and started the race. Wendell did not run Bob Colvin's track for one reason. He's a Negro. You may be interested to know that I am white, but I have more respect for Scott than I do for a lot of white people I know . . . If any other driver who was ninth in the Grand National point standings was turned away from any race you would have really heard some grumbling. Scott was knocked down at least two positions in the points, and it is not likely he will be able to get back in the top ten before the season is over."

On October 18, Scott was running eleventh of forty-four cars in Charlotte's National 400 when he blew a front tire and hit the wall. He drove slowly down the road behind the pits, the fender crushed against the shredded tire, the car spewing sparks and gravel. He jumped out, grabbed a crowbar, and worked frantically to pry the fender off the tire. Finally the metal gave way, and Scott put on a new wheel, only to realize that his suspension had been knocked severely out of alignment. He crawled under the car to look at the damage and came out shaking his head. He was out of the race.

Sportswriter Tom Higgins of the *Charlotte Observer* saw the potential for a poignant feature in Scott's problem. He watched the four attractive young women sitting directly above Scott on a scaffold, cheering on "the bright Fords of more illustrious pilots — Fred Lorenzen, Ned Jarrett and Bobby Johns — while completely ignoring the plight of the solitary figure with the crow bar."

He wrote about Scott's faded gray coveralls, his stoic disappointment, and the frustration of "competition with the millions [of dollars] of the factory-backed Ford and Chrysler" teams. "I don't want to sound like I'm crying, though," Scott told Higgins. "Just 'cause they've got it and I haven't, I don't wish them any misfortune." Since his damaged Ford wouldn't roll straight, he wasn't sure yet how he'd get it home. He still didn't have a trailer. He towed his race cars on their wheels with just a tow bar. Up on the scaffold, the women cheered for the handsome Lorenzen, on his way to another victory. "As the bowed little Scott faded into the crowd," Higgins wrote, "a feminine voice was heard to yell, 'Come on, Freddie.'"

During a race at Savannah's dirt track, Scott rolled over in the Ford. The car came to rest on its side, and Scott scrambled out while it was still rocking slightly. He pushed on the car to keep it rocking. "I kept rocking it and rocking it and finally rocked it back on its wheels and jumped in and took off," he said. Like all drivers in that era, he wore an open-face helmet. "I had lost the windshield. I run the rest of the race with no windshield, and the sand was like somebody shooting buckshot. It like to tore my face off. That sand beat me to death. I'd never do that again." At least, that's what he said many years later; at the time, quitting wasn't considered — someone from Ford might be watching the race.

The season's racial troubles weren't over. Twice that fall, Scott successfully confronted groups of white men who menaced his teenage sons for trying to use bathrooms at North Carolina tracks. At Harris Speedway on October 25, more than a dozen spectators blocked the bathroom door. "They were heckling us, talking about cutting our balls off," Frank Scott said. His father, who had just finished a practice session, walked up to the men, still wearing his helmet. "He told them in no uncertain terms, 'Don't bother my family,'" Frank went on. "'Leave my sons alone, or you got to kill me.'"

At the Jacksonville speedway on November 8, the boys hurried to an outhouse while their father unloaded the race car. Wendell Jr. went in first. Frank was waiting outside when a group of men began making threats.

Frank ran to get his father. Wendell Jr., unaware of what was happening, "pushed the door open, and all I saw was these rednecks with beer cans and a Confederate flag, and they're saying, 'Yeah, we're going to drop the nigger down into the shitter.' And they meant it. I was scared to death in that little wooden toilet.

"Then all of a sudden, Daddy was there, and he was screaming, 'You sons of bitches, that's my son — I'll kill all of you!' And they got scared of him, and they left me alone, and he brought me out of there through the crowd." Wendell Jr., sometimes resentful of his father, appreciated his bravery in these incidents. "Nothing took precedence over that race car — up to a point. But if you started messing with his family, you were in the wrong, and the man was there for us."

But Scott had a good deal less confidence, some friends said, about promoting himself to the corporate types who controlled racing budgets. Nothing in his background as a black high school dropout, born in a southern mill town in 1921, prepared him to deal easily with self-assured, educated white men from the world of big business. "They intimidated him," said Scott's friend and admirer Leonard Miller, an urbane northerner who became one of the sport's black pioneers in the ownership of racing teams during the 1970s. Scott felt that his vocabulary and his country way of speaking were a handicap, Miller said. "He didn't talk up among people who had that intimidating Wall Street big vocabulary and very authoritative manner about them." Scott "never understood the white corporate world and how it worked. You had to spend money doing brochures and calling people, and no one in NASCAR ever came forth to help him with that."

Late that year, one of Scott's supporters, a South Carolina clergyman and political activist who would later be elected as the first black member of the Greenville County Council, traveled to Dearborn to give Ford's racing program a presentation advocating sponsorship for Scott.

Bishop Johnnie M. Smith had met Scott by chance one evening a year or two earlier in Greenville. Scott had stopped there on the way home from a race, dirty, tired, and hungry. Smith had never heard of Scott or seen an automobile race, but he liked Scott right away — "a very humble, nice guy" — and invited him over for dinner. They quickly became friends. When Smith went to races, he was struck by the financial gulf between Scott and the factory drivers. "These guys had uniformed mechanics all around them, a spare car, all kinds of parts, big trucks to carry everything, and Wendell didn't have any of that. I said to myself I'd do everything I could to try to get someone with the money, like Ford, to sponsor him."

Smith, who ran churches in Chicago and Atlanta as well as Greenville, knew nothing about the business world of racing, but he was a personable, confident go-getter accustomed to seeking out the man in charge and making a pitch. He wangled an appointment with Jacques Passino, the executive who oversaw Ford's NASCAR program for Iacocca, and drove out to the Glass House, Ford's Dearborn headquarters, in his Cadillac.

Like Ned Jarrett in his earlier meeting with Iacocca, Smith pushed the idea that if Scott were racing in a competitive Ford, his successes could boost the company's sales to black customers. Fast cars appealed to many potential black buyers, Smith said, and Ford had just introduced the Mustang. Passino was courteous, attentive, and noncommittal.

On December 4, Smith followed up with a letter: "It was good of you to listen to Wendell's case. I hope that he will get full sponsorship this year so that he might be able to give his best. Any consideration that you might be able to give to him in your 1965 budget will be greatly appreciated."

Smith said his trip didn't leave him hopeful. His talk with Passino, he said, had the feel of a "polite-but-no" conversation.

At the end of the 1964 season, Bobby Fleming's prediction proved correct — Scott hadn't been able to get back into the top ten in points. He had run fifty-six races, scoring one win, eight top-fives, and twenty-five top-tens. He placed twelfth in points. Still, that was three spots higher in the standings than last year. And he was racing now with some kind of backing from Ford, though the support was small and vaguely defined. Despite all his difficulties, this had been his best Grand National season yet.

# 20

## "We used to be the cleanup boys."

After Scott's crash at Charlotte, a fan, Peter Davis of Raleigh, sent him a letter of praise and support. "It is an inbred characteristic of Americans to pull for the underdog," he wrote. Scott's appeal, he said, reflected the struggles of the unsponsored drivers against the factory teams. "You and other independent drivers show courage by continuing against these hardships and heartbreaks," he said, adding that NASCAR racing "is going to suffer in the long run from this practice of favoring a certain few."

The letter lifted Scott's spirits — he kept it for the rest of his life — and it offered a partial explanation for a new, somewhat surprising development in his career.

Despite the South's embattled racial atmosphere, despite the fact that most NASCAR fans were working-class white people, Scott was becoming one of the circuit's most popular drivers. At the pre-race driver-introduction ceremonies, the applause for him was getting more and more enthusiastic. When his turn came to run his qualifying laps, crowds now cheered him loudly.

This was a big change, of course, from his first Grand National four years earlier, when the announcer was ordered to fudge his name so that spectators wouldn't realize that the field included a black driver. "By about 1965, Wendell would draw almost as much applause as the top drivers," said Roy Moody, an ardent NASCAR fan who watched Scott race at many tracks. Often, the crowds cheered almost as loudly for Scott as they did for Junior Johnson, Fred Lorenzen, and Richard Petty, Lorenzen recalled. Sometimes only Petty got a bigger response, said Scott's crewman Ray Arnold.

At Bristol, Tennessee, on May 2, 1965, applause for Scott during the driver introductions "was as great as that received by the pre-race favorites, Johnson and Lorenzen," the *Danville Commercial Appeal* reported, even though he qualified only eighteenth. In the race, Scott slowly worked his way forward in the thirty-three-car field. When he got up to fifth, where he would finish, his car number, thirty-four, flashed onto the scoreboard for the first time. "As soon as it did, the 20,000 fans stood and roared their approval."

Scott's perseverance as an independent, however, wasn't the only reason for his growing fan support. Clearly his status as NASCAR's first black driver also figured strongly in his appeal, as did his choice to avoid any public comments on racial matters. The white independents, drivers such as Tom Pistone, Roy Tyner, Neil Castles, and G.C. Spencer, had their admirers, but Scott got far more crowd reaction. NASCAR fans understood perfectly well which driver was the underdog among underdogs.

At a time when many white southerners felt maligned and stereotyped by civil rights activists and journalists, Scott presented the image of an integration pioneer who nevertheless was quiet, polite, hardworking, and nonaccusatory. He had the rough, scarred hands of a workingman, and he understood blue-collar things such as bearings and bushings and valve-spring compressors. For the first time in their lives, thousands of white spectators were beginning to find themselves rooting for a black man to outperform white men. Journalist Morris Stephenson, a racing buff who became a friend of Scott's, summed up the phenomenon, with a broad stroke of hyperbole, in a profile that focused on Scott's growing popularity with white fans. "In his own way," Stephenson wrote, "a Danville Negro has done as much for race relations in the deep South as Dr. Martin Luther King and all the marchers . . ."

Stephenson saw this happening not only at speedways but also at the trailer park in Rocky Mount, Virginia, where he lived with his family. Often Scott dropped by the Stephensons' place on his way to or from a race, towing his stock car, sometimes with his own family along. He would stop outside the park entrance and beep his horn, and the Stephensons would go out to talk with the Scotts alongside the road. After a couple of visits, Stephenson realized that their chats were happening at the roadside because Scott didn't want to come into the trailer park.

"I invited them in and they declined," Stephenson said. "He kept repeating this — he'd come by and blow the horn; my wife and I would go out and talk with them. Finally one night I told him and Mary, 'Y'all come on in — now.'

"He says, 'No, no, we can't.'

"I said, 'We stand out here every time you come by — come on in the house. Let's fix some sandwiches.'

"He said, 'No, I don't want to get you in trouble. People don't like black folks visiting a white place.'

"I said, 'Hey, this place is mine. You're not going to get me in trouble.'"

Actually, Stephenson was just renting the trailer, and the landlord did get upset when he heard that a black family had been visiting. But the neighbors' reaction wasn't at all what Scott had anticipated. The residents welcomed the Scotts as visiting celebrities. Dozens of people would converge on Stephenson's trailer to talk about racing with NASCAR's only black driver and, sometimes, get his autograph.

"The word spread, and every time Wendell and his race car and his family hit that park, and it was a rather large park, our mobile home would fill up," Stephenson said. "Everybody wanted to talk with Wendell. It got so you couldn't hardly move around."

Stephenson would complain jokingly that he should never have insisted that Scott come in. "We didn't have hardly any money, and we were footing the bill for all the sandwiches and drinks for half of this trailer court."

Most of the visitors came back again and again, Stephenson said, because they found Scott likable and without pretense. As a NASCAR racer, Scott was doing something far beyond the capabilities of most people, but he never put on airs.

"He was a diplomat," Stephenson said. "At that time in the South there was a lot of racial unrest, and he wasn't a Martin Luther King kind of crusader, but he was out there as an example that blacks could race with whites and have a good relationship. He was a good, shining example for blacks in the racing profession. He wasn't a troublemaker, he wasn't a rebel, he wasn't saying, *Hey, I'm black — you owe me this and you owe me that, just because I'm black.*"

To what extent Scott's fan support would continue if he got a competitive ride, stopped being an underdog, and began defeating white competitors regularly — well, that would be a problem he would be glad to face. A week after the Bristol event, Scott was allowed to run his first Darlington race, the Rebel 300. He passed the rookie test easily, turning laps at 126 miles an hour. As usual at superspeedways, his speed was about twelve miles an hour slower than the leaders. He finished fifteenth, twenty-one laps behind the factory-sponsored Ford of the winner, Junior Johnson. Fans crowded around him for autographs.

Typically, Scott said nothing publicly for years about what happened next. After victory celebrations ended and the fans left, many of the unsponsored drivers stood in line at a track office near the garage area, waiting for their travel money. "It was the guys who were racing more or less in my bracket — the ones with no financial backing," Scott said.

"Bob Colvin was handing out $150 or $200 apiece to these guys to get back home on. Colvin would give them their money and have them sign their name for it. I went over and got in line.

"When my turn came at the window, Bob Colvin looked up and said, 'Nigger, you better git yo' ass back up that road.'

"I walked away." The incident was almost an exact replay of promoter Enoch Staley's treatment of Scott eleven years earlier, which had prompted Bill France Sr. to promise that from then on Scott would be treated like any other NASCAR driver.

The boost that Scott's fan support could have added to his efforts to impress Ford Motor Co. was undercut by the deteriorating condition of the race car that the company had furnished him the previous year. Engine failures, broken differentials, and other mechanical woes in the much-used Ford would force Scott to drop out of eighteen races during the 1965 season, more than a third of those he started.

By now Scott had become a well-known and admired figure in Danville, perhaps the city's most famous resident since Jefferson Davis. For several months, Danville radio station WBTM ran a fund drive to buy Scott a new engine. "His friends among racing enthusiasts here and elsewhere fear Scott is waging a losing battle to make his mark" against the "favorite sons" of the factory teams, a WBTM editorial said, despite his "guts and a supreme self-confidence that few among us possess." Hundreds of employees in beauty shops, car dealerships, banks, taxi companies, and other businesses contributed a dollar apiece. The drive raised $620.

As in the past season, the Holman-Moody racing shop and some factory-backed teams would give parts to Scott, or sell him some at bargain prices and throw in others for free. Author Tom Cotter, who wrote a book about Holman-Moody, said Scott got much more help from the company than other independent drivers. Ralph Moody "had a soft spot in his heart for Scott."

The generosity of Leonard Wood of the Wood Brothers team, which won many races, particularly stood out. Often he'd tell the Scotts to bring their truck to the team's shop in Stuart, Virginia, fifty miles west of Danville. "Leonard would tell us, 'Y'all come up on Tuesday, and I'll have some used stuff for you out back,'" Wendell Scott Jr. said.

Many times, they would find new parts mixed into the pile of used ones. Often those new parts would be exactly the ones that were nearly worn out on Scott's car, and they would realize that Wood had put a lot of observant attention into figuring out just what they needed most. Sometimes the pile would include a nearly new differential with precisely the right gear ratio for the next race.

"Frankie and I would look at each other, and we almost felt like we were stealing. 'Did he mean for us to get this? This is new.' And he'd have put it amongst bent fenders and so on, so it looked like discarded stuff. When you went into the shop to thank him, he didn't want to hear it.

"He really looked out for us. He cared. You could be around Leonard Wood for a week and not hear ten words, but whatever ten he chose to speak were out of respect and decency."

Even with such help, keeping the Ford going remained a struggle. Before Atlanta's April race, Scott towed his engineless car to Holman-Moody's shop in Charlotte. He'd been forced out of the past three events by engine troubles, completing only seven laps in the last one. He came away with assorted engine parts, drove to Atlanta, scrounged more parts from the Ford teams of Lorenzen and A.J. Foyt, and assembled the motor. It lost oil pressure after only twenty-nine laps. He headed back to Holman-Moody to dicker for more parts.

Sometimes Frank Scott accompanied his father to Holman-Moody's fifty-thousand-square-foot facility. He felt like a child visiting Santa's workshop. He would marvel at the wealth behind Ford's racing operation. All over the complex he saw new engines, new cars, sophisticated chassis components, so many things his father could never afford. For every part that an independent driver would replace from the junkyard, Holman-Moody had a stack of lighter, stronger, state-of-the-art versions of that part sitting on a spotless shelf.

Frank Scott's appreciation for the company's help was mixed with some resentment: "It was better than nothing. But whenever we got something, it was already obsolete, and they had already found something better. They sold us old stuff that they weren't going to use anymore." As promoter Humpy Wheeler observed, "It was a little like giving your old clothes to the maid."

Tom Pistone, one of the first northerners to race in Grand National, thought he knew better than most what Scott was going through. A Chicago native of Italian descent, Pistone experienced his own versions of Scott's problems, both as an independent and as an outsider trying to break into the culture of NASCAR in the 1960s. For a long time after he moved from midwestern racing to Grand National, Pistone said, "all I heard was 'Yankee, Yankee, Yankee.'" He was called a wop or a dago many times. "It was very hard to move in with these people down South. Very hard." Like Scott, Pistone felt that he had the driving talent for a factory ride but that being an outsider was a major obstacle. "I put myself in the same category as Wendell, which was that they just didn't want us around, for some reason or another."

Many times, he said, he and Scott stayed late at the tracks to scavenge for parts the factory teams left behind. "Wendell and I, we were always the last ones to leave. We used to be the cleanup boys. All this stuff that these teams left in the garage area, we'd take it and put it in our cars and run it in the next race. They'd leave windshields, bearings, seals, gaskets, air cleaners — all good stuff." Sometimes they ate food that the teams hadn't finished.

When Scott's car didn't break down, he managed to put together some top-five finishes on short tracks. Besides his fifth place at Bristol, he scored another fifth at Beltsville, Maryland, and two fourths, at Spartanburg and Nashville. He also scored good finishes at two superspeedways. He came from deep in the field to place ninth at Atlanta, in his first race with the engine bought with Danville fans' contributions, and to finish tenth in his first Southern 500 at Darlington. He ran fifty-two events and scored twenty-one top-ten finishes, which meant that when his car didn't fail, he came in tenth or better in nearly two-thirds of his races. He placed eleventh in points for the season, his best result yet, one spot ahead of last year.

Scott's four top-five finishes, however, represented only half of the top-fives he'd scored in the previous season, when his car was fresher. He didn't come close to another win. His top-tens reflected not competitive speed but his gift for squeezing the most performance out of an inferior car, often on worn tires, without pushing it hard enough to break something.

This wasn't a skill that caught the eye of auto manufacturers, and Scott didn't hear anything to suggest that Ford might consider him for a factory team.

To be sure, it's unclear if better results could have changed anything for Scott. The 1965 season was particularly unfavorable for independents seeking factory rides. Chrysler pulled out of NASCAR for much of the season over a rules dispute. Chevrolet produced only a weak effort. Ford dominated the circuit with the formidable talent it had already hired: Lorenzen, Johnson, Foyt, Marvin Panch, Curtis Turner, Cale Yarborough, Ned Jarrett.

Attendance fell sharply on the circuit as Ford won thirty-two consecutive races from February through July and forty-eight of fifty-five for the year. The company had become the Microsoft of Grand National. It had no reason to hire any more drivers. Another respected independent, G.C. Spencer, believed he'd had an agreement locked up to drive for Ford, but when Chrysler pulled out, he said, "suddenly there was no deal. The Ford man said their present setup of drivers would be sufficient for 1965." With Ford's overwhelming success, it would have been hard for any company executive to argue for changes in the racing program, particularly something as controversial as a black driver.

After one of Scott's good finishes, a sixth place at Winston-Salem, the *Charlotte Observer* ran a story that illustrated, inadvertently, how Scott still felt obliged to lie about his experiences and feelings. He told the paper he had only one "bitter racial memory": that an unnamed driver had wrecked him in 1955 in Morehead City, North Carolina. He volunteered nothing about Darlington or Jacksonville. The story also showed how readily such dissembling was accepted. "Scott is not an angry man, far from it," the story concluded, quoting his straight-faced assertion that "as far as this race business is concerned, it's never bothered me."

In late September, a few days before the Klan staged a large rally outside Danville, Scott got what seemed to be a major break in his career. The management of Charlotte Motor Speedway, hoping to reverse the attendance slump caused by Ford's domination, arranged for Scott and several other drivers to run its National 400 in Chevrolets. Speedway officials said the Chevrolets would be new, fully competitive race cars.

The supposed chance-of-a-lifetime opportunity for Scott became a central theme in the speedway's pre-race promotion. "'This could be the best thing that has ever happened to me,' Scott said humbly this morning," reported the *Charlotte News*. Promoter Richard Howard told the newspaper: "We're happy to see Wendell in first-class equipment. I have always thought he is a good driver, but he never has had a chance to prove himself because of inferior equipment."

At the time, the Charlotte facility operated under the supervision of a bankruptcy court after years of financial woes. Not surprisingly, on race day the Chevrolets turned out to be not very competitive. "That weren't no good car," Scott said. "It lacked a whole lot." Howard acknowledged many years later in an interview that "we had Chevrolets in the field, but some of them wouldn't run so fast." After eighty-nine laps the driveshaft broke in Scott's car, and he hit the first-turn wall.

The episode brought Scott some sour publicity. The *Charlotte Observer*, probably the most-read newspaper in NASCAR racing, suggested that the wreck was simply what anyone should have expected of Scott. His crash "didn't surprise anybody, perhaps, but Scott." One anonymous "wag," the reporter wrote, had this comment: "Ain't that something. Wendell finally gets a car and wrecks it in the first race."

Describing Scott as "a thin man with a narrow face who shows every one of his forty-four years," the story noted that the seat of his racing suit was badly worn. "Fellow racers might say the coveralls were worn that way because careful Wendell sits so tight. Anyway, his seat showed more wear than his shoe soles." The reporter's meaning wasn't hard to translate: Scott was too old, was afraid to go fast, and didn't push the gas pedal very hard.

After his difficult season, Scott suffered major ulcer problems in December that were serious enough to leave him worried that he'd have to quit racing. The attack forced him to do what he probably should have done years earlier. He went into the hospital for an operation to remove the ulcerated parts of his stomach. "I'd been sick all my life and didn't know it because I thought that was the way you were supposed to feel," he told a reporter. The surgery was successful; for the rest of his life, stomach troubles were infrequent and minor. While recovering, he got a satisfying reminder of his popularity with fans. "You should see the cards and letters I got when I was laid up, people asking if they could help," he said. "Made me feel good."

For Bill France, the idea of building NASCAR's next major superspeedway in the Spartanburg area wasn't working out. He and his friend, promoter Joe Littlejohn, had not been able to put together enough land for a track that would be bigger than Daytona.

Since September 1964, however, France had been examining another possible site — a project that would lead NASCAR and its founder into a long, friendly, and mutually beneficial alliance with a political figure who had become the predominant voice of southern racism in the 1960s: the governor of Alabama, George Corley Wallace.

# 21

## "I'll get it done, Bill."

During the 1965 racing season, Bill France came to George Wallace's office at the state capitol in Montgomery to promote his plan for the next big phase of NASCAR's expansion. France hoped to build the nation's largest, fastest speedway outside the small Alabama city of Talladega. He had little more than a broad, rosy vision of the huge facility when he sat down with Wallace, yet he wanted the governor to give him a multimillion-dollar commitment for major highway spending and other state subsidies for his venture.

Aides to both men were struck by the strong personal rapport that emerged almost immediately between NASCAR's founder and the wily, cigar-chomping politician. From their first meeting in the historic capitol, birthplace of the Confederacy, France and Wallace developed a tight relationship, their aides said. Their bond would grow into a personal friendship and would lead to France playing important roles in Wallace's later campaigns for the presidency.

Jim Foster, a senior aide to France, recalled, "Bill was telling George Wallace, 'I'm going to build a track that one of these days is going to be bigger than Indianapolis, but I need you to build me, off the interstate out there, I need six lanes to get the people in and out on race day.'"

The proposed track in northeastern Alabama would sit alongside Interstate 20, the region's main east–west highway. The speedway would be forty-five minutes from Birmingham and ninety minutes from Atlanta. "George listened to him and said, 'Yeah, that sounds good. You build the track, and then I'll build the road.'

"Bill said, 'No, I got to have the road before I start trying to raise money to get this thing going.'

"They had a little more conversation, and then Wallace said, 'Yeah, well, I'll do it. I'll get it done, Bill.' Just like that."

Charles Snider, a close aide to Wallace, said: "The governor called the highway director over and told him what he wanted to do, and the highway director said, 'If we put those roads in, Governor, how do we know that Bill France is going to put that track in?'

"The governor's exact words were, 'Because, damn it, he said he would.' That's how the governor felt about Bill. He just had a lot of credibility here."

After another meeting among France, Wallace, and other state officials, the governor fired off a short, blunt memo to his director of industrial development: "Let's get this done soon." Wallace ordered plans drawn up for several highway projects for the track, including Speedway Boulevard, essentially a seven-mile, four-lane driveway for France's facility, costing the state two million dollars.

Wallace wrote to France: "I am very grateful for your interest in Alabama . . . We are going to work with you to bring this fine attraction and addition to our state." Plans aren't pavement, however, and many other issues remained on the table — tax exemptions, sewage, water, the possibility of a state-funded racing hall of fame at the site — and those matters, along with their personal affinity, would keep France and Wallace closely involved for years.

On the surface they seemed quite different, but in many ways they weren't. France had the polished charm of a corporate leader and deal maker. Wallace had a cruder persona, raw and elemental, still a crafty country boy. But they shared some fundamental qualities: dominating personalities, immense ambition, tireless energy, an audacity of long-range vision about what they could accomplish, and a deep disdain for Washington bureaucrats and liberalism.

By 1965, the fiery and polarizing Wallace had emerged as the South's most prominent public official in the effort to preserve segregation. At his inauguration two years earlier, berating the "tyranny" of federal support for civil rights, Wallace had delivered some of the most famous words in the annals of white supremacy, written by his favorite staff speechwriter, Asa Carter, a Klan organizer:

"Today I have stood, where once Jefferson Davis stood, and took an oath to my people. It is very appropriate, then, that from this cradle of the Confederacy, this very heart of the great Anglo-Saxon Southland, that today we . . . send our answer to the tyranny that clanks its chains upon the South. In the name of the greatest people that have ever trod this earth, I draw the line in the dust and toss the gauntlet before the feet of tyranny, and I say, 'Segregation today, segregation tomorrow, segregation forever!'"

The following year Wallace gave his presidential ambitions their first test. He ran in Democratic primaries in Wisconsin, Indiana, and Maryland, attacking liberals, Washington, and what he called the "civil wrongs" bill. He surprised many pundits, winning enough votes to establish himself as a credible national candidate. His candidacies in the next three presidential elections — all including France in significant roles — would help push American politics to the right.

In defiant, sometimes half-snarling speeches, Wallace masterfully exploited and defended the hatreds and fears not only of some white Alabamians but also of the close-knit ethnic and working-class white neighborhoods across the South and North that "shared the same deep and visceral apprehensions," historian and Wallace biographer Dan T. Carter wrote. As the civil rights movement helped to inspire protests over the Vietnam War, sexual freedom, and women's rights, Wallace broadened his message to portray those activists, too, as elitists trampling on traditional values of God and country.

When France became friendly with Wallace in 1965, the governor was embroiled in controversy over one of the era's most notorious episodes of police violence against blacks. Some officials, including the head of Alabama's state police, said Wallace had personally ordered the clubbing and tear-gasing of peaceful demonstrators marching from Selma to Montgomery, seeking the right to vote for blacks. In private conversations, Wallace regularly referred contemptuously to "niggers" and to their inferiority as a people. Pollsters found that Wallace's racial views gave him an approval rating among white southerners, NASCAR's primary audience back then, of about 80 percent.

France, however, felt that Wallace had been labeled a racist unfairly, according to Charles Snider, who became a top Wallace campaign official as well as a close friend of France. Snider said the NASCAR founder "was convinced after sitting with George Wallace that he was far different from the way he had been perceived by the American public and others — that he was a very compassionate individual."

France thought Wallace did not deserve "the segregationist reputation that he had," Snider said. "The fact of the matter is that George Wallace had to take the stand he did, or he could never have gotten elected governor. And Bill knew that." Moreover, Snider said, France "just liked George Wallace personally, very much so. I would say on a scale of one to ten, it was probably seven personal, three political."

France's political support for Wallace wasn't about race, Snider said. "Bill's issue was that the liberalism in this country was going to destroy us, if you didn't get some conservatism in there that would respect and look to businessmen to run their businesses and do the things necessary to make this economy go . . . He thought there was a lot of things in government that needed to be changed."

Under Wallace, state government in Alabama was openly and pervasively corrupt. His friends and political backers, including Klan officials, prospered from a freebooting system of sweetheart contracts, kickbacks, and other graft. Right after Wallace's election, his brother Gerald, a lawyer, made it widely known that anyone seeking state business would first have to make private money deals with him. He "put the word out all over the country that to do business in Alabama, with the state of Alabama, you had to go through Gerald Wallace," said journalist and author Wayne Greenhaw.

Gerald was "a crook, a bag man — very corrupting guy," said attorney Tom Turnipseed, a former Wallace campaign director. Nobody doubted that he was acting with the governor's approval. The previously modest income of Gerald's one-man law firm quadrupled. Asphalt deals became a lucrative sideline among Wallace cronies. One company in which Gerald Wallace owned an interest sold the state $2.9 million in asphalt during his brother's first term, despite charging $2.50 per ton over the going rate. Biographer Dan T. Carter said in an interview: "Nothing came through Wallace's office that didn't go through Gerald, certainly nothing that involved money. He didn't make any bones about it. He told anybody who dealt with the state in any way that they had to come through him."

Another insider profiting from state actions was entrepreneur Oscar Harper, one of the governor's closest friends. Harper shared interests in various companies with Gerald Wallace. Among other ventures, Harper sold the state $2.4 million worth of asphalt. Often Harper bragged about being a good friend of France, journalist Greenhaw recalled. "One of the things that might have sold Wallace [on France] in the beginning would have been Oscar's okay."

It was a time when the normal routines of Alabama government and politics included businessmen buying influence, state officials accepting gratuities, and politicians operating campaign slush funds where the line between contributions and payoffs remained deliberately murky. During the 1960s, Charles Snider said, France "on several occasions invited the governor's staff down to Daytona to watch the races and some of us accepted and went down . . . courtesy of Bill France. I remember one time he sent up a DC-3 [airplane] and loaded up about thirty of us, and it was all the governor's cabinet and everybody around. It was just a gesture on his part — 'I want you guys to come down as my guests.'"

Turnipseed, who said the bigotry and graft he saw under Wallace inspired him to become an anti-racism activist, recalled another France-financed junket. "He flew us, the whole campaign staff, down to the Daytona race and put us up for the whole damn weekend. Everything was on the house . . . Thirty people or so. He was lobbying Wallace." France's expenditures were "smart," Turnipseed added, "because Wallace helped him with the Talladega thing." The governor told Turnipseed "The good folks that drive stock cars and love stock car racing, they're going to elect me president of the United States."

Seymore Trammell Jr., the son of Wallace's state finance director, worked in Wallace's political campaigns and had his own state job with Alabama's tourism agency. France was a big contributor to Wallace, said the younger Trammell, whose father eventually went to prison on federal tax and corruption charges. In those pre-Watergate years before campaign-finance reforms, money often changed hands with no paperwork, he said.

"It was such a haphazard thing back at that time. Nobody kept records. Sometimes they would give checks. Sometimes, particularly if George or Gerald was around, people like France would just pull out a handful of hundred-dollar bills and give it to the governor to stick in his pocket . . . They provided a great deal of what today we'd call soft money. We didn't know what to call it back then, except just under-the-table stuff."

The selling of influence, of course, was hardly unique to Wallace's state, but some of the details had a distinct Old South flavor. At one fifteen-hundred-dollar-a-plate fund-raiser in Alabama's vast, white-columned governor's mansion, the waitresses serving dinner to France, Harper, Gerald Wallace, and the other guests were inmates from the nearby Julia Tutwiler Prison for Women.

As the Talladega project took shape, journalists at the *Montgomery Advertiser*, which exposed numerous corruption scandals during George Wallace's reign, heard scuttlebutt that Gerald Wallace had "a piece of the action," recalled former political writer Bob Ingram. "That was the rumor. If there was money to be made, Gerald was in the front row waiting to get his. Gerald was notorious." But no evidence confirming the allegation ever became public. The newspaper's former editor, Ray Jenkins, said Gerald "had his hands into everything and his fingerprints on nothing."

The intricacies of Alabama influence-peddling, the strategic alliances behind NASCAR's expansion plans, the political and financial support France gave to Wallace — these were matters that, in Wendell Scott's day-to-day world, might as well have been unfolding in another galaxy.

Scott was working in his backyard garage, hoping to coax a few more miles an hour out of his arthritic race car, moving around gingerly after his ulcer operation. But as word got around about France's Talladega plans, Scott realized that this new venture added another question mark to his prospects for a competitive Grand National ride, at least concerning any role NASCAR might play in those prospects. Would Wallace spend millions of dollars of taxpayers' money on France's project if NASCAR's program included any realistic possibility of a black driver winning a race in Alabama?

As anyone with even a fraction of Bill France's savvy would have understood, Wallace's abhorrence of integration extended to many activities, including sports. An incident a few years later made that point quite explicit. When Wallace wanted a prestigious running mate for his 1968 presidential campaign, his closest aide, Seymore Trammel Sr., recruited the popular Happy Chandler, former Kentucky governor and US senator — and former national baseball commissioner who had supported Jackie Robinson's admission to the major leagues.

Wallace immediately objected. "You know, he's the one, the commissioner, that integrated baseball," Wallace told Trammel. Even though Chandler's offense against segregation had happened twenty-one years earlier, it was the first thought that came to Wallace's mind when he heard Chandler's name. At first, briefly and uneasily, Wallace accepted Chandler for the ticket. Then he acted on his first instincts and dumped him.

Chandler's support had given Robinson his opportunity to outperform many white players. To Wallace, that was an abomination. He wanted nothing to do with anyone whose leadership of a sport allowed such a thing to happen.

## 22

### "You're not gonna miss that li'l ol' wheel."

Another season, another cross-country tow to California, another costly setback. Strapped into his race car, Scott sat waiting on Riverside International Raceway's pit lane on January 23, 1966, warming up his car, when suddenly the engine blew. He had no spare engine, which meant he'd miss the race. He'd be towing the broken car back to Virginia with no prize money in his pocket. Once again the tired Ford had failed him.

During practice that day, Fred Lorenzen had crashed in one of the factory-sponsored Fords he drove for the Holman-Moody team, rolling the car over several times. Scott examined the crumpled Ford after a wrecker hauled it back to the pits. The accident had destroyed the body, but the chassis might well be better than what he had now. Probably the engine was, too — right now, almost any engine would be. After a morning like this one, even the wreckage of a factory-team car looked desirable.

Scott decided to attempt some of the most ambitious scrounging of his career. He walked up to Lorenzen's team owners, John Holman and Ralph Moody. They were talking with their driver and Jacques Passino, who ran Ford's NASCAR racing program for Lee Iacocca.

"Wendell said, 'Mister Ralph, that car's in awful bad shape,'" Lorenzen recalled. "'You wouldn't want to take that all the way back to Charlotte and fix it. You just give it to me, and I'll get it ready for Daytona.'

"Ralph said, 'Naw, we can fix that.'

"Wendell said, 'Naw, it'd be awful hard to fix that. I'll just fix it, and I'll put FORD on it.'

Nobody would give him an answer, and eventually Scott headed back to Virginia with his old car and some lukewarm hopes. At least they hadn't said no.

The next morning, Moody said, "a little meeting" took place to consider Scott's request. "I asked Ford, what about it? Let's give that thing to

Wendell. He's got all the bodywork to do; we just give him the stuff and go with it.

"They said, 'Do what you want with it.'"

A week or so later, Scott met with Moody at the team's complex in Charlotte. It was obvious, Moody said, how badly Scott wanted the car, a 1965 Galaxy with a 427 engine.

"He said, 'How much do you want?'

"I told him, 'Ten thousand dollars.'

"Boy, he walked around, shaked his head awhile, wanted to know if I'd take five or four. Finally I agreed on something foolish like thirty-five hundred or something. Hell, the engine, the wheels and the tires were worth more than that.

"So he said he'd be back, and I said, 'Damn, you better leave a deposit on that thing if you really want it. Somebody might come and get it.'

"He walked around and looked a little bit more and said, 'Will five dollars be all right?'"

Moody told Scott he could take the car. Moody never expected, he said, to get the rest of the money. "He never finished paying for it. Nobody ever bothered him about it. We knew damn well we were going to give it to him."

As with the Ford that Scott had gotten from Holman-Moody two seasons ago, exactly what had happened in this transaction remained somewhat murky, perhaps deliberately. Perhaps Ford Motor Co. had given Scott a car; perhaps Scott defaulted on a payment agreement to Holman-Moody; perhaps reality lay somewhere in between. In any case, nobody could say that Ford was sponsoring a black driver — or, for that matter, refusing to help a black driver.

Determined to impress the company — and to make some money, after his financial misfortune at Riverside — Scott resolved to rebuild the Galaxy in time for the Daytona 500, less than two weeks away. Scott, his sons and a rotating crew of friends worked virtually around the clock in his garage, dismantling the car to the bare frame, discovering more damage than expected, fitting an entire new body. One friend, Jack Cousins, recalled that Scott got the Ford with no camshaft or carburetor, two parts so critical to making horsepower that companies considered their exact designs to be high-level corporate secrets.

Outside the garage, a heavy snowfall was melting. Little streams of water ran across the floor. As Scott and his friends used power tools and an arc welder with their feet in the water, they got some electrical shocks. "Everything on that car was twisted," Ray Arnold said. "That's the only reason they gave it to him. Scott and them, they got the heating torches and chains and jacks and finally got all of the wheels to sit on the ground."

For years afterward, the car would be known to all involved as the Twelve-Day Wonder. Scott made it to Daytona. He placed thirteenth of fifty starters, the first of the owner-drivers, although crashes and breakdowns left only five other cars still running at the finish.

NASCAR acknowledged Scott's growing popularity with an upbeat, respectful profile in its official newsletter. The article, spread across the front page with a large photo, carried the headline: "Those Cheers Are Louder Now For Wendell." The newsletter, which had run no story about Scott's win at Jacksonville in 1963, described the enthusiastic crowd applauding him at Columbia, South Carolina, where he finished ninth.

"Today Scott, the only Negro in stock car racing, is cheered by the thousands of fans who attend races . . . ," the newsletter reported. "It had not always been that way. 'They used to cheer like that and I knew they were making fun of me,' he said seriously. 'Now they're for me. It makes you feel real good. Twenty years is a long time to work for something. Yes! It makes you feel real good.'" While Scott still dreamed of winning a five-hundred-mile race, the article said, the "odds are stacked against him because his equipment is not the best. But the fans notice him now. They respect his driving. The cheers are louder."

One of the country's best-known black magazines, *Ebony,* published a laudatory, four-page profile of Scott, praising his determination. "'All I need is a little luck,' says the nation's only big-time Negro driver, 'and I could really reap a harvest . . . With a little better equipment, I know I can come out on top.'" A Newspaper Enterprise Association feature on Scott said he was "a good, consistent driver and undoubtedly would do better with first-class equipment." Even Darlington Raceway's program included a positive blurb about Scott, acknowledging that he was "very popular."

The good publicity, support from fans, and occasional positive remarks from Ford's Jacques Passino gave Scott some glints of hope about his sponsorship prospects. According to Ray Arnold, Passino "would always be at the track, and he'd say, 'I'll see if I can get something done for you. If you can hang on until the end of the year, we're gonna figure something out there that you can use.' He always talked as if he might be able to shake it loose for you."

Scott expressed some private despair, however, in a letter to his friend Mel Leighton, who had been one of auto racing's best-known black pioneers before Scott. Leighton drove open-wheeled race cars on the West Coast in the 1930s and '40s but was never able to realize his dream of racing in the Indy 500. Scott wrote of his lack of success in finding support from either white- or black-owned companies. "I just can't get a good ride," his letter said. "The colored people that could help a colored man that can drive a race car are just not interested. It looks like I have carried this sport about as far as I can alone. You can wear out race cars faster than you can pay for them."

Another cloud in the sponsorship picture was the turmoil that season in Ford's NASCAR program. Chrysler's ultrapowerful Dodges and Plymouths with their new hemi engines were trouncing the Fords easily. Ford hadn't been able to negotiate enough rules changes to make its cars competitive, so on April 15 the company announced a boycott of NASCAR. "We can't be competitive under these new rules," Henry Ford II said. The company, Bill France retorted, was "acting like children."

With the factory Fords on the sidelines for the time being, Scott's results immediately improved. He placed third, fourth, and fifth on North Carolina short tracks in April and May. He finished regularly in the top ten throughout the summer. He managed seventh-place finishes at both the Charlotte and Atlanta superspeedways, even though the Twelve-Day Wonder was ten to twenty miles an hour slower than Chrysler's dominant hemi-powered cars.

In June, Scott lost a key crew member — Wendell Scott Jr. was drafted into the army. He left for basic training dreading the experience, he said, because his father had talked so often about hating his own army years. "It wouldn't have been nearly as intense if I hadn't heard it all my life," Wendell Jr. said.

Ford returned to NASCAR in late August, its boycott having failed to win any concessions. Now, with more factory-sponsored cars in every race, the odds of a win for Scott became much steeper. The company's return did help him, however, in one important way. Once again the well-funded Ford teams were at the racetracks with large supplies of the spare parts Scott needed to keep his own shoestring operation going. His style of asking for handouts combined politeness, persistence, and a touch of guilt provoking.

When he'd approach Holman-Moody, Lorenzen recalled, Scott would slip in references to the team's wealth. "We had millions of dollars, he'd say. 'You're not gonna miss that li'l ol' wheel. You done run that wheel twice already. You got lots of 'em — you got a whole truckload, and I have none of 'em.'

"I liked him. He was a very kind-spoken person. He spoke with sincerity. When he asked for something, you knew he needed it. He'd say, 'You got that whole stack of tires over there, twenty-two tires. Now, those two on the bottom, they're almost wore out. They'll run me for a while.' So you'd give it to him."

Scott went into the season's final race at Rockingham, North Carolina, with a chance for a top-five finish in the points. During practice, however, his engine failed. His friend Tom Pistone let Scott drive his car in the race. Pistone's car was considerably faster than Scott's. Starting fortieth of forty-four cars, Scott charged up to about tenth place early in the race, Pistone said. "He came through that pack like a tornado. He showed people right there and then that he could drive a race car." Then Pistone's motor blew, and Scott's day was over.

Still, his overall results for 1966 kept Scott's sponsorship hopes flickering. He finished sixth in the points, breaking into the top ten for the first time. He scored seventeen top-ten finishes, including three top-fives, in forty-five races. He won $23,051, more than ever before. His age, to be sure, wasn't among his assets. The *NASCAR Newsletter* article had noted that, "like the great Satchel Paige, who was accepted by baseball after he passed his prime, the quiet, soft-speaking Wendell is feeling the years. At forty-five, he's one of the oldest drivers in racing."

On the other hand, some drivers in their forties had just proven that they could still run up front. Buck Baker, two years older than Scott, scored seven top-fives in 1966. Marvin Panch, at forty, won the World 600 at Charlotte and had three other top-fives. Darel Dieringer, also forty, won three races, including the Southern 500, and finished in the top five four other times.

Some top drivers agreed with Ned Jarrett's assessment to Lee Iacocca — that Scott could drive competitively if he had a fast car. Richard Petty said: "I have no doubt in my mind that he could have drove a good car and won races with it." Marvin Panch said: "If Wendell had had the equipment, he would have been very competitive. He was real good." Junior Johnson said: "Wendell's driving ability was as good as anybody's out there. He just never had a good enough car to prove it." Lorenzen said Scott would tell him, "'I know I could run right with you if I had the same equipment.' And he was right — he probably could have."

Some other prominent racing people, however, felt that Scott hadn't proven himself worthy of factory support. Buck Baker said: "I don't think Wendell had the killer instinct that would make a factory say, 'Not only is he the only black driver, but he's got enough killer instinct.' I think they felt that he would be a nice guy, and let's face it, nice guys have their place." Smokey Yunick, who knew all of the sport's major players and worked at various times for the racing operations of Ford and General Motors, said he believed that Ford executives thought Scott lacked the ability to win and didn't have the outgoing, upbeat personality that would make him a public relations asset. "I think that Wendell was given a damn good looking-over [by Ford] . . . And I got a feeling that, in their observation of his driving talents, he didn't qualify. I don't think they felt that he handled himself well enough in public that he could represent them." Banjo Matthews, a driver who became a leading builder of cars for factory teams, considered

Scott "mediocre, nothing exceptional and not bad. He was just an independent that made a living racing." Scott's equipment, Matthews said, looked like "a typical nigger rig."

Some weeks after the season's end, Scott drank coffee in his kitchen with his friend Morris Stephenson, the journalist whose trailer-park neighbors always came over whenever Scott paid a visit. On the table sat a letter that a Ford Motor Co. executive had written to a friend of Scott's, one of the many who'd contacted the company advocating sponsorship for him.

Scott stared at the letter. "Man, they done closed the door right in my face," he said.

The letter, Stephenson would write later in an article, "stated that [Ford] couldn't help Scott because the company had decided against giving assistance to any driver over forty years of age."

Typically, Scott had gotten the news secondhand; nobody from the company had spoken to him.

"I know I'm colored," he told Stephenson, "but that should be all the more reason they would want to help me . . . A lot of colored people come to the races, and I had a good year."

He sipped his coffee. "They helped me a lot in the past, and don't think I don't appreciate it. Ever since I've been driving a Ford I've gone up in the point standings. Every year has been better than the last."

By this time, Scott said, he hadn't really expected Ford to make him a full-fledged driver on a factory team, but he'd still been hoping for some kind of support deal that would make him more competitive. "I was just wishin' they'd give me a little help, like parts to build a new racer and a new engine at a good price."

The details of Ford's decision-making process could not be determined. Iacocca declined to be interviewed. Both Passino and his boss, Leo Beebe, who headed all of Ford's racing programs, said they didn't recall Iacocca ever speaking with them about the idea of Scott driving for the company. The role of Henry Ford II, if any, remains unknown. Ralph Moody said the fact that Ford already had an armada of talented drivers under contract probably hurt Scott's chances. "They had so many on the hook — Christ, they didn't need one more."

Stephenson, who later became a speedway promoter, said Ford's decision wasn't surprising. Scott's participation hadn't brought large numbers of black spectators to NASCAR events, and except for the *Ebony* profile, he got little coverage from black publications. "You're asking Ford to support a black race car driver when there weren't many black fans in the stands, and radio and television coverage, all this exposure, just wasn't there. I could see why Lee Iacocca probably didn't act on it. That wasn't the thing to do at that particular time. NASCAR was regional, it was white, and it was redneck."

At Scott's kitchen table that day in 1966, Stephenson pressed his friend for more comment on this setback — what was the future of his racing program now? Scott fidgeted with the letter, looking glum, shaking his head slowly. "I don't know what I'll do," he said.

# 23

## "I'm going to show them."

Scott's mother, still sprightly and cheerful in her midseventies, often searched her backyard for a four-leaf clover to give her son before a race. Each leaf, Martha Scott would say, was supposed to bring its own kind of luck: "One leaf is for the highway; another for a safe race; the third is for the money and the last is for a safe trip home."

One sunny afternoon in March 1967, Scott's truck and race car sat on the shoulder of Route 85 in northern Georgia. He'd been driving to Atlanta International Raceway when the truck's engine blew at 5 AM. His two volunteer helpers sprawled in the cab, weary and bored. They hadn't seen Scott for several hours. He'd hitchhiked to the speedway, 130 miles away, to borrow somebody's truck and come back for the race car. He got to Atlanta just in time, but the result was hardly worth the effort. He qualified forty-first of forty-four cars. Ten laps into the race, his engine blew. The clover hadn't brought any luck, and that would be the story for much of his 1967 season.

Up to now, despite troubles and disappointments, Scott often had managed to run among the top independents and to finish occasionally in the top five. The factory teams, however, fielded dramatically faster cars every year. The top Daytona 500 qualifying speed, which had been 175 miles an hour in 1966, would jump to 180 in 1967, to 189 in 1968, to 194 in 1970. Some of the younger independents got used cars from those teams that easily ran away from Scott's. His sixth place in the 1966 points would turn out to be a high point of his career. "That was the only year we really showed a profit and had some cash money at the end of the year," Frank Scott said. "Things got rougher after that."

Scott had put a junkyard engine into his truck to get home from Atlanta. But on his way to the April race at Richmond, the truck's crankshaft snapped, thirty miles from the track. Once again, he got his race car to the speedway in time for the race. Once again, the Ford's engine failed early. He wound up twentieth of twenty-four cars. Only his knack for improbable temporary repairs allowed him to get home. He dropped the truck's oil pan, carefully welded the crankshaft together without removing it, and drove back to Danville very slowly.

The many ways that cars and trucks can betray their owners, the small sounds or smells that can signal these betrayals — that sort of knowledge was so ingrained in Scott's consciousness, his sons came to believe that not even sleep could shut down his awareness of the mechanical karma of whatever motor vehicle was transporting him. One night after a race, Frank Scott was driving the truck home. His father slumped in the passenger seat, eyes closed, head drooping, apparently in deep slumber. Suddenly, without saying a word, Wendell Scott reached out and shut off the ignition. "We just burned out a bearing," he said as they rolled to a stop. Scott had smelled the failure in his sleep before the bearing made any sound. They had no food with them, but during the many hours they spent stranded on that deserted stretch of rural highway, a white couple stopped and made them sandwiches of baloney and egg salad.

Despite Scott's popularity, his family still endured bigotry and threats at some tracks. At Darlington, spectators in the notoriously rowdy infield, often drunk, regularly harassed Scott's teenaged daughters with racial and sexual taunts. Mary Scott warned the girls to stay near the family's truck, but that wasn't always possible. Deborah Scott, who traveled all over the South with her father, said Darlington was the only track where she often felt fearful. "If we'd run down to the bathroom, these white men always started bothering us, picking on us, calling us 'little nigger gals,'" she said. Once, her little sister Cheryl kicked one of those men in the ankle and ran away as fast as she could.

Darlington's president, Bob Colvin, forty-seven years old, died of a heart attack that year in his office. (His funeral, the newspapers noted, featured a big floral reproduction of the Confederate flag.) For the Scotts, his absence didn't change much. Spectators leered and shouted at the girls from the roofs of their campers, Sybil Scott, the youngest daughter, recalled. "We were lucky to come out of there alive. Their favorite term was *chocolate*

— that's what they'd always call my sisters and I. 'I see some chocolate over there. We gonna have us some little chocolate Fudgesicles today.' All kinds of crazy loud tones. There'd be a chain reaction from camper to camper, them up on the roofs, just going berserk."

One evening at Montgomery Motor Speedway, Wendell Scott sent Frank to the concession stand to buy him a pack of chewing gum. In Montgomery that night, black residents were demonstrating for civil rights, which angered some spectators at the Alabama track, as Frank quickly found out.

"Daddy always chewed gum when he raced," he recalled. "They didn't have a concession stand in the infield, so I had to go across the track and past the main grandstand." Spectators began shouting at him. "I thought I wasn't going to get out of there. They were calling me nigger. 'Kill him. Hang him!' All of that. 'Why you not up there [at the demonstration] with your friends?' I just kept walking."

Frank bought the gum. As he walked back, the spectators' shouting started again. "I was afraid. We had been trained that people calling you names wouldn't hurt you, as long as they didn't put their hands on you. But I ran. It wasn't like I was super-brave. I knew he needed that gum, so I had to get it."

Ford's racing program for 1967 raised a question about whether the company's decision not to give Scott any direct support really did result from a new company policy against sponsoring drivers over forty. If Ford had such a policy, somebody apparently forgot to tell Junior Johnson and Darel Dieringer.

Johnson had retired from driving and now owned a Ford-sponsored team. Dieringer, who turned forty-one that season, drove for that team. His support from Ford continued, and his performance could have been the script for a commercial promoting forty-something drivers. In the eighteen races Dieringer ran that season, he finished second three times, third twice, and at North Wilkesboro became the first Grand National driver ever to win a race by leading every lap.

The well-connected Smokey Yunick said he believed Ford officials had come to regard Scott as ungrateful. "When Ford had decided to help him and they were giving him last year's stuff, which was still pretty damn good stuff, he didn't exactly sound to me like a guy who appreciated the hell out of it," Yunick said. "He was still playing that song of 'If I had good equipment, I could run with them.' And maybe he could have. But I think that Ford deal, he undone it himself by not being as appreciative as he should have been."

Mechanical problems, mostly engine failures, knocked Scott out of sixteen races during 1967. More often now, he finished in the middle or back of the field. On the short dirt tracks, where in recent seasons he'd often raced near the front-runners, his best results were three sixth-place finishes. He wound up tenth in points for the season, with eleven top-tens, six fewer than last year, and no top-fives.

Even more than in the past, Scott often had to drive conservatively to make sure he'd collect enough prize money to pay the bills. Frank was a freshman at North Carolina State, and Scott's teenage daughters were talking about college, too; Wendell Scott Jr. was still in the army. Ralph Moody and Richard Petty saw the compromises Scott had to make between showing his talent and making a living. "He was a good driver," Moody said. "I've seen him, on some short tracks, run the tail off those people. Thing is, he didn't have equipment good enough to run hard all day on the big tracks. He'd put too high a gear in [his car], make sure he could run all day, get the best finish he could get."

Petty said: "He drove according to what he thought his equipment was. If he felt he had a good car, or he had a new motor, he'd run hard. If he knowed that thing had a bunch of laps on it already, then he'd pace himself. He'd say, 'Okay, this is the pace that I'm going to set, and I can run all day at this pace.' He had to make do with what he had."

Often, Scott said, the cost of tires determined how hard he could drive. He always had to try to figure out if he might win enough additional prize money to pay for new tires. Often the economics forced him to run on old tires, knowing he'd be slower. Scott and his racing friends felt he wasn't treated fairly by Goodyear, a leading tire supplier for the circuit. One such critic was Scott's close friend Leonard Miller, who later became an owner of racing teams and an activist for more opportunities for black drivers.

Miller said that Goodyear for years denied Scott the support it customarily gave other drivers.

At the time, Goodyear had an unofficial policy that Grand National independents who finished in the top ten got some free tires. According to Miller, "If an independent driver was getting in the top ten, at the next race he could go up to them and get a free set of tires. Wendell couldn't get any tires at all. There were no exceptions made for him during his racing, and that hurt him very badly."

Also, Goodyear wouldn't allow Scott to buy tires on credit at the track and pay for them after the race from his winnings, a convenience routinely given to other drivers, noted Scott's friend and crewman Ray Arnold. When a new white driver would join the circuit, Arnold said, "after about a month, he could get tires on credit from the Goodyear truck at the race-track. But Scott would still have to pay up front for tires, and he'd been running for years before that boy ever got started."

Scott's unhappiness with Goodyear wasn't a secret — he talked about it openly in a newspaper interview. "I can remember lots of times," he told Tom Kelly of the *St. Petersburg Times,* "when there'd be forty or fifty cars in a race and I'd be the only one who was payin' for tires."

William Neely, head of public relations for Goodyear's racing program at the time, confirmed that the company often provided free tires to independents when they performed well. But he questioned the criticism of Goodyear. He said he believed that "there were times when they gave Wendell tires . . . I would like to think that Wendell benefited from it." Goodyear spokesman Chuck Sinclair explained that the company currently has no way "to either substantiate or refute the notion that Mr. Scott had not been accorded the same treatment as any other drivers . . ." Goodyear, he said, "has been working with NASCAR [for] the past several years to help try and advance the NASCAR diversity program. We plan to continue that support in the future."

Bill France, whose business depended on its also-ran drivers as well as the stars, made a point of knowing what his racers needed and sometimes used his position to help them get it, racing people said. "He knew a little bit about everybody, Big Bill did, and he knew what they needed," recalled racing photographer Pal Parker. "Anybody that needed something, needed help, could go to him, and he would be like a big benevolent judge, and he would decide whether or not they needed that, and so forth . . .

"You'd see Big Bill walking around before the race, going through the garage, and he'd stop and talk with them. He'd sit down and talk with Wendell for a few minutes." But as with Scott's earlier problems with Darlington, there is no evidence that his situation with Goodyear ever made it onto France's to-do list. Eventually, Scott stopped buying Goodyears and switched to Firestones, not for financial reasons but "because the Firestone man just treated me nicer."

Mechanical breakdowns took Scott out of twelve races in the 1968 season. Typical of these trouble-plagued events was the Asheville 300 on May 31. Preparing for the race, Scott had worked on his car late into the night. He looked worn out the next morning at the kitchen table as he drank coffee with a magazine writer, David D. Ryan, who would spend the weekend with him. Ryan noticed how the sunlight highlighted the gray in Scott's hair and the deepening lines in his face.

"Sometimes I have been at a point where I thought I would have to quit," Scott said. "But now I'm in it and can't back up." He dug into his pocket for spending money for Deborah, eighteen; Cheryl, sixteen; and Sybil, thirteen. Without sponsorship, he said, "This is a rough game . . . They tell me my age is holding me up, but they didn't try to help me when I was young enough."

On the 230-mile trip to Asheville, many white motorists and workers along the highway, recognizing the race car on the back of Scott's truck, waved at him and shouted "Good luck." Five miles from the speedway, his truck broke down. Scott pulled over — stranded in almost the same spot where the truck had failed a year earlier and caused him to miss the Asheville race.

Several race drivers stopped to offer help. One of them, David Mote, rigged a pipe and chain to the front bumper of Scott's truck and towed it, very slowly, to the track. They arrived in time for the race. Scott was running seventh, challenging for sixth, when a plume of smoke trailed out behind his car. The differential had lost its lubricant and overheated. Seventeenth place paid a hundred dollars.

"It's times like this that I wonder why I keep racing," Scott told Ryan as he loaded up equipment and considered his broken vehicles. It was early the next morning before he could get the truck repaired, load up the race car, and start his trip to the next day's race in Macon, Georgia. Everyone else had left hours before.

Sometimes keeping the race car and truck going took as much as two-thirds of his income. The Scotts put up their house as collateral for a $1,620 loan from Sears ($9,854 in 2008 dollars) — the eighth time they had remortgaged their property or taken out other loans since he'd started racing.

Scott's mother, who had been been living with the family, died in the spring of 1968. On her deathbed, Martha Scott made him promise to give up gambling. "I used to gamble, right much," he acknowledged. "Poker. I played poker." He speculated that perhaps he'd inherited his love of gambling. Besides his father's compulsion for numbers betting, Scott said that according to family lore another ancestor "was supposed to have been a riverboat gambler. They think that's where I got my gambling from." He said he kept his promise to his mother — mostly, though he still bought state lottery tickets.

During 1968, France focused intensely on his Talladega speedway project. Ground was broken, the Alabama legislature had passed favorable measures, and France talked with state officials about plans for a state-subsidized racing hall of fame at the track, which was to open the following year. Across the country, this was a year of bitter turmoil over Vietnam, civil rights, racial riots, and the deepening cultural war between left and right that still divides American politics. In April, Martin Luther King was assassinated. Two months later, Robert Kennedy was assassinated. Alabama's best-known politician, George Wallace, was between stints as governor. He ran for president that year as a third-party candidate, railing against integration, attacking the liberals, intellectuals, and Washington bureaucrats he said were destroying the nation.

France used his political connections in Florida to provide significant help to Wallace's presidential campaign, said Charles Snider, a key Wallace aide and political operative. Florida officials were raising questions about signatures on documents the campaign had filed to get Wallace on the state's ballot for the presidential election. His campaign strategists asked France to use his considerable political influence in Florida, NASCAR's home state. France made some calls, and the problem went away, said Snider. "He helped tremendously with his efforts to help the governor get on the ballot, which we did."

At Darlington on Labor Day weekend, France orchestrated the pre-race festivities to provide maximum boost to Wallace's campaign. Wallace got ten minutes to address the crowd and then rode in the open pace car during the traditional parade laps, waving to the spectators, trailed by a carload of Secret Service agents. Scott "stood silently as George Wallace . . . got a thunderous ovation from the 70,000 spectators gathered for the Southern 500," the *Charlotte Observer* reported. "The years, however, have taught Scott to conceal his feelings. When he's asked about his reactions to the enthusiastic reception Wallace got, Scott's guards slip into place, and he answers in five short words: 'Everybody has his own politics.'"

That summer Wendell Scott Jr. completed his two years as an army draftee and resumed his place on his father's racing crew. Scott told his sons to say nothing to the press or anybody else about George Wallace or France's political activities. "Those were his emphatic orders," Wendell Jr. said. "He said, 'Anything we say about that can't do nothing but hurt us.'" Wallace's campaign had enthusiastic support from the White Citizens' Councils, Ku Klux Klan leader Robert Shelton, the John Birch Society, and other far-right elements. In the violent climate of 1968, Scott wondered occasionally if his own name was on somebody's assassination list. "I used to think about it," he would admit years later. "I was a little bit afraid at Darlington, places like that. I always hoped there were no snipers — no folks with high-powered guns out there somewhere."

Scott placed ninth in points for 1968, but his status among the independents slipped down a couple more notches. In forty-eight races, he scored no top-fives and ten top-tens, one fewer than last season. Five independents, one more than last season, finished ahead of him in fourth through ninth places in the standings: Clyde Lynn, John Sears, Elmo Langley, James Hylton, and Jabe Thomas.

Sometimes Scott talked about quitting racing and running an auto-repair shop full-time in Danville, but his friend Ray Arnold learned to disregard such talk. "He'd say, 'Well, if I can make it through this week, I'm going to get in my shop full-time and forget about all this and make me some money.'"

But racing's grip on Scott, Arnold said, always brought him right back. "The next thing, you'd look up, and here he comes again, wants to try again.

"I'm saying, 'What are you doing? I thought you weren't going to run anymore.'

"He says, 'Well, I'm going to give them another shot. I'm going to show them I ain't going to give up.'"

## 24

### "The funds was just not there."

Wendell Scott Jr. was twenty-two when he came home from the army in the summer of 1968. People noticed he often seemed dark and troubled. They weren't seeing the quick, mischievous sense of humor that had offset his stormy moods during his younger years. Resentments flared up often. Good fortune had taken him to Germany rather than to Vietnam, but he fumed over the army's refusal to grant him leave for Martha Scott's funeral. He began feeling the same sort of ulcer symptoms that had plagued his father. "He came out of the army a very angry, bitter person," his aunt, Guelda King, said.

He went to work at the local Goodyear plant as a tire builder. Most weekends he traveled to races to work in his father's crew. He got his own apartment, a car, and a circle of friends who liked to party. He brooded over what he should do about his future. He felt like the family's "pain child," the one who couldn't deal with life's annoyances and setbacks as comfortably as the others. His father was a racer with thousands of fans, his brother and sisters were planning to be college graduates, and he was just a factory worker. Some of his friends smoked pot, and he tried it, but it just made him sleepy.

Over the years his father often had spoken about both of his sons following in his footsteps and becoming NASCAR drivers. But Scott's own racing schedule was so arduous that nothing happened to advance that idea beyond the talking stage. No specific plans for their driving apprenticeships had taken shape. During periods when Scott had a second, older Grand National car that was still usable, Earl Brooks drove that car and shared the prize money with Scott; the arrangement was part of Scott's business. There was no beginner-level car for Wendell Jr. or Frank to try his skills in local races. Their father always had another race just a few days away, always something he had to repair, always the compulsion to chase his own dream.

To outsiders, Scott might look like a journeyman long past his prime, scraping together a living in an aging car. At forty-seven, he was the circuit's oldest driver. But Scott still knew — not hoped, *knew* — that he could win one of NASCAR's superspeedway races, that he could still put himself into racing's history books, if he could get the break that put him in a competitive car. That wouldn't happen unless he was out there grabbing at the brass ring with every turn of the NASCAR merry-go-round. The longer his odds got, the more often he had to play them.

For Wendell Jr. and Frank, Scott could be a demanding boss at the racetrack, quick to criticize, sparing with praise. Mike Sykes, a family friend who became a NASCAR technical inspector, noted that Scott expected his sons to work as hard as he did — always. Frank often traveled from college to help his father on racing weekends. "They were Wendell's slaves," Sykes said. "From when he'd get to the track at seven in the morning, you didn't see anything but asses and elbows all day long."

When their work didn't satisfy Scott, sometimes he chewed them out forcefully in front of others. "He would jump them — 'I told you to do it this way, or that way.' He would get harsh at them," Sykes said. This would irritate Wendell Jr., just back from two years of sergeants barking orders, much more than the even-tempered Frank. Wendell Jr. "didn't like to be scolded in front of everybody," Sykes said. "That would piss him off right away."

Scott's mediocre results and money problems as the 1969 season unfolded did nothing to lift the morale of anyone in the family. He had to borrow two thousand dollars from Bill France (interest-free) after finishing twenty-ninth in the Daytona 500, thirty-two laps behind the leaders. In the season's first twenty-five races, his average finish was seventeenth. In May, the Scotts had to refinance their home yet again, this time to borrow $3,840. "Daddy renewed his [mortgage] notes so many times it was pathetic," Wendell Scott Jr. said. "When we'd have the bad weekends, on the way home he'd always say, 'I gotta renew that note in the morning.'" He used Danville's black-owned First State Bank, the primary lender to local African Americans since 1919.

At the season's second Daytona race, in July, Scott was the last driver to attempt to qualify. Wendell Jr. watched from atop an oil drum, convinced the engine was simply too weak. "He ain't gonna make it," he told a sportswriter. "The car just won't turn fast enough." To bump the slowest qualifier from the forty-car field, Scott had to average 156 miles an hour for two laps. As he crossed the finish line the first time, the public address announcer delivered the bad news: "First lap: 149.825. Scott's really going to have to go to make the field."

Wendell Jr. jumped down, spit disgustedly, and walked toward the garage, not bothering to watch the second slow lap. "Damn!" he said. "They're paying $600 just to start this one, and we can't even qualify. Damn!"

But as he struggled with these problems, Scott got some news that revived his hope of finally racing in a competitive car, and soon he could think of little else. The encouragement came from the director of Chrysler Corp.'s racing program, Ronney Householder. He told Scott he was planning to put him into a factory-sponsored Dodge built by Ray Fox, one of the sport's top car builders. "He assured me I would get the car. I just couldn't even sleep at night, just had it on my mind so much."

Chrysler's main competitor, the Ford racing operation run by Holman-Moody, had heard about Householder's plan, Ralph Moody said. "Householder figured that it would be a good thing to draw [black] people and sell cars to those kind of people, and that's why he got into it."

Weeks went by, however, and nothing seemed to be happening, leaving Scott plenty of time to worry about the intense competition and politicking that always occurred when drivers learned that any factory ride might become available. One likely competitor was Neil Castles, thirty-four, an independent driver from Charlotte. He was running faster than Scott that season and had some Chrysler connections.

At this point in Scott's career, his troubles with other drivers had largely ended. By all accounts, most drivers liked and respected him, and those who didn't seemed content to ignore him. Scott considered Castles one of the last throwbacks to the old days, someone who still could be counted on for dirty driving tactics and hostility with a racial edge. "He used to wreck me all the time, or try to anyway," Scott said.

Off the track, Castles never confronted Scott directly, but he made a point of using racial slurs and telling stories about how bad things happened to blacks who didn't know their place, Scott said. "He'd tell me about how a black guy moved in near him, and right away his house burned down." Castles added, smirking, that nobody could link him to the fire because he'd been at a bar that night.

Castles knocked Scott around on the track because he knew Scott wouldn't retaliate, according to Buck Baker. "It made Neil look a little bigger in somebody's eyes, certainly not in mine . . . He wasn't as good a driver as Wendell was, and I think that kind of brought on a little resentment." Castles denied ever deliberately trying to wreck Scott. "I have never hit nothing that wasn't in the way . . . I mean, come on — hell, it's a race. If you can't accept it as a race, then you shouldn't race." He considered their relationship friendly: "Me and him got along."

Castles carried large-caliber pistols, made sure people knew it, and often talked about violence. The Grand National circuit raced occasionally at the Bridgehampton Race Circuit on Long Island, New York, a road course more often used by amateur sports-car racers. As some of NASCAR's good ol' boys saw it, these were sissy Yankee drivers in sissy cars. One weekend when both groups were racing there, Castles towed his Chrysler stock car to the registration shack and sauntered up to the counter. "Welcome to Bridgehampton, Mr. Castles," said one of the volunteer registrars, a pretty secretary in a jacket covered with racing emblems.

Castles grunted, filled out some forms, and gave the woman a cold stare. "We 'un goin' to git a chance to race with them sporty car boys?" he asked.

"No, Mr. Castles," she replied. "They will race separately in the preliminary events. You'll just be racing with the other stock cars."

"Aw shit, that's too bad," said Castles. "I was fixin' to kill me a couple of them little gentlemen." He turned and walked away, unsmiling, leaving the volunteers to wonder if he meant it.

Castles didn't just talk about violence. In a fury after a Darlington qualifying race in 1969, he used a wax can to slug driver Bob Ashbrook, whom he felt had blocked him and cost him a victory. NASCAR fined Castles two hundred dollars and put him on probation. In other incidents, Castles roughed up a racing reporter, and he was convicted of assaulting two white teenage boys who were shooting rifles near his house.

Nevertheless, Castles had some beneficial relationships among influential people in NASCAR. One of his connections to Chrysler was Buck Baker, who had driven for the company for many years and was Castle's longtime racing mentor. Castles was friendly, too, with Richard Howard, president of Charlotte Motor Speedway. "Howard was a very powerful man, and Soapy was his boy," driver Frank Warren said. "If there was anything to be given away, or to be had, Soapy was going to get it." Chrysler hired Castles to drive for Ray Fox's factory Dodge team in 1969, but the arrangement was short-lived. Fox didn't get along with Ronney Householder, the director of Chrysler's racing program. Fox decided to quit racing and gave all the team cars back to Chrysler.

Householder, meanwhile, kept telling Scott that soon he'd be driving a Fox-built Dodge. Scott remained optimistic and excited — he seemed to be closer to a factory ride than he'd ever been able to get with Ford.

Driver Ed Negre, a low-budget independent who drove Chrysler products, was skeptical about Scott's chances: Householder had repeatedly given him the same sort of assurances. As a native of Washington State, Negre felt like an outsider in NASCAR's southern culture. Some drivers razzed him, Negre said, because his name, pronounced *neg-REE,* was only one letter different from *Negro.* "Householder made promises to a lot of people . . . ," Negre said. "I'd been promised [Chrysler backing] for three years and never got any." After many such conversations, Negre overheard Householder telling Don Tarr, a physician who raced part-time in Grand National, that he would be getting factory support. "I said, 'Don, don't wait on this guy to give you any help. He's standing here lying to you.' Boy, I'm telling you, old Householder got mad. I knew I wasn't going to get any help then." Junior Johnson shared Negre's opinion of Householder: "You couldn't believe nothin' he said. He was the lyingest person I ever seen."

Ultimately, the skeptics turned out to be right — Scott's hopes weren't realized. The car Scott had expected to drive, Ray Fox said, wound up going to Castles. Fox didn't know why Scott was passed over, except that

Householder "had people, you know, that he took care of a little better than others."

Bill France's friend William Neely, who was in charge of public relations for Goodyear's racing program, said Chrysler probably had consulted France about whether to support Scott. The auto manufacturers often sought France's confidential opinions about which drivers they should sponsor, Neely said. "That happened a lot. There were so many conversations with car companies that nobody ever knew about." France's advice to Chrysler, Neely added, would have reflected his judgment about whether NASCAR's fan base was ready for a competitive black driver.

Ralph Moody and driver Sam McQuagg said they believed Householder had been sincere about wanting to support Scott. "I guess the people higher up [in Chrysler] just decided they didn't want to spend the money on somebody like that . . . ," Moody said. "All of a sudden it stalled out." McQuagg noted that Householder had planned to finance Scott's ride from a Chrysler "contingency fund" separate from the regular racing budget. "The contingency fund was kind of low, and the money just wasn't there like Ronney thought it was. I definitely know it wasn't a thing that they just wouldn't give it to Wendell, but I think they maybe made some promises a little prematurely that they financially couldn't take care of . . . When Ronney promised Wendell a car, the funds was just not there that time."

In any case, Scott's prospects for a competitive ride seemed now to have slid from shaky to hopeless. He'd been passed over by both Ford and Chrysler, and General Motors was no longer in racing. It was particularly irksome to lose out to Castles. To the Scotts he seemed a distillation of every redneck who'd ever given them trouble.

As in the past, Scott got no clear explanation of what had gone wrong. "So many times we had prospects and promises made, and they always fell through," Frank Scott said. "I heard so many people faithfully tell my dad, 'Next year you'll be in a factory car; you're going to have this,' and when the time came for it to be produced, it never was." The absence of explanations, he said, gave the disappointments an insulting quality. "No one felt that they were obligated to explain anything to us. It was never anybody who was really in charge who came to us and assured my father of anything. It was always some second- or thirdhand person who would tell him you're going to get this or that . . . It was never done on a professional basis, like I believe it was done with other people."

This was a difficult time for Wendell Scott Jr. Often he could lull himself to sleep only by rhythmically bumping his head against the headboard of his bed, over and over. His love for his father was mixed with anger. "He was the only man I've ever known who I was second fiddle to. No other man dominated me." A friend, Anne Blair, said: "I guess he felt there was this great big person over him, and he felt like, *What am I going to grow up to be?*"

Although his father talked about both of his sons becoming racing drivers, Wendell Jr. understood that the focus was mostly on him. He was the first son, the namesake. He knew his father considered him a meaner person than his brother, and thus more likely to be competitive. "He wanted Wendell Jr. to be a driver more than Frankie," Scott's friend Leonard Miller said. "That's a fact. He confided in me with that."

Could Wendell Scott Jr. live up to this expectation — and did he even want to? Did he want the life he saw his father leading — fifty races a year, hundred-hour workweeks, sleeping in the truck, crashes, blown engines, one setback after another? And if his father couldn't get a competitive ride after all these years and all this effort, how would life be any better for NASCAR's next black driver?

One night Wendell Jr. got together with a few friends at an acquaintance's apartment. On the coffee table sat a dish full of white powder. "He hands us this dollar bill, rolled up. 'Try some of this,' he says."

Nobody, Wendell Jr. said, asked what the powder was. "We snorted that stuff, and I ain't never felt so much better in my life.

"I ain't never loved everybody so much in my life. I ain't never knew that anybody could be so free of any pain, just total."

Soon, he said, "I started looking forward to that dish being on that table. And then I asked him, 'Man, I want a little of that stuff to take over to the house.'"

# 25

## "I know my place now."

One sure way for a driver to have a bad day at the racetrack was to get on the wrong side of the Gazaway brothers. In his powerful position as NASCAR's technical director, Bill Gazaway supervised the inspection officials who decided at every event whether or not a driver and his team were allowed to take part in a race. Joe Gazaway worked as a technical inspector in his brother's fiefdom. For Scott and his sons, dealing with the Gazaways became an ongoing aggravation in the late 1960s.

Often, they said, Joe Gazaway gave Scott a hard time over his car's appearance. To be sure, Scott's cars often did look rougher than those of the sponsored teams, and NASCAR was also pressing other low-budget drivers to spruce up their cars. Gazaway, however, went out of his way to use the appearance issue to cost Scott as much track time as possible, the Scotts said. Sometimes Scott would be ordered to spend entire practice sessions in the garage, he said, touching up blemishes in his car's paint while the other drivers tested their cars on the track and improved their chassis setups.

Joe Gazaway, asked about such incidents, replied that Scott was lazy. His cars looked like something from "a scrap yard," he said. "Wendell didn't like to work . . . You could look at his appearance and his automobile — that'd tell you right quick . . . You don't run scrap iron."

With disputes over Vietnam and '60s lifestyles joining the civil rights conflict as issues polarizing the country, Bill Gazaway became increasingly repelled by long hair, beards, and other manifestations of the counterculture. "The hippie generation was getting started, and we had all these long-haired folks trying to force theirself on you," Gazaway said.

Both of Scott's sons had beards. They were working with their father on the race car at the Bristol, Tennessee, speedway in 1969, hurrying to get ready for qualifying, when one of Gazaway's subordinates came over. "He says, 'Your boys got to cut them beards off if you want to race on Sunday,'" Wendell Scott Jr. recalled.

"'Daddy said, 'What are you talking about, man?' I thought he was going to hit him. 'Don't come over here fuckin' with me!'"

Wendell Jr. knew when his father's temper was close to exploding. "He had a way that his nose flares, and his eyes turn from blue to gray-green, and he'll hit you when he's like that — I know it. He just went crazy."

Scott rushed off and confronted Bill Gazaway. Wendell Jr. watched from a distance. They were making angry gestures. His father "was cussin' and raisin' hell. He come back to the car, and he said, 'Goddamn it, load this son of a bitch up.'

"Frankie said, 'What you talking about, Daddy?'

"'Them crazy sons of bitches tellin' me you all got to shave the beards off.'

"He was throwing stuff. He was mad. Whatever we were doing, the preparation, all of that stopped. Frankie said, 'What you think, brother?'

"I said, 'Man, we're gonna cut 'em off.'

"We said, 'Daddy don't worry,' because he looked like he was getting ready to shoot somebody. 'We'll go in the bathroom and do it now.'

"He said, 'Y'all ain't cuttin' off nothing. I'm tired of these motherfuckers fuckin' with me.' He was screaming.

"That's when Richard Petty walked by and asked what the hell was going on. Daddy says, 'These sons of bitches are telling me that my boys got to cut their beards off before they let me race.'

"Richard says, '*What?* Hell, half my pit crew got beards. I wonder if they got to cut theirs off.'

Gazaway's subordinate, Wendell Scott Jr. said, "says to Richard, 'You might need to talk to somebody else. You might not need to get involved in this.'

"Richard said, 'The hell I don't. I'm gonna race, and ain't none of my pit crew going to cut their beards off. Who told you to tell Wendell that?'

"He said, 'My boss.'"

Petty, probably the circuit's most popular driver at that time, went off with Scott to talk to Bill Gazaway. When they came back, Wendell Scott Jr.

said, "It was all fixed. The beards stayed. The last thing Richard said was, 'Hell, I might grow me a beard for next week.'"

Smokey Yunick and others described the Gazaways as openly prejudiced. The Gazaways, however, denied any racial motives for their treatment of Scott. Bill Gazaway said they were merely enforcing a NASCAR policy that "everybody shaves and everybody has a haircut." A NASCAR spokesman, however, said no such policy ever existed.

In Alabama, Bill France orchestrated the development of his mammoth new Talladega speedway and of the political relationships that were moving it toward completion. He juggled problems and negotiations with officials from Washington to Montgomery to the Talladega City Hall, bestowing honors and favors on the venture's political benefactors.

Federal agencies, including the Defense Department, had authority over some parts of the project, proposed for a site that included a former army air corps base. France had influential Washington connections, ranging from powerful members of Congress to senior officials of the FBI. His old friend L. Mendel Rivers had become chairman of the House Armed Services Committee, and Alabama's congressional delegation supported the Talladega venture. The cutting of federal red tape proved to be no problem. With that accomplished, France appointed Rivers as NASCAR's new national commissioner. Rivers, still an impassioned civil rights opponent, became the first appointee to NASCAR's top advisory post to know little about motor racing, or even how an automobile worked. Regardless, France said, Rivers had been "a staunch supporter of stock car racing."

France negotiated with Alabama officials for a state-subsidized auto-racing hall of fame as an additional attraction at the Talladega facility, a proposal his friend George Wallace would approve after winning another term as governor in 1970. Talladega mayor James Hardwick, influential in mobilizing local support and approving governmental measures for the speedway, became a member of the board of directors of the Frances' International Speedway Corp., which owned both the Talladega track and Daytona International Speedway. France also appointed Hardwick, a physician, as the new speedway's official doctor. In that paid position,

Hardwick would run the track's emergency hospital while continuing to serve as Talladega's mayor. France named the facility the Dr. J.L. Hardwick Medical Center.

Scott's poor results on the circuit continued through the summer. Often car problems ended his races early or he finished many laps down, one of the last cars still running. His disappointment over the lack of support from Chrysler sometimes added a barbed edge to his comments. He talked with journalist Tom Kelly about his Jacksonville victory six years earlier. "After I won that race I had the ambition to win some more, and I almost went to the poorhouse trying. I guess you might say I know my place now."

But a strong performance in a non–Grand National race at Atlanta's Lakewood Speedway helped to boost Scott's confidence that at age forty-eight, his driving skills remained sharp. Lakewood was the track that wouldn't allow him to race in 1955 until a separate "black ambulance" could be found. This time, no such problems came up. Promoter Ernie Moore "paid me good to come down there," Scott said, for the hundred-mile, late-model sportsman race on August 31, 1969.

Qualifying was rained out, so drivers drew for starting positions on the fast, treacherous one-mile dirt oval. "I started thirty-seventh," Scott recalled. "Halfway into the race, I was leading." In the closing laps, driver Eldon Yarbrough spun in front of Scott. "I hit him, knocked my fender and bumper in on my tire, and I lost three laps. Bobby Allison won, but I had that race in the bag. Ernie Moore came over to me — you talk about praising somebody — he said he ain't never seen nobody drive a car like I did that day."

Both of Scott's sons wanted to race, he told the Associated Press that summer, but he couldn't afford to let them learn with his race car. "Wreck it and we're out of business," he said. "I've got to keep it going so as to pay the bills and feed the mouths."

When Wendell Scott Jr. wasn't helping his father at races, he and his hard-partying friends often hung out at the apartment with the dish of white powder on the coffee table. Their host was a local drug dealer. Sometimes, Wendell Jr. said, he and others in their circle would sit around the kitchen, some of them helping the dealer to pack the loose powder into hundreds of capsules for customers.

For a while, he said, all they knew or cared about the powder was how it made bad feelings go away. Eventually, he learned the hard truth he'd been avoiding: It was heroin.

"I said, 'Well, as long as we don't shoot it up, we're all right.' That was my dumbness at the time."

The Goodyear plant fired him in June for missing seven days of work without an explanation. But soon he got a more challenging job. At Central Florida Junior College, administrators had read about NASCAR's Scott family, and they offered Wendell Scott Jr. a faculty position. He would teach auto mechanics and take classes toward his own college degree. At this point, he had been snorting heroin for about six months.

He loved his new job but quickly discovered that the powder had become a need, not an optional recreation. The Danville dealer began mailing him bags of heroin. "Before you knew it, I was strung out. I was twenty-three years old, with every success in the world right there at hand, and these damn letters coming in the mail, full of dope."

Eventually he had to admit to himself that he needed help. He took a leave of absence, came home, and admitted his addiction to his father, who helped get him into the veterans' hospital in Salem, Virginia. Withdrawal took sixteen agonizing days, and he was able to resume teaching in Florida. For weeks he'd been afraid to confide in his father, he said, but "I was able to face the man, and I told him, and Daddy came to my aid."

# 26

## "We will not forget."

Few events in NASCAR's history have been roiled by as much angry conflict as the opening of the new Talladega superspeedway in mid-September 1969. Several top drivers had tested the huge, high-banked track during the summer. They found its surface surprisingly rough, and they expressed concern over whether tires would survive the punishment of high speeds on such bad pavement. France was adamant, however — the race would run as scheduled, and drivers would have to deal with whatever conditions existed.

As France had hoped, Talladega quickly proved itself to be the nation's fastest speedway. In opening-day practice, the factory-backed Dodges and Fords ran at unprecedented speeds, almost two hundred miles an hour, at least ten miles an hour faster than at Daytona. But the bumpy, abrasive asphalt chewed up their tires, making them blister and lose chunks of rubber. On many of the faster cars, tires that normally lasted eighty to a hundred miles came apart after a few laps. Goodyear flew in batches of new tires with different rubber compounds, but the flawed paving damaged them, too.

Drivers began speaking out. "The track is just too rough," said James Hylton, one of the best independent drivers. "Somebody is going to get killed here if something isn't done." Coincidentally, several weeks earlier some drivers had formed a new organization, the Professional Drivers Association, to press NASCAR for a pension plan, better purses, and a voice in scheduling. Richard Petty, president of the fledgling group, urged France to postpone the Talladega 500. Otherwise, he warned, drivers might boycott.

France rejected any postponement. Talladega's inauguration represented one of the biggest events ever held by NASCAR. A delay would hurt his organization's credibility. The audience, which would total sixty-two thousand, was to include not only politicians such as L. Mendel Rivers, George

Wallace, and the current Alabama governor, Albert Brewer, but also top executives of many major corporations with which NASCAR did business, or hoped to. They included Chrysler, Ford, Permatex, Falstaff Brewing, Colt Industries, and PepsiCo — more corporate dignitaries, said the speedway's promotion director, Roger Bear, "than have ever been to any stock car race in history."

Also, France badly needed the revenue from the event, said NASCAR historian Bob Latford: "The word was that he had a big payment on the construction loan due the day after or the week after the race."

At a meeting between drivers and France, one driver, LeeRoy Yarbrough, asked: "Bill, how would you like to attend a couple of funerals next week?"

"I'll take my chances on that," France replied.

Besides the Grand National racers, France had a second field of cars at the track for the preliminary race on Saturday, September 14. These lighter, less powerful Camaros and Mustangs of NASCAR's Grand Touring division had not experienced tire problems. Neither had the unsponsored Grand National drivers like Scott, whose cars also ran substantially slower lap times than the factory machines. If necessary, France could put together a mixed field of Grand National independents and Grand Touring machines for Sunday's Talladega 500.

"There will be a race tomorrow, and we will pay the posted purse," France told the Grand National drivers. "If you aren't going to race, then leave."

In response, the drivers' group led by Petty called for a boycott. The possibility of compromise was over. Some Grand National drivers began loading up their race cars and gear.

Caught in the middle of this dispute, Scott found himself awash with mixed emotions. As always, he had financial worries. He'd come to Talladega with little money, counting on prize winnings to buy the gas for his trip home. His consistency in finishing had gotten him into tenth place in the season standings. As a point of competitive pride, he didn't want to be bumped from the top ten by missing this race. "I needed to run it — bad."

On the other hand, he felt the pressure of loyalty to his driver friends, and he thought about the possibility of paybacks if he angered them. "It had taken me a long time to gain the respect of the drivers," he said. If he didn't join the boycott, "I'd have been right back where I used to be. Every time I went to the track somebody would have been beating and banging on me. I would have gotten blackballed by the drivers."

In his jumble of conflicting feelings, too, were the dreams he could not let go, and that would not let go of him — that he still might somehow get a competitive ride, that someday he'd be able to show what he could really do. Alienating Bill France could hurt his chances. If Sunday's field was mostly independents and Grand Touring Camaros, maybe he should stick around. This might be his chance — at last — to win a prestigious superspeedway race.

Both Petty and France made personal appeals to Scott, as they did to other drivers. Petty approached him after the first day of practice. Scott and his sons were leaving the track in their Dodge truck, which Scott had bought from Petty. "We were on our way out of the gate," Wendell Scott Jr. said. "We didn't know anything about the proposed boycott. Richard says, jokingly, 'Stop my truck!'

"So Daddy stopped, and he jumped up on the running board, and he says, 'Wendell, I need you with us.'

"Daddy said, 'What are you talking about?'

"Richard said, 'Have you heard about them tires blistering on us?'

"Daddy said, 'Yes, on the *fast* cars.'

"Richard said, 'We need to boycott it with the slow cars, the fast cars, everybody.' He told Daddy that 'You would be looked on in a bright light by your competitors.'

"He said, 'Now, I ain't gave nobody else no money yet, but here's some for you — think about it.'" With that, Wendell Jr. said, Petty handed Scott a few hundred dollars.

France came over to Scott while making the rounds of the garage area, lobbying drivers to break with Petty's group and run the race. "Bill France made Daddy a gray-area promise that 'If you drive in this race, your future could get a whole lot better.'

"He probably told a lot of other people the same thing, but that's what he told us."

France didn't say that Scott's future would get worse if he didn't race, Wendell Jr. said, "but it was like an implied ultimatum. He was real careful — he didn't just talk off the top of his head."

Scott decided that he had to support his driver friends and join the boycott. He loaded up his race car. In all, thirty-two Grand National cars were withdrawn from the field. Only thirteen would start the race, joined by twenty-three Grand Touring cars. As Scott drove his truck toward the gate, rolling along slowly in a line of departing racers, something surprising happened.

Former driver Jack Smith, who had been one of Scott's worst nemeses in the early '60s, suddenly jumped up on the truck's running board. Scott, startled, thought for a moment that Smith wanted to fight: "I was fixing to knock him down with the door." Then Scott saw three twenty-dollar bills in Smith's hand. Smith had heard that Scott was short of money, he told Scott, and he wanted to congratulate Scott for joining the boycott. "He handed me the sixty dollars, and he told me what a hell of a man I was," Scott recalled. Smith's gesture marked the beginning of what became a friendly relationship between the two former antagonists.

Soon afterward, however, Scott's mixed feelings pulled him in another direction, France's close aide Jim Foster recalled. After driving away from the speedway, Foster said, Scott phoned France and said he'd changed his mind. Foster, who was in France's office, said he heard the whole conversation.

"Wendell said, 'Mr. France, I didn't want to walk out. Now I'm going to come back. I want to race.'

"Bill said, 'Sorry, Wendell, I can't let you do that. You walked out, and I can't let you do it.'"

Foster said: "I stopped him and said, 'Come on, Bill — let Wendell come back.'

"He said no, and he said good-bye to Wendell.

"Then he said to me, 'Jim, those guys could have talked Wendell into coming back over here and causing a wreck or something else. We can't take a chance on that. Anybody that left out of the gate can't get back in.'"

The inaugural weekend at Talladega, whose existence owed so much to George Wallace, would take place with an all-white field of drivers. Although Scott had hoped to run competitively with so many faster cars missing, the outcome of the weekend's main race on Sunday made it clear that his chances to win in his Ford would have been minuscule. There were no crashes; most of the cars were slow enough that the track didn't damage their tires. But the walkout had given a little-known driver, Richard Brickhouse, the chance to drive one of the fastest Grand National cars at the track, a new, winged Dodge Daytona owned by a factory-sponsored team. Brickhouse cruised at a comfortable pace for most of the race to avoid tire trouble, then cranked up his lap speeds to 198 miles an hour to take the lead eleven laps from the finish. He won $24,550. "All my life I've dreamed about driving a factory-backed car," Brickhouse said. "I couldn't pass up this opportunity."

As Wendell Scott Jr. saw it, his father's position on Bill France's mental list of people and situations deserving his attention — a list on which Scott had never ranked very high — dropped to a new low after the Talladega weekend. "The boycott turned Bill France against him," he said.

After the race, driver Bill Ward said, France angrily vowed to get back at all the drivers who had walked out. Ward, a part-time racer who had found the Talladega site for France and helped him win local political support, drove a Grand Touring–class Camaro in Sunday's race, finishing eleventh. Afterward, he visited France in his office at the track. "He said, 'I'll break every one of those drivers,'" Ward recalled. Two weeks later, Ward got a letter from France and Bill France Jr., who had become a NASCAR vice president, thanking him for taking part in the first Talladega 500. "You may rest assured we will not forget your loyalty," the Frances said.

## 27

### "It was about wore out."

Maybe it had something to do with the Talladega boycott, or maybe not. In any case, 1970 and the following season seemed to bring a significant upswing in Scott's problems with NASCAR's officialdom, sometimes in situations reminiscent of the discrimination he'd faced in the 1950s and early '60s.

Scott had finished ninth in the 1969 standings, scoring eleven top-tens in fifty-one races. It was his third season without a top-five finish, but the press still described him as one of NASCAR's most popular drivers.

Nevertheless, Scott said, NASCAR officials harrassed him increasingly during pre-race technical inspections. Joe Gazaway and some fellow tech inspectors, clearly acting on instructions from higher up, would repeatedly tell Scott that his car's appearance didn't meet NASCAR standards, or that the car needed a particularly intensive examination, and he would lose valuable practice time while he tried to satisfy their objections, the Scotts said. "He'd have me going around my car with a spray can, touching up little spots," Scott said. "Or he'd make me jack the car up again — he wanted to look back under it again.

"I said, 'Well, you've been under it already.'

"'Jack the car up — I didn't check it good.'"

Frank Scott said the treatment his father received was "discrimination — just blatant, blatant stuff."

Former NASCAR official Mike Sykes said: "Joe Gazaway was a real prejudiced, heartless person. If he could find anything to keep Wendell out of a race, he would." Gazaway said he was simply enforcing NASCAR's appearance standards. "If he's going to run, he's got to look after his self," Gazaway said. "Nobody picked on Wendell Scott."

By the early 1970s, it was clear that Bill France Jr. was being groomed to take over NASCAR. "He's the one who dropped the hammer on Daddy about car appearance," Wendell Scott Jr. said. "He put the inspectors on Daddy." France, however, said NASCAR never singled Scott out for any negative attention. "In those days we were trying to get everybody to get their cars looking better, to clean up their acts," he said.

Wendell Scott Sr. found the younger France chilly toward him, almost hostile. Often he would walk by without saying a word. "I had a good relationship with Bill France Sr.," Scott said. "Then Bill France Jr. came along, and he was different. I don't think he ever thought too much of guys like me. He'd turn his head and walk away rather than talk to me."

On May 31, 1970, Scott suddenly found himself banned from one of NASCAR's tracks — the first time this had happened since his exclusion from Darlington ended six years earlier. The track, Martinsville Speedway in Virginia, was owned by promoter H. Clay Earles and a partner: Bill France Sr.

Earles ordered Scott to leave the track after they had a disagreement, and told him he'd never race there again. In interviews, Scott and Earles, who had also held a NASCAR executive position as field manager, gave strikingly different accounts of how Scott's expulsion occurred.

The speedway's Virginia 500 had been postponed twice by rain during the previous week. For low-budget independents from other states, spending those extra days at Martinsville had been costly, and some felt the management should pay them some extra expense money. As Scott recalled the dispute, Earles approached him outdoors after the race and brought up the money question himself. "I was just standing there, and he walked up behind me and said, 'How you doin', Scott?'

"I said, 'I'm doing okay. How are you, Mr. Earles?'

They chatted a bit, Scott said, "and then he says, 'See all them guys standing up there at my office?'

Scott said he saw several unsponsored drivers waiting to talk to Earles. "I said, 'Yeah, I see 'em.' They were guys like Frank Warren, Cecil Gordon, guys what didn't have no money. They had been there all week and got rained out, and now they had to go back home.

"He said, 'You know what they want me to do?'

"'I said, 'No, sir.'

"He said, 'They want me to pay 'em some money, or loan 'em some money. What you think about that?'

"'I think you ought to give 'em some.'

"He said, 'You do?'

"I said, 'Yeah, I do.'

"I wasn't asking for money myself. I wasn't but thirty miles from home. He asked me, and I gave him my honest opinion."

Earles, sitting in his office in front of a large Confederate flag, recalled a sharply different version of how the dispute began. "Wendell brought about five or six white drivers up here — brought them up here to confront me. He said, 'I think you should give me and every one of these fellows five hundred dollars apiece.'"

Scott and the other drivers, Earles said, reminded him of a union making demands, a disturbing image for speedway owners in the aftermath of the Talladega boycott. "Once you give in to something like that, you're stuck," Earles said.

"I said, 'Wendell, if y'all all had come to me one-on-one, not come to me as a group, demanding so much, I would have helped every one of you. But since you've done it like this, there's nothing for any of you.'"

However the dispute got started, both Scott and Earles's top aide, Dick Thompson, the speedway's vice president for public relations, gave identical accounts of how it ended. Pointing to Scott's race car, Earles told Scott, "You can load that shitbox up and take it home and never bring it back."

The white drivers who had asked for expense money were not told they couldn't come back. This was the first time Scott had been banned from a racing facility in which France had a direct financial interest since his exclusion from Bowman Gray Stadium in the early 1950s. The ban on Scott continued for Martinsville's fall event in 1970, but the track did allow him to resume racing there in 1971. Thompson said Earles got over his anger and relented.

Scott's income took another hit from a run-in with NASCAR officials in June 1970 at California's Riverside International Raceway. At the previous week's race in Michigan, Scott's engine cracked a cylinder wall. He'd expected to tow his race car to Riverside from Michigan. Now that plan wouldn't work. He didn't have another engine, and he didn't have time to go back to Danville, build a new engine, and return to Riverside for the race.

This setback, he said, threatened to knock him out of NASCAR's so-called deal-money program. Scott depended heavily on deal money to stay in racing. As long as he ranked in the top twenty in points, he said, he would get five hundred dollars in deal money — a payment for showing up and starting the race — at tracks of one mile or longer. At shorter tracks he'd get $250. To discourage drivers from skipping the long haul to Riverside, Scott said, NASCAR warned them that missing the race would mean they'd be bumped from the deal-money program.

Scott called another black driver, George Wiltshire, a former New Yorker struggling to make a racing career on the West Coast, and asked him if he could borrow his car. First, he said, he got NASCAR's assurance that driving a different car at Riverside wouldn't be a problem. At least, he thought he did. "I called NASCAR, and they told me that as long as I had my number, thirty-four, on the car and my name, it was all that's necessary."

Scott completed only fifteen laps of the Riverside race before Wiltshire's engine failed. NASCAR, he said, refused to pay him the five hundred dollars in deal money because he didn't own the car. Frank Scott, who crewed for his father at Riverside, supported his father's account. To the Scotts, NASCAR's explanation seemed far-fetched. Factory-team drivers had far more lucrative appearance-money deals than Scott, and they didn't own the cars they drove.

Scott had gotten another well-used race car from Holman-Moody for the 1970 season, a '66 Ford with a '69 Torino body. To the press, Scott continued to talk hopefully about racing careers for his sons. "Maybe because of what I went through it'll be easier for my boys," he told a reporter. "Maybe they could even get a contract like Richard Petty. Then they can take over and give me a little rest." There were no clear plans for how any of that would happen, however, and with friends Scott was more pessimistic. He told Leonard Miller that his sons, after their long involvement in his own career, didn't want "the years of hand-to-mouth where you don't see anything in return."

---

On July 12 at Trenton, New Jersey, Scott had a violent crash. During a qualifying session on the fast 1.5-mile speedway, his car lost traction in turn one. The Torino climbed the steel guardrail, rolled over on top of it, slammed back down onto the track, rolled again, and came to rest with the chassis and body badly mauled. Alarmed by the force of the wreck, Leonard Miller ran to see if Scott was hurt.

"I said, 'Wendell, how did you get through that?'

"He said, 'Leonard, I was so worried about the car catching fire, I turned off the key while it was upside down in the air.'

Miller expressed surprise that Scott had the presence of mind to do that while undergoing such a battering.

"He said, 'There was no way I could get to the next race if I didn't.'"

Earl Brooks offered Scott his car for the race. Scott dropped out early with a mechanical failure but was able to hold onto twelfth place in the points.

He drove another event in Brooks's Ford, then ran eleven races for Don Robertson, Jabe Thomas's car owner, in their backup car. The results ranged from mediocre to poor, and that pattern continued when Scott finished repairing and resumed racing the Torino.

His friend Bobby Fleming, who'd helped with the repairs, said it was clear that the car would never handle properly again. Well before Trenton, Fleming said, "it was about wore out. It probably had about two hundred races on it. Then it was in the rollover, and the frame rails got warped. The right front was cocked up, and the left rear, and you could never get the weight on those wheels right, to make it handle."

The drama and flair of drivers broadsliding around dirt tracks was soon to vanish from Grand National racing, a casualty of NASCAR's evolution into the modern superspeedway era. The 1970 season would mark the end of Grand National racing on dirt. Even on his favorite type of speedway, Scott could produce only another lackluster performance in the circuit's last dirt race on September 30 at the Raleigh half mile. He qualified thirteenth of twenty-three and fell out early with transmission failure. For a driver who'd scored a win, a pole, and fifteen top-fives in Grand Nationals on dirt, the day was another sad landmark in a fading career. Neil Castles, enjoying one of his most successful seasons after getting the Ray Fox Dodge that Scott had hoped to drive, came in second behind Richard Petty.

The August weekend at Talladega brought a reminder of Bill France Sr.'s ability to effect dramatic change in the careers of drivers he wanted to help. For this event, France used his influence to make a long-held dream come true for Bill Ward, an occasional racer, now forty years old, to whom he owed a substantial favor. Ward, who ran an insurance agency in Anniston, Alabama, had used his many business and political contacts to give France some important assistance with the Talladega venture. When Ward located the property that would become the speedway's site, he took France to look over the land. Immediately enthusiastic, France "picked up the phone and called Texas," Ward recalled, "and he said to me, 'Do you know Clint Murchison?'"

Ward knew that Murchison was the controversial oil tycoon who'd provided the key financing for the Daytona speedway, but they had never met. "I said, 'Hell, no — I don't know Clint Murchison.'

"France said, 'Well, you're going to meet him.'" France told Murchison's top real estate executive, according to Ward, "that 'I got a man here with the most wonderful piece of land in the world, and we can get it.'"

Then Ward introduced France to Talladega mayor James Hardwick "and the city council and all the powers that be in Talladega." The city owned most of the acreage that France wanted. France flew the officials on a promotional junket to a race at Daytona, where they realized the economic impact a superspeedway could have on their community. "They had never seen that many people at one event," Ward said. "Mr. France came back, we all got together, and he cut a deal with the City of Talladega." During the speedway's opening weekend, Ward earned France's further gratitude by driving in the Talladega 500 despite the boycott by many other drivers.

Soon Ward learned how a few phone calls from France could change a driver's fortunes. France arranged for Ward to drive a state-of-the-art Ford race car, built by Holman-Moody, in the 'Bama 200 at Talladega. He bought a five-thousand-dollar engine from Smokey Yunick. Then

France had Tom Pistone install the engine and prepare the car, deliver it to Talladega, and serve as Ward's crew chief for the race on August 22, 1970, which was part of the Grand American series.

Ward had a spectacularly successful day. He was the last competitor to make a qualifying run. His Ford turned out to be the fastest car in the field, and Ward took the pole position away from the renowned David Pearson. He went on to win the race. He beat other nationally known drivers besides Pearson, including Buck Baker, Tiny Lund, and Jim Paschal. For Ward, this superspeedway victory was the pinnacle of his racing career, and he owed it all to Bill France.

Later, when Ward bought a former Junior Johnson Chevrolet to race at Talladega, France used his connections again. Ward's phone rang, and a secretary told him to hold for Vince Piggins, a senior executive and engineer in General Motors' racing operation. "Mr. Piggins came on and said, 'Bill, I just want to congratulate you on buying a Chevrolet. Mr. France told us that you had purchased this car, and we are adding you on our list.'

"I said, 'What list is that, Mr. Piggins?'

"'You'll be furnished cams, engine parts, and sheet metal for your car from General Motors.'

Soon a GM camshaft expert called. "He said, 'Bill, your name's been added to the list. Every time Junior Johnson decides what cam to run at Talladega, you'll be shipped two of them.'

"I said, 'I may not be able to pay for those things.'

"He said, 'We'll worry about that later.'"

Then Piggins called again. "He said, 'Bill, we're giving you a brand-new engine. We just want to show our thanks.'"

It had been a striking demonstration, Ward said, of France's ability to reward a driver. "Bill France could do anything he wanted for anybody."

Other drivers remembered getting similar help from France. Bobby Allison had planned to skip the Daytona race in July 1966, he recalled, because he didn't have a competitive engine. "Bill France Sr. called me and said, 'I'll give you a 427 to put in that thing so you can come to Daytona. You go to Junior Johnson's shop; he's got some 427 Chevy engines there, and I'll have him give you one.'"

Dr. Don Tarr, the first physician ever to compete in Grand National, said France made the connections that resulted in his driving for Ray Fox's Chrysler team. France's efforts benefited both Tarr and NASCAR, putting Tarr into highly competitive cars and generating considerable promotional publicity for the races he entered. "I was a doctor," Tarr said, "so I was a gimmick" — just as Scott had been a gimmick, useful to promoters, when he started racing.

Bill Ward said France could easily have arranged a competitive ride for Scott. France and John Holman of Holman-Moody "were very personal friends," Ward said. "I've been in Bill France's office at Talladega when he'd pick up the phone and call John Holman. He could have called Holman, if he had wanted to, and said, 'I want one of your cars and one of your engines for Wendell to run Talladega.' He could have done it for anybody, like he did for me."

Ward and others, however, said they doubted that putting Scott in a position to win during those years would have been good business for NASCAR. "I don't think it would have helped France for Wendell to be out there winning races," Ward noted. "He needed Junior Johnson to win races, Curtis Turner to win races. That sold tickets in the South. Wendell wouldn't have sold tickets."

Veteran newspaperman George Smith, who covered the early years of Talladega racing as the *Anniston Star*'s sports editor, agreed with Ward. "A certain segment of the Old South would still resent it today," Smith said. "There were others who would have supported Scott. But overall, I don't think it would have done NASCAR much good."

28

## "I'm gonna wreck him."

Ironically, the highlight of Scott's 1971 season came about because his car was too slow to qualify for the Atlanta 500 in April. One of NASCAR's first races on network television, the event attracted an extra-large group of competitors for the forty starting spots. Instead of just sending away the drivers who failed to make the field, NASCAR gave them a consolation race.

Right from the green flag, Scott drove around the 1.5-mile superspeedway with his right foot planted on the floor, taking the lead on the first lap. Not far behind, a new driver on the circuit, Doc Faustina, chased Scott in a Plymouth he'd just bought from Richard Petty. Faustina, a Las Vegas dentist driving on a high-banked track for the first time, had the faster car, but he drove with a touch of caution at first.

"Last three laps, Faustina caught on to that Plymouth, and boy, he was coming. I seen him, but I couldn't do nothing. I held that thing on the bottom, and his car was gaining on me every lap. But I beat him — I won the race," Scott said.

It was far from the superspeedway victory of Scott's dreams, this obscure triumph in a consolation race. But it had been many years since he'd felt elation from any win at all, and he thoroughly enjoyed the rest of the day. There are no official victory festivities for consolation winners, but Scott and his crew made their own party. They had a big fried-chicken meal at an infield hospitality tent while country music star Marty Robbins sang for the crowd. Ralph Moody enjoyed the unusual sight of Scott proudly celebrating a win. "They had a hell of a time that afternoon."

Otherwise, Scott had the sort of season that makes racers struggle to recall why they love racing. The components of his arthritic race car took turns breaking down. The engine, the ignition system, the clutch, the rear end, the cooling system, the transmission — each knocked him out of at least one race, and some failed repeatedly. Besides the Atlanta 500, Scott missed both Daytona races and the World 600 at Charlotte. When he did finish, he was often many laps behind, one of the last cars still running.

A new development in NASCAR's business world, meanwhile, clouded the career picture for Scott, as well as for other independent drivers and aspirants like Wendell Jr. As the 1970s began, the auto companies cut their racing budgets abruptly and severely, in preparation for ending motor-sports sponsorship completely. The money, auto executives said, could be spent more effectively on other promotional efforts. The cutbacks threw many teams into financial crisis. Holman-Moody went out of business; Scott would get no more hand-me-down Fords. Few other corporations sponsored NASCAR racing at the time. Among the teams, there would still be the haves and the have-nots — racing had always been that way — but now the have-not drivers could no longer dream of the factory ride that might turn them into stars.

To some spectators, Scott's pace suggested a loss of motivation, ability, or both. Those who worked on his ill-handling Ford, however, saw how often he had to drive on the ragged edge simply to make the field. As his car became more uncompetitive, his sons said, Scott would take bigger chances during qualifying, pushing his car harder in the turns. After every practice session, he'd immediately ask, "What was my time?"

"We'd tell him," Wendell Scott Jr. said, "and he'd ask us, 'What's G.C. Spencer running? What's John Sears running? What's Elmo Langley running?' That would let him know how dangerous it's got to get.

"Then we'd set the timing up as far as we can go without burning a hole in a piston. We'd put as much air as we can in the tires without it really being on ball bearings. Now he's got to go in a little bit deeper, and he always believed there was a half second he could gain."

That half second proved elusive. "It didn't matter what we did," Wendell Scott Jr. said. "Daddy would work and work and work, and come up with this idea and that idea, and I knew it was the car, the chassis — it was kaput. Bent and warped. The tires were actually sliding on the track as he drove down the straightaway."

The Scotts also didn't realize that some of their fellow independents were outqualifying them through a new method of cheating. They had tanks of nitrous oxide — laughing gas — concealed in their cars. When the driver pushed a hidden button, the engine inhaled an invigorating jolt of the gas and produced a burst of extra horsepower. Scott didn't know his rivals were using the gas. "Guys that I should outrun, they would outqualify me, and I couldn't understand what was happening," Scott said.

At the time, Ralph Moody said, NASCAR officials knew that many independents, struggling to make the field, were using nitrous to boost their qualifying times but chose to ignore the cheating as long as only independents were involved. "They'd let them do it, let them get in, make a few bucks, fill out the field." But nobody tipped off Scott. Much later, he said, he learned that even Earl Brooks, one of his closest friends, had used the gas.

The evening before a race at Atlanta, all of the drivers had invitations to dine with then Georgia governor Jimmy Carter at the governor's mansion. "As usual, Wendell Scott had worked all day the day before at his garage in Danville, Va., driven all night to the racetrack and then worked all day on his race car," the *Charlotte News* reported. "As other drivers left the messy work of mechanics to their crews and headed for the governor's reception," the story said, Scott labored on until he was exhausted. "As the other drivers shook hands with Jimmy Carter and ate his fine dinner, Wendell Scott fell asleep on the front seat of his battered truck."

Scott started thirty-seven races in 1971. Mechanical breakdowns knocked him out of seventeen. He had no top-five finishes and only four top-tens. At the Southern 500, he finished 125 laps behind the winner. Once again, he and Mary had to remortgage their house.

Except for his Atlanta consolation win, the season brought only one other obscure point of personal satisfaction, this one involving the belligerent Neil Castles. At North Wilkesboro Speedway in North Carolina on November 21, Scott blew an engine in practice and wasn't able to qualify. He hated the prospect of falling behind Castles in the season's point standings, and that would probably happen if he missed this race.

Scott began asking other drivers if he could borrow their car. At first, Ed Negre agreed. He got along well with the Scotts: Wendell Jr. and Frank occasionally served as Negre's pit crew when he had nobody to help him. But when word got around that he planned to loan Scott his car, Negre said, Castles "come over and told me, 'If you let Wendell drive your car, I'm gonna wreck him.'" Negre, aware of Castles's animosity toward Scott, said he took the threat seriously. Reluctantly, he told Scott — without an explanation at first — that he had to withdraw his offer. "Boy, was he upset. I said, 'Wendell, don't be mad at me.' He thought I was against him."

Negre hadn't wanted to get drawn into controversy, but eventually he explained to Scott that somebody had made a threat. "I don't want to get my car tore up," he said. Without any name being mentioned, Negre said, Scott immediately knew that the threat had come from Castles.

Scott told Negre there would be no hard feelings. Scott then asked Earl Brooks if he could borrow his car. By that point in the season, Brooks's own ranking in the points was assured: This race would make no difference. "So he let me drive his car. And he told Neil, 'You better not touch that car,'" Scott said.

Scott drove an uneventful race, finishing seventeenth. He got no trouble from Castles, who came in twelfth. Brooks's favor allowed Scott to stay ahead of Castles in the points. He placed nineteenth in the season standings, three spots ahead of Castles. As racing accomplishments go, this didn't amount to much, but it helped to salvage Scott's pride — as did another event that day at North Wilkesboro.

Before the race, the track announcer noted that Scott would be driving Earl Brooks's car. A white fan got Brooks's attention and called him over to the grandstand. "The man gave Earl a hundred dollars," Scott said, "for letting me drive that car." After this season of troubles and mediocre results, Scott enjoyed the reminder that he still had some devoted fans. He would always remember this gesture of support from a complete stranger.

## 29

### "A chance to win one."

During the Daytona 500 qualifying race on February 17, 1972, a driver blew a tire at high speed, and suddenly thirteen cars were spinning, dodging, and crashing in front of Scott. He swerved into the infield at more than a hundred miles an hour, missing the pileup. His car bounced over a series of drainage ditches, knocking the front wheels so badly out of line that just his slow drive back to pit lane scrubbed most of the rubber off his tires. The impacts left the chassis of his ill-handling Ford even more twisted, well past the point where adjustments could fix it. But he was alive.

One of his friends wasn't as fortunate. A car slammed into Friday Hassler's red Chevrolet, bending it like a horseshoe, killing him on impact. Hassler, quiet and modest, became the tenth Grand National driver to die of crash injuries, mostly on superspeedways, since Scott had joined the series eleven years before.

For NASCAR, the 1972 season brought major changes. Bill France Sr. had recruited R.J. Reynolds Tobacco Co. as NASCAR's primary sponsor. The Grand National circuit became the Winston Cup series. NASCAR cut the schedule from more than fifty races to thirty-one, each of them 250 miles or more, a package R.J. Reynolds considered more promotable. With that accomplished, France, now sixty-two, turned over NASCAR's presidency to his oldest son, Bill Jr., thirty-eight. The elder France announced he would work in an active advisory role with NASCAR while remaining the president and chairman of International Speedway Corp., which owned and operated Talladega and Daytona. He had taken one hand off the steering wheel, but not both.

That spring, Scott failed to qualify for most of the Winston Cup events. He turned to a minor-league circuit NASCAR had recently created. The new Grand National East series had taken over some of the short-track races cut from the Winston Cup calendar. The series featured a mixed field of Winston Cup–style sedans, mostly second-rate or worse, racing against smaller coupes such as Mustangs and Camaros. These shorter races on slower tracks seemed to offer Scott a better chance to make a living with his decrepit Torino.

The season's first Grand National East event took place on March 14 at the circuit's only dirt track: Jacksonville, Florida, the same half-mile speedway where Scott had won in 1963. Scott arrived for the hundred-mile race with worn-out tires and little hope. Driver Tiny Lund tried to boost his spirits with an upbeat pep talk. Like most men called Tiny, DeWayne Lund was of bouncer proportions: six foot four, 270 pounds, a cheerful extrovert who liked pranks and good times. His presence in Grand National East reflected his up-and-down career. He had won the Daytona 500 in 1963, but top-flight rides had mostly eluded him.

The Scott family had long been friendly with Lund. He admired Scott, he told his wife, Wanda, both as a racer and a racial pioneer. "He'd say, 'You know, Wendell really is a hell of a driver,'" she said. "'I'd really like to see what he could do if he had top-notch equipment one time.' Tiny felt Wendell could run with the best of them, or outrun them even." Her husband, who came from Iowa, told her that Scott had "a lot of courage to get into racing at this time in our history, with the black and white problems."

Though Scott liked Lund, he also held an old, small grudge against him from eight years before, when NASCAR had changed Scott's finishing position from third to fourth at Valdosta, Georgia, because of Lund's claims that he'd finished ahead of Scott. That was back in 1964, when Scott, hoping for a factory ride, was hungry for every point and every scrap of recognition he could get.

Typically, after so many years of avoiding confrontations about his troubles in NASCAR, Scott had never discussed the incident with Lund. Lund had confided to Wendell Jr. that he'd long felt badly about Valdosta and wished, in hindsight, that he'd never challenged Scott's third-place finish.

As they got ready to race at Jacksonville, Lund tried to boost Scott's morale. He told Scott his 427 engine might well overpower the Camaros and Mustangs. "Tiny said, 'Why don't you put your good tires on and go out and win this race? You can outrun these little cars.'"

Scott told Lund he was broke. "I said, 'Tiny, I ain't able to buy no tires.'" Lund took four of Scott's extra wheels and walked over to the Goodyear truck. He brought the wheels back with four brand-new tires mounted.

During the race, the lighter coupes had a considerable advantage, and they captured the first three positions. But thanks to the tires Lund had bought for him, Scott finished a strong fourth, intensely proud that he'd beaten every other Grand National sedan in the field. Later, he reflected that Lund had chosen a perfect time to do him a favor, a day when his spirits were dragging. Maybe Lund had given him the tires as a way to apologize for Valdosta, Scott reflected, but in any case, it was time to put aside the old grudge and accept Lund as his friend.

With fewer daily responsibilities in NASCAR, Bill France Sr. became deeply involved in Alabama governor George Wallace's latest presidential campaign. Seeking the Democratic nomination to challenge President Richard Nixon, Wallace took to the primary trail, attacking "permissiveness in this society," the federal government's role in integration, and the idea of busing to desegregate schools. Wallace no longer spoke out publicly for "segregation forever" — a lost cause by 1972 — but his private conversation remained laced with racial jibes and slurs. More than any other national political figure of the time, he made himself a symbol of angry resistance to racial change. As governor, he called the Civil Rights Act "rotten" and "monstrous" and refused to enforce it.

During his presidential campaign, NASCAR featured prominent publicity appearances by Wallace at its major events. Wallace appointed France as his campaign chairman for Florida, where a primary victory could be crucial for him. France also worked as a major fund-raiser for Wallace's national campaign. He loaned the campaign his airplanes, traveled extensively with Wallace's staff, and became a friend and close adviser to campaign manager Charles Snider.

France and Wallace "were in close agreement on political philosophy," journalist and author Jerry Bledsoe wrote. "'Christ,' says one of France's former employees, 'the old man [France] is so conservative he's the John Wayne of the South.'" With Wallace as president, insiders speculated, France could be the next secretary of state.

Wallace won every Florida county in the March 15 primary, swamping his opponents, far exceeding expectations. Florida voters also overwhelmingly approved two anti-busing measures. Wallace's success forced Nixon to condemn busing. *Newsweek*'s cover story proclaimed: "They Have to Listen Now." France's leadership, Snider said, had been vital in pushing the national political agenda in Wallace's direction. The Florida results "really gave us tremendous credibility nationwide."

Wallace won four more primaries, but a would-be assassin, Arthur Bremer, shot him on May 15 at a campaign stop in Laurel, Maryland, paralyzing his legs and derailing the campaign. "We were going great guns until he got shot," Snider said. "I think we had scared the pants off the national Democratic Party. Without Bill France, very little of that would have happened. Had we not won Florida, we would never have gone as far as we did. Had we not had Bill France as our chairman in Florida, we'd never have won Florida."

There is no public record of racist statements by France. Former friends and top aides who were close to France for years say they never heard him make a single prejudiced remark. "Bill was very complimentary of Wendell Scott," Snider said. "He said on several occasions that he hoped, in the future, there would be more minorities involved in the sport."

Still, France's devotion to the cause of putting a segregationist into the White House could not help but make an implicit statement about the nature of NASCAR. His campaigning for Wallace was consistent with his choice of L. Mendel Rivers as NASCAR's national commissioner. Clearly, NASCAR remained an organization where the old ways of the South were not viewed as something dishonorable, and where the politicians who fought so fiercely to preserve segregation were still treated as figures of respect.

The next major episode of Scott's career would raise again the old question of the boundaries of his acceptance in NASCAR. For Scott, his first Winston Cup event of the 1972 season, the spring race at Martinsville, began with a typical bout of car trouble and aggravation. Scott had spent the previous week putting together an engine from used parts. As he was unloading his race car from the tow truck, the engine blew. Frank Scott had driven up from college in North Carolina to help his father. They pulled the engine from Frank's street car, a 1966 Ford, and put it into the race car. Scott qualified thirty-fourth of thirty-six cars.

On the Sunday of the race, all of these problems were overshadowed by some momentous, completely unexpected news — the biggest career opportunity, apparently, that Scott had ever gotten in racing. The news came from one of the sport's most prominent figures, millionaire Richard Howard, the promotional impresario who had rescued Charlotte Motor Speedway from bankruptcy. Howard was the speedway's general manager, and his other business enterprises included one of Winston Cup's best racing teams, managed by the legendary Junior Johnson.

In just one month, Howard announced, Wendell Scott would be competing in Charlotte's World 600 in a car capable of winning the race: a state-of-the-art Chevrolet from the Johnson-Howard racing team. "I feel sorry for Wendell," Howard told the press at Martinsville. "I took a look at his old car and realized how much trouble he's had. He's never had a chance to win a race. Well, I decided to give him a Chevrolet and a chance to win one."

Howard had approached Scott that morning. "He asked me would I consider driving a Junior Johnson car at Charlotte in the World 600." Astonished, elated, Scott gave Howard an immediate reply: "I told him, 'God, yes! Lord!'"

Thanks to heavy attrition in the Martinsville race, Scott managed to finish sixteenth, sixty-four laps behind winner Richard Petty. Afterward, reporters crowded around the fifty-year-old Scott and his threadbare race car. For the racing press, this was a Hollywood-style underdog story with an intriguing racial subplot, one so obvious it didn't have to be explicitly stated: Was southern stock car racing really ready for a black winner? Certainly Scott had achieved considerable popularity among many fans. But for some others, just as certainly, any do-gooder scheme aimed at Scott's winning a race would be considered an abomination.

Scott thanked Howard for giving him the chance he'd almost lost any hope of attaining. "It will be by far the best car I've ever driven," Scott said.

"I just wish I could have gotten a car like this Chevrolet fifteen years ago . . . I'm just looking forward to the chance to run with the best of them . . . That new car will be like a Cadillac to me."

Right now, Scott said, he was seven thousand dollars in debt. "Everybody in Danville who's got any confidence in me, I owe. Maybe I can make that back in one race." Long after the crowd had left, the Scotts worked late into the night, putting the engine back into Frank's car so he could make it to the next day's classes at his college.

Howard's announcement accomplished a goal he'd openly acknowledged all along — a blizzard of favorable anticipatory publicity about the World 600 and Scott's prospects. Howard was a favorite of the racing press, which often described him as the P.T. Barnum of NASCAR. A North Carolinian who owned several furniture stores, he was cheerful and unpretentious — "a jolly 300-pounder," as the Associated Press described him. He didn't act or look wealthy. He wore discount-rack sport coats and loafers with worn-down heels.

His promotional stunts made for colorful copy, and he made a point of doing favors for journalists who would accept them. "The press, if they need furniture," Howard said, "I don't give a thing, but they can buy furniture from me at about half price. Well, that gets you good relations with 'em . . . they're working people, and they need some extra."

But no promoter's charm or petty payola can give a story much resonance if the basic idea isn't plausible, and over the past few years Richard Howard had established himself as someone to take seriously when he said he'd put a driver into a competitive car. His association with Johnson gave Howard's credibility a solid boost. Johnson, perhaps NASCAR's best-known figure, had been immortalized as "the Last American Hero" in Tom Wolfe's famous essay. Brilliant and tough, an ex-bootlegger with a prison record, Johnson was a figure of considerably more renown than his team owner. He'd won fifty Grand Nationals as a driver, retired from driving in 1966, and would go on to win six championships as a car owner.

Howard had backed some highly competitive race cars in recent years, both from his own Johnson-managed team and in his other recent "chance of a lifetime" promotions to boost attendance at Charlotte. In what he called his Big Chance program, Howard would arrange top-quality rides for popular drivers who hadn't run competitively for a while and then extensively promote the prospects for their dramatic victories.

Twice in the past two years, such victories had almost taken place. Howard had talked Fred Lorenzen out of retirement for the 1970 World 600 by providing him with a front-running Dodge Daytona. Lorenzen was leading when the engine blew. To promote the 1971 World 600, Howard put up the money for Johnson to build a Chevrolet for Charlie Glotzbach, whose fans loved his hard-charging driving style. Glotzbach won the pole and led the race four times before another driver's mistake took him out.

To be sure, Howard's promotions hadn't always proven successful, and he'd disappointed Scott once already in the 1965 incident when he chose Scott to drive one of four supposedly competitive Chevrolets he was backing. The car turned out, of course, to be far from a front-runner. "Some of them wouldn't run so fast," Howard acknowledged years later, "but they were there, you know?" He said he hadn't gotten involved in the details but merely gave a friend some money "and told him to get me some Chevrolets and get them in the field."

That fiasco, however, took place when the Charlotte speedway was still in the aftermath of bankruptcy. Now Howard's corporate pockets were much deeper. So far in the 1972 season, the regular driver for Howard's team, Bobby Allison, was Winston Cup's top money winner, with two wins and five second-place finishes. The team included Junior Johnson's longtime ace mechanic, Herb Nab, whose ability was seen as another boost for Scott's prospects in this year's race.

Also, Howard was demonstrating this year that he was willing to do some major spending. In another promotional flourish, he persuaded Jim Paschal, who'd twice won the World 600, to come out of semi-retirement for this season's event. As an inducement, Howard paid eighteen thousand dollars to buy a competitive Chevrolet from the Allison brothers' shop in Alabama for the forty-five-year-old Paschal to drive.

These promotional schemes produced a gusher of favorable press attention. An Associated Press story published in newspapers all over the South reported that, thanks to Howard, Scott would be able to "rocket away in a Chevrolet capable of running alongside the superstars." Every knowledgeable NASCAR fan understood that a "Junior Johnson car" was a likely winner. Story after story referred to the car Scott would drive as "Johnson-built," "Johnson-engineered," a product of the "Johnson stable."

"I was born poor and have always been an underdog man," Howard told the AP. "I get a kick out of doing stuff for poor folks, and I don't know anybody poorer than Wendell." The article added: "It also happens to be good business. Howard freely admits that Scott's sudden appearance in a competitive machine will juice up his World 600 attendance. 'We'll top 80,000 for sure,' said Howard. 'Wendell Scott may be our biggest drawing card . . . He's got the deal of a big-timer, and I'll be pulling like the devil for him.'"

In this publicity crescendo, however, a couple of discordant notes went unreported. Howard began talking privately to the regulars in the NASCAR press corps, asking if they thought it really would be a good idea to put Scott into a fully competitive car. Howard expressed concern that Scott "would hurt himself," journalist Gene Granger said. "Richard ran it by a group of us writers in the press box long before it happened — what did we think? Every one of us had concerns about Wendell at his age, whether he should even do this, period."

Howard asked the reporters to keep his concerns off the record. "He says, 'I don't want you to write that because that really makes Wendell look bad,'" Granger said. Since none of these writers had ever driven a race car against Scott or anyone else, it seemed more likely that Howard was planting an idea, one that might shape the spin of future stories, rather than seeking expert opinion. Making a reporter feel like an insider and trusted adviser is a basic co-opting technique understood by every savvy publicist.

At the Talladega racing weekend in early May, three weeks before the World 600, a friend of Howard's, a man he trusted for occasional items of confidential business, quietly made the rounds among the unsponsored, low-budget teams that ran Chevrolets. He took people into his motor home for private talks.

Would they be interested, he asked, in renting out their car for Wendell Scott to drive in the Charlotte race? Richard Howard would pay generously — as much as a few thousand dollars. The Junior Johnson crew would spruce up the car and install an engine. In these negotiations, two points came through clearly. First, the definition of a "Junior Johnson car" had evolved into something quite different from the ultracompetitive machine that had been described on dozens of sports pages. Second, Howard planned to spend on the race car for Scott only a fraction of what he'd spent to put Lorenzen, Paschal, Allison, and Glotzbach into their World 600 cars.

As in 1965, Howard had delegated to one of his buddies the assignment of obtaining the car that was supposed to fulfill Scott's hopes of a superspeedway win. Back then, Buck Baker had obtained the mediocre car that went to Scott. This time, Howard had given the job to Scott's longtime nemesis Neil Castles.

## 30

### "Just dreaming."

From the moment Wendell Scott Jr. first saw the Chevrolet in the pits at Charlotte, he realized it wasn't what his father had been promised. Even from a distance, he could see that this freshly painted Monte Carlo was no Junior Johnson car. For years, Scott's sons had observed the numerous differences between the race cars of the independent teams and those with money. At first glance, the Chevrolet looked sharp in its glossy metallic-maroon paint. But this car, Wendell Scott Jr. quickly concluded, obviously had been obtained from some low-budget team. The more details he noted, the angrier he got.

"You could see the wrinkles in the sheet metal as you walked toward it," he said. "You could see that the contours of the car weren't that of a factory car." Fender dents had been smoothed over with body filler. A Johnson car would have gotten new fenders. Even the new yellow lettering promoting one of Richard Howard's businesses, Howard Furniture, didn't fit the available space properly and had a hasty, sloppy look.

Wendell Jr. slid under the Chevy to inspect the chassis. Everywhere he looked, he saw components that appeared second-rate. The shock absorbers didn't seem securely mounted. The welding looked mediocre. Along the bottom edge of the bodywork, he spotted some remnants of the former paint scheme, and that told him exactly where Richard Howard had gotten this particular Monte Carlo. "I was under that car less than a minute, and when I came out, I was fighting mad," Wendell Scott Jr. said. He knew this car's history. It had never come close to finishing on the lead lap of any race.

Frank Scott examined the car and agreed with his brother. "It had a nice paint job and a motor that was better than what we normally had, but that was the extent of it. It was just a hoax." A real Junior Johnson car and this imitation, Frank Scott said, were "as different as a Mercedes and a Chevy."

Wendell Scott Jr. had left his Florida teaching job and again was deeply involved in his father's racing, working as a crewman at most races. He confronted his father, arguing fervently that he shouldn't drive the car. He said that the Chevrolet gave him no real chance to win, that he was being exploited to sell tickets, and that he could only hurt his reputation. He tried to persuade his father that "all his fans, they don't know that Daddy ain't in no Junior Johnson car. He wasn't supposed to take that exploitation and gamble his future with it."

Scott, his expression stony, shook his head as Wendell Jr. talked. He wasn't going to take his son's advice. He'd seen the car already, a couple of days ago, and he, too, had recognized its shortcomings right away. But for several reasons, he'd decided to keep quiet and run the race. First, he urgently needed to make some money, and this race car had to be faster than his own. The Chevy did have some sort of Junior Johnson engine, though Scott wondered about its quality. In any case, Scott felt that all of the publicity made it impossible to back out now, just a week before the race. The press was still churning out upbeat stories about the "Junior Johnson car." He could be branded a malcontent, an ingrate, maybe even a has-been who was afraid of a fast car.

The most primal reason, though, came from that reservoir of pride, hope, and stubbornness still at the core of Scott's identity as a racer. As the oldest driver in Winston Cup, Scott still held the unshakable belief that he could drive as well as the circuit's stars. This car didn't look capable of winning the World 600, but with luck he might manage a top-five finish, and somehow that might get him a sponsorship deal for a competitive car in future races.

There was nothing surprising about Scott's decision. This was the same approach he'd taken since he'd begun racing: make the best of things, don't complain, keep on hoping. Nevertheless, his oldest son was furious. "I said, 'Daddy, you're making a mistake.'" Wendell Jr. left the speedway, after telling his father he wouldn't be back for the race. "I fell out with the family about it. I would not go to the race. I admire the hell out of Daddy, but I don't admire him for what he did at Charlotte."

His father clung to the idea that Howard had started out with a sincere plan to put him into a bona fide Johnson-built car. But whatever Howard's intentions, his approach had a basic flaw from the beginning: He hadn't cleared the idea with Johnson. "He just thought he'd tell Junior, 'Let him drive one of the cars,'" Scott said.

Although Howard owned the team, Junior Johnson wasn't a man who jumped just because somebody wanted him to do something. Years later, during a NASCAR banquet weekend in New York City, the maître d' at the swanky restaurant 21 tried to get Johnson to put on a necktie. Johnson walked out, bought a hot dog from a vendor, and ate on the sidewalk. Howard, though rich and influential, would never be profiled as the Last American Hero. As Johnson saw it, decisions about the team's cars and strategies were his prerogative, not Howard's.

"I was running my own team," Johnson said. "It was just called Howard's team — you know what I'm saying?" Johnson's priority was to win the Winston Cup championship with team driver Bobby Allison. When Howard belatedly approached him about putting Scott into a team car, Johnson told his team owner they had no spare car available, at least none built for superspeedway racing. He felt "there wasn't an extra Chevrolet in the Johnson stable that [the team] could afford to wreck," *Stock Car Racing* magazine later reported.

Some racers privately bristled at the idea of Scott getting any kind of special help, and Howard did some public backpedaling to appease those concerns. Racing writer Bob Myers of the *Charlotte News,* a friend and confidant of Howard's, wrote that the promoter's initial announcement of his plan to put Scott into a first-class car had provoked considerable "racially prejudiced" criticism within the sport. "Some drivers naturally resent Howard offering a car to a 50-year-old black man . . . instead of to them." Others considered it "degrading" for Scott to be treated like a teammate to a white star such as Allison, Myers reported. Howard quickly clarified in public statements that although both Scott and Allison were driving for him, they shouldn't be considered teammates.

In any case, Howard's choice of Neil Castles to locate and rent a car for Scott — along with the modest amount of money Castles apparently had been authorized to spend — did not suggest that the promoter had really put any urgent priority on finding Scott a competitive ride. Castles's prejudice toward Scott was well known in NASCAR. At the Talladega event, Castles approached a low-budget, beginner team from Tennessee and made them a low-budget offer. "Neil called us over to a Winnebago that he had on the grounds, and he cut the deal with us," the car's owner, Charlie McGee, said. McGee's driver and racing partner, David Sisco, recalled Howard paying them only "a couple of thousand" dollars to rent their Chevrolet.

Their team, McGee said, was a struggling two-man operation. McGee, a tire salesman, supplied most of the money, and Sisco provided the labor. In the past two seasons, they'd run only eight races. They had one respectable finish, a seventh at Daytona, fourteen laps down. "We were not a front-runner," McGee said. "We were new on the block. We were just trying to get started. We'd carry our engine to the motel, tear the thing down, wash the parts in the bathroom. That's the kind of deal we were."

By May 20, McGee's Chevrolet had been prepared at Junior Johnson's shop, and Scott went to Charlotte to test it for the first time. One of Scott's white friends, George Henderson, came with him. Henderson, a Danville police officer and racing enthusiast, often worked as a volunteer crewman for Scott. On Scott's fastest laps, he averaged just over 149 miles an hour. The Chevrolet was much quicker than Scott's own car — this was the first time he'd lapped Charlotte at more than 140. But 149 was far from a competitive time. The top cars were expected to qualify for the World 600 in the mid- to high 150s.

As Scott drove, Henderson stood with the men in Scott's pit as they timed his laps and talked about him. "Bobby Allison was there, Junior Johnson, Herb Nab, some other people, and they were kind of laughing, snickering about Wendell driving the car — that they had got him a competitive car, and he was scared to drive it," Henderson said. "Wendell made four or five laps and came in and asked Bobby Allison to drive it and see what he thought about it. So Allison went out. He drove it wide open, too, and it ran 149.

"So then the snickering kind of stopped.

"Herb Nab said, 'Scott, don't worry — we'll get you a couple or three more miles an hour out of it before qualifying.'" After a few adjustments, Scott turned a practice lap the next day at 151.685, still significantly slower than the front-runners.

For a *Charlotte News* feature story about Scott, reporter Myers drove several slow laps in the much-publicized car. Though he wasn't an expert on race car construction, Myers said years later in an interview that "I knew it wasn't a Junior Johnson car . . . It just didn't look right. You can tell — the workmanship and everything. The car just didn't impress me as being a very good car." However, the story he wrote on deadline didn't reflect those observations, describing the car simply as "Richard Howard's $20,000 Chevrolet."

Ralph Moody had volunteered to be Scott's crew chief for the race. Moody took the job, he said, after others refused because Scott was black. "I understand they tried some other people who said, 'Hell, I ain't gonna crew-chief this damn thing,' which was kind of stupid — what the hell's the difference what color he was?" For a while, Moody said, "Nobody wanted to be crew chief on it. So they called me up and asked, and I said, 'Yeah, I don't give a damn if he's black.'"

Scott was determined to make the field on the first day of qualifying, when the top twelve of forty starting spots would be awarded. On the first lap of his two-lap run, the Chevy's transmission lost second and third gears, slowing his acceleration. On the second lap, trying too hard to make up lost time, Scott bobbled slightly on the bumps of turn four, losing a fraction of a second. Despite these problems, Scott improved on his practice times. He ran 152.810 miles an hour and took eleventh place on the grid. Qualifying just ahead of Scott, beating him by only a sliver of a percent, were two NASCAR superstars: Fred Lorenzen at 152.883 and Richard Petty at 153.061.

However, the other two cars fielded by Richard Howard ran much faster than Scott's. Allison took the pole position at 158.162. Paschal, qualifying later in the week, set the field's third fastest time at 156.037. At his motel that night, Scott pored over the day's results while Myers interviewed him. "If I had only beat Petty," Scott said. "I would have liked that, beating a real big name."

Scott tiptoed diplomatically around the issue of the car's mediocrity, hinting at it only obscurely. "The race has been built up so big, there's been so much publicity about Richard Howard giving me this good car to drive, I just had to try as hard as I could . . . I guess lots of Chevrolet fans are disgusted with me . . . But I don't think I let myself down or anybody else. I still think I am a better man than the car was."

He still believed that this race could rejuvenate his career, he told Myers. "I've kept looking for something all these years [and] that could happen Sunday. I've always wanted a chance to prove I'm as good as the next man in my field. Maybe I will Sunday, maybe I won't. Except for three or four cars, I know I can run with the leaders, run hard . . . And there is some hope that maybe this'll lead to a better car."

Myers covered the story of Scott's experience with Howard more extensively than any other journalist, first in the newspaper, and later in a long profile of Scott for *Stock Car Racing* magazine. Eventually, Myers said, Howard admitted to him that he'd deliberately made sure Scott's Chevrolet was significantly slower than the cars he entered for Allison and Paschal. "Howard did tell me they had felt like Wendell would really hurt himself if he got a strong car and had a strong engine like Junior Johnson's regular drivers had," Myers said. "And so that's why they toned it down and gave him something else." Nab made a similar acknowledgment, Myers said. "The words that Herb used were, 'Well, we detuned the engine.' Whatever they did, it just didn't have the horsepower of a normal Junior Johnson engine." Before the race, Scott learned from crew members that the engine hadn't even been freshly rebuilt, something a top team would do routinely for such a major event as the World 600.

On race day, as spectators crowded into the grandstands, Howard savored the spectacular results of his promotional efforts. This would be the most successful World 600 in the event's thirteen-year history. About 81,500 fans packed the speedway on this warm, sunny afternoon — 3,500 more than last year. More than five thousand of the spectators, Howard noted, were black. "I never seen so many black people on the back grandstand in my life." Although some press corps insiders had come to realize that the Chevrolet didn't match up to Howard's promises, the pre-race coverage stuck with the appealing story line that Scott had a competitive ride and a chance to win. The *Charlotte News* listed him as a "dark horse" favorite. The *Charlotte Observer* called him a "legitimate contender."

But after the green flag waved, Scott's fans were quickly disappointed. He could keep the Chevrolet in the bottom half of the top ten, but the leaders lapped him on the twenty-fourth of four hundred laps. For many laps, Scott battled closely with Lorenzen, a four-time winner at Charlotte. Lorenzen had publicly estimated that his own car was about seventy horsepower short of being competitive. He would pass Scott on the straightaway, but Scott could get by him going into the turns. The car that Howard had furnished for Scott, Lorenzen said, had "about 70 or 60 percent" of the performance that the crowd had been led to expect.

As the race went on, the handling of Scott's car deteriorated. The car developed what racers call a "push" — a tendency for the front end to lose grip in the turns and plow toward the outside wall. Scott was running ninth on lap 283 when the engine began to miss. He pulled into his pit. His crewman Ray Arnold ran to the window. "What's it doing?" Arnold yelled over the ragged engine noise.

"It's popping through the carburetor," Scott shouted.

Arnold and Frank Scott, each on one side of the engine, took turns pulling off and replacing spark-plug wires, one at a time. One cylinder, they discovered, had stopped functioning. Later, broken parts were found in the valve train. Then they spotted the cause of the poor handling. The brace supporting a right-front shock absorber had broken off the chassis, making the car too crippled for any quick repairs. Scott's day was over.

Right after the race, Lorenzen recalled, Scott came over and told him proudly, "'I was running right with you, Mr. Fred.' He was, too. He was running right close to me."

Although Scott had placed only twenty-second, Howard stuck to the event's promotional script. He had created a career-honoring award for Scott, called the Curtis Turner Achievement Award. Turner, a driver much admired by Scott and many others, had died two years earlier in a plane crash. At a special ceremony after the race, Bunny Turner, his widow, presented the plaque to Scott.

The assignment of giving Scott a congratulatory kiss went to Toy Russell. As southern stock car racing's first and only black race queen, she understood perfectly well why she'd been chosen for this particular ceremony. "There was no problem with me kissing the white drivers, but there would certainly be a problem with a white girl kissing him," she recalled wryly.

In the typical way that men of influence in NASCAR dealt with Scott, nobody ever explained to him why he had gotten an inferior car. In interviews, Howard and Johnson said they'd wanted to put Scott in a competitive ride but ran out of time. "We tried, and then we couldn't," Howard said. "We had to do it the way we did it." Johnson said: "We was trying to get Wendell a car that was capable of doing the same thing as the other two cars we had, and we never could get it all together in time."

Racial prejudice, Johnson said, didn't play any part in the situation. "I don't think there's a single soul in our racing who didn't like Wendell Scott. He was a great person, a great competitor." Johnson said he'd asked his chassis builder, Banjo Matthews, known as one of NASCAR's best, about assembling a car for Scott, but they'd run out of time. Matthews declined to comment, except to offer his opinion of Scott: "Typical nigger — you'd give him something, and you'd look again, and it would be all wore out."

After the race, with the crowd leaving and the late-afternoon sun sinking low, Richard Howard sat on the porch of the old house on the grounds where the speedway had its offices. He was relaxing with another of his racing-writer friends, Tom Higgins of the *Charlotte Observer.* They were sipping bourbon and enjoying the shade of the elm trees when Scott suddenly came around the corner of the house, walking quickly, looking intense.

"Man, he's striding purposefully," Higgins recalled, "and Richard said, 'Oh, Lord, here comes trouble.'"

Scott had been in Charlotte for several days, taking part in practice sessions, qualifying, and promotional activities. At Howard's request, he'd stayed at a motel near the speedway.

"Wendell said, 'Mr. Howard, I got to have a little getting-home money to get back to Danville.'

"Richard said, 'Well, my goodness, Wendell, I gave you five hundred dollars.'

"Wendell said, 'Yeah, but that motel room cost me fifty dollars a night. I ain't ever paid that much to stay nowhere in my life.'

"Richard said, 'Well, fifty dollars is not that much.'

"Wendell said, 'If I'd known it was going to cost that much, I'd have done what I always do. I'd have slept in my truck.'

"Richard sort of laughed at that, and he said, 'Wendell, you did a good job for us. You're a good fellow. You tried real hard.'

"Richard reached in his pocket and pulled out a rather sizable wad of bills and peeled off five hundred-dollar bills and gave them to Wendell. I don't think I've ever seen Wendell grin wider in my life.

"He said, 'What's the chance of me getting that Big Chance again next year?'

"Richard said he would see about it, and they shook hands, and Wendell left to go home."

After they resumed relaxing and drinking the Jack Daniels, however, Howard began to wonder if Scott had made up the story about the motel bill, Higgins said.

"Richard got to thinking about it, and he said, 'You know, I bet that rascal did sleep in his truck.'"

After a career of stepping aside from confrontation or controversy, Scott spoke out about the Charlotte race with unusually bitter candor in an article Myers wrote for *Stock Car Racing* magazine the following year. Scott called the event "the most humiliating experience in my Grand National career, perhaps since I've been in the sport." Howard had started out with good intentions, Scott said, "but somewhere along the line, somebody who counted resented my being in a Junior Johnson Chevrolet, and Howard yielded to the pressure."

Howard "promised I'd make a lot of money, maybe $2,000, out of the deal, and I needed that." Instead, he said, he got home with about four hundred dollars and the new sport coat the speedway had given him for promotional appearances.

Far worse, Scott said, was the knowledge that he'd compromised his reputation as a driver. "There's hardly a day passes that some smarty doesn't walk up to me and say that I was in a Chevrolet like Bobby Allison and couldn't outrun anybody."

He'd persuaded himself that if he did well in the race, he might attract sponsorship, maybe even work out a deal with Johnson to drive one of his cars. Now he wished he'd taken his son's advice and walked away from the deal. "I've been sorry many a day that I didn't refuse the ride," he said. "Wendell Jr. warned me about it. He said I was being exploited, and I was."

He had been racing for twenty years, and during those decades the civil rights movement had brought about some significant political changes for black Americans. But in the world of NASCAR, where important people still dwelled on which beauty queen could be allowed to kiss him on the cheek, apparently the time still wasn't right for a black driver to compete in a first-class car. When he looked back on his hopes for the World 600, Scott said, "I realize now I was just dreaming."

## 31

### "And the crowd laughed."

After the Charlotte race, Scott's troubles on the circuit got worse. Every event seemed to bring some new blow to his pride. Promoters told him he wasn't worth the $250 appearance fee he requested. "I couldn't get anybody to give me any appearance money," he told journalist Bob Myers. Ever since his boyhood exploits on bicycles and roller skates, his talents for speed and competition had been a bulwark of his self-respect. Now, as sometimes happens with addictive pursuits, his passion for racing seemed to be turning against him, bringing more humiliation than rewards. One promoter promised he'd mail a hundred-dollar check, which never arrived. Another, Myers wrote, simply "told him he didn't need his junk in his race." Some drivers with better equipment, Scott said, "laughed and made fun of my operation."

At Daytona, Bill Gazaway came up with a particularly insulting way, Scott said, of excluding him from the Firecracker 400 race on July 4. After his car passed technical inspection, Scott said, he drove toward the track to take part in a required practice session.

"They had a rule back then that you couldn't go out to qualify unless you had practiced first. Bill stopped me at the gate and said, 'Go back in there and jack your car up. I want to look up under there.'

"I said, 'You done looked up under there once.'

"He said, 'I forgot to look at something. I want to look up under it again.'"

Scott returned to the pit area, he said, jacked up the car, and waited for Gazaway. "He never did come back to check my car."

After practice ended and Scott had lost his chance to qualify for the race, he said, Gazaway returned to give him a brusque order. "He told me, 'Well, you can let it down and load up and go home.'"

Two decades after Scott had broken the color barrier in southern stock car racing, he still couldn't come to a NASCAR race confident that he'd be given the fair treatment Bill France Sr. had promised, even at a track that France owned. Asked about Scott's account of the Daytona incident, Bill Gazaway said, "I don't recall," and changed the subject. A NASCAR spokesman said the organization has no information on the matter.

As the Labor Day weekend approached, Scott decided to try to run Darlington's Southern 500, but that trip brought him more misfortune and embarrassments. While towing his race car to South Carolina on the Wednesday before the race, Scott stopped for a meal at a truck stop. That night, in a little motel that catered to blacks, he became violently ill, apparently with food poisoning. He'd hoped to arrive at the track early and make some improvements to the old Ford, but the illness left him too weak to work on the car or to try to qualify until Saturday, two days before the 500.

This was the final day of qualifying, with twenty-three drivers vying for the last nine starting spots. For the rest, there would be a consolation race. The grandstand was full of fans who'd bought two-dollar tickets to watch these slower competitors battle to make the field. Scott's car ran poorly and, with its bent frame, handled even worse. The right-rear and left-front wheels barely touched the track. He couldn't get anywhere near a competitive time. Of all of the race cars at Darlington that weekend, the slowest turned out to be Scott's. He would start the consolation race in last place.

Jerry Bledsoe, a North Carolina writer working on a book about stock car racing, took a lot of notes on this obscure race. He was intrigued by NASCAR's underdogs, the drivers who sacrificed much for little reward, and he knew he'd be writing a chapter about Wendell Scott. Some drivers in the fifteen-lap consolation race planned to run only one or two laps. Then they'd pull in, load up, and go home. Everybody who started the race would get a hundred dollars, and winning paid only two hundred. As they saw it, there was little point in pushing hard, wearing out tires, risking a blown engine or a wreck, in a race that meant nothing.

Bledsoe's book *The World's Number One, Flat-Out, All-Time Great, Stock Car Racing Book,* one of the sport's classics, would capture Scott's struggle with the shame of being so uncompetitive, so easy to dismiss as a has-been or never-was. Before the consolation started, Bledsoe wrote, "the track announcer, a guy with a melodious voice who tried to wring the maximum drama out of every word, began the introductions. When he got to the last one, he said, 'And star-ting in the scratch po-si-tion, the un-o-ffic-ial mayor of Dan-ville, Virginia — Wendell Scott!'

"It was the only introduction to draw any real response from the crowd, but the response included a lot of jeering and mocking laughter. Then somewhere up in the stands, some guy boomed out: 'GI'EM HELL, WEN-DELL!' And the crowd laughed."

The faces of Scott's sons, his crew for the weekend, showed their stress and embarrassment. After the first few laps, they saw that their father could not keep up with anybody on the track. They signaled him to pull in. He ignored them. On the next lap, they tried again to wave him in. Scott kept on driving. Finally, they gave up and walked away from the pit wall, shaking their heads but hardly surprised. Scott ran the entire race, finishing last among the cars that had stayed out.

Bledsoe asked Scott why he hadn't pulled in early. Scott replied tersely: "I don't race like 'at."

"For him," Bledsoe wrote, "it had been a matter of dignity." Scott managed to qualify for only six Winston Cup races in 1972, failing to make the field at many others. His results for the season were his worst ever: no top-tens, fortieth in points, only $5,830 in prize money. On the minor-league Grand National East circuit, Scott's only top-five was his fourth place on the new tires from Tiny Lund. Otherwise, the best finishes he could manage were an eighth, a ninth, and two tenths. He won only $3,005. His income fell far short of expenses. He and Mary refinanced their mortgage yet again, borrowing $9,193 ($46,557 in 2008 dollars).

Neil Castles, driving his winged Dodge, won the Grand National East championship. He thanked Chrysler's Ronney Householder for "helping me land a first-class piece of equipment." He also thanked the Charlotte Motor Speedway's Richard Howard, who'd provided crucial financial assistance. For Scott, it was galling to be beaten so thoroughly by someone who held him in contempt and didn't mind saying so publicly. As Castles would tell one writer, he considered Scott "just more or less a joke." Scott raced only because "he was making more money than the average nigger."

Scott's race car sat untouched all winter. Fixing other people's cars took up all his time as he tried to catch up with the family's bills. Bledsoe, researching his book, came to Danville in the spring of 1973 to spend time with Scott. He found Scott wrestling with the question of whether it made any sense for him to continue racing, his mood darkened by second thoughts about the past.

Over the winter, Scott related, he "had almost reached the conclusion that it was all futile, that no matter how hard he tried, a black man just couldn't make it in this business." He'd lost all hope of sponsorship by now, and he wondered if he'd been too nice, too deferential, in trying to win support from the auto companies.

"The reason I think I didn't get no factory backin'," Scott said, "was because I was a black man and the people that was over charge of the factory racin' business just wasn't goin' to help a black man in racin'." Maybe, he said, he should have made the auto companies worry that he'd stir up public controversy if they passed over NASCAR's only black competitor. If Jackie Robinson had been in his position, he'd probably have spoken out.

"If I'd been demandin', if I'd a went about it in a different way, to where I could've prob'ly hurt different car manufacturers through talkin' or demonstratin', or somethin' like 'at, there is a possibility I would've got some factory help, but I didn't go about it the right way, I guess."

He considered the possibility that he was through with racing. He felt no itch to go to Riverside in January or to Daytona in February. But when spring came to Danville, Scott's old desire returned, so strongly he knew he couldn't resist.

"We gonna give it one mo' try," he told Bledsoe as he worked in the small, cluttered cinder-block shop he'd built years ago, now surrounded by the rusty carcasses of his old race cars and trucks. Scott hoped to race next weekend in Hickory, North Carolina. He squatted down, peering under the Ford with its dull paint and wrinkled bodywork, trying to come up with a strategy for straightening the chassis.

"Now, if I jack dis right here and cut dat right dere — naw, dat ain't gonna do it."

He decided to get some advice. With Bledsoe, Scott drove his old pickup over to Bobby Fleming's body shop. Fleming, a racer himself and one of Scott's closest white friends, regularly helped Scott with his race cars. Scott pulled up out outside the shop, and he sat talking with Bledsoe for a few minutes.

Fleming came out and walked over to the driver's side of the truck. "What the hell you waitin' on, curb service?" he asked, grinning.

"We're just talkin'."

"You got yours ready to go?"

Scott shook his head, looking pained. "You know, I just got that jack under that thing and I been thinkin' and tryin' to figger. That's what I came up here — to ast you somethin'."

Scott began sketching the chassis on a scrap of paper. "I ain't did a thing but just been trying — okay, now dis wheel over here, dis is right rear . . ." The conversation became deeply technical. They talked about an approach that involved cutting a couple of chassis pieces. "See, it's squirrelly behind," Scott said. The crippled car clearly needed some sort of surgery.

Eventually, Fleming said, "You waited too late to start doin' shit like this."

"I know it," said Scott, despair in his tone, "but what can I do? I spent two days —"

"You shoulda brought that car up here the other day like I told ya."

"I didn't want to bother y'all, I swear I didn't."

"We'da had that damn thing ready to race by now."

"You got your hands full," Scott said. Fleming had four customer cars to paint by Friday.

"I know that, but I'd never stop you from racing."

"I know, I know."

"Hell, we gotta race."

They talked more about the chassis. "Cut them bars aloose now," Fleming said. "If you don't cut them bars aloose, you workin' against yourself."

"I know it."

"If you need any help, hollah." If necessary, Fleming said, he could stall a couple of customers.

Scott started his truck. "I'm goin' back," he said. "And if I don't get it right, I might not bother you till Saturday."

On the way home Scott talked about Wendell Jr. and Frank — that they, too, wanted to race but weren't willing to accept the conditions he had. They weren't willing, he told Bledsoe, to take any shit. He parked outside his garage and shut off the truck. He sat awhile, staring into space.

"But *I* ain't taking no more shit," he said finally.

Inside the garage, amid his piles of scratched and grimy tools and the stacks of old car parts that a poor man couldn't bring himself to throw away, Scott hunched down and scowled at the underside of the car. He pondered the chassis, running a hand through his graying hair. He talked as he worked, mostly to himself. "Now, if I bend it right there . . . naw, that ain't gonna work, he done told me wrong. I swear, I don't know what to do."

All winter, Scott had persuaded himself — almost — that he'd had enough of the racing life, that it was time to quit. Retiring had seemed like a commonsense decision — almost. His sport required racing for five hundred miles inside a sweltering race car without power steering on humid, hundred-degree days in the Deep South. His Ford was shot, and he was fifty-one years old.

But spring had arrived now, and the urge to go racing was back, powerful as ever, and he couldn't forget that last year, people had laughed at him.

# 32

## "He put all his chips on the table."

Scott showed up for the five-hundred-mile race at the Talladega speedway in May 1973 towing a race car that astonished his competitors. Somehow, NASCAR's perennial underdog had arrived at America's fastest superspeedway with a thoroughbred machine far superior to his old cars, those backyard rehab projects with patches of brush paint that fans had come to associate with Scott. "The car was the most beautiful car there, beyond a doubt," Frank Scott said.

Even from a distance, the other racers could see that Scott's gleaming Mercury had the crouching, predatory look of a front-runner. The car had been raced only a few times since Holman-Moody built it for Ford Motor Co.'s corporate racing operation. Under the hood sat a fresh, ultrapowerful 429-cubic-inch V-8 from one of the sport's renowned engine builders. The color scheme — red, white, and blue — suited its role as a vehicle for an American dream. "It was immaculate — inside, underside, outside, immaculate beyond description," Frank Scott said. "This was our dream car."

His father's manner had a noticeably sharper edge. "He was excited, ready for the challenge, confident," Frank said. His sons noticed that other drivers, amazed to see Scott's new race car, seemed somewhat cool toward them. They didn't appear pleased to see the Scotts with such a competitive-looking machine. It reminded Frank and Wendell Jr. of 1962 in Savannah, when their father had qualified on the pole and some drivers acted as if he'd violated an unwritten rule of his acceptance.

Now, eleven years later, they felt the same sort of chill. For a while, Frank said, "no one would come around us. Even people we had been friendly with, they wouldn't come around. Everybody was keeping their distance. It was just us working on the car."

Scott didn't acquire the Mercury because he'd gotten any help from NASCAR or found a generous sponsor. He got the car by taking on the largest burden of debt he'd ever carried. He'd decided to borrow every dollar he could for one more attempt to prove he could run with NASCAR's best.

Wendell Jr. helped to seal that decision. He'd advised his father either to quit racing or somehow buy a competitive car. "You are right," his father replied. "Let's get us a damn race car."

Mercurys built by Holman-Moody had proven consistent winners, helping drivers such as Bobby Allison and David Pearson attain their star status. The aerodynamics were near perfect for superspeedways; Mercurys had won the last two Talladega races. Scott found one for sale in Michigan with no engine. Ralph Moody helped Scott to locate a state-of-the-art engine by Waddell Wilson, a former engine-building wizard for Holman-Moody.

Then Scott took the financial plunge into heavy debt for most of the next decade. He took out a $13,306 mortgage from Danville's black-owned First State Bank and got more loans from friends. By the time the Mercury was ready to race, Scott said, he'd spent about $22,000, nearly all of it borrowed — the equivalent of $104,893 in 2008 dollars.

One of Scott's old friends, journalist Morris Stephenson, came to see him shortly after he brought the Mercury home. That day, Scott's garage looked like a class reunion of his volunteer crewmen. "Every black friend who'd ever helped him was there," Stephenson said. "There were people there who hadn't helped him in a long time because they'd gotten tired, disgusted. Now all the guys that worked with him one time or another, everybody was there again, ready to go get 'em. They were just like bees in a hive on that car."

Scott talked excitedly about his hopes. "He looked at it as his big, big chance," Stephenson said. "It was first his real opportunity to do something, his big break for a great showing. This was going to be the car that was going to bring him the recognition that he deserved. He was just walking on cloud nine."

"This is it!" Scott told him.

"He put all his chips on the table, and he was just waiting for the last card to be dealt. He knew he was going to be successful with it."

The Talladega race happened to fall on the same day as his daughter Deborah's graduation from Virginia State University. There was no discussion of Scott skipping the race for the ceremony, family members said. His children knew that he loved them deeply but that racing was overwhelmingly important. Instead, Deborah, who had helped her father at many races, skipped her graduation to go to Talladega.

"I was all excited about it," she said. "I felt like this was going to be Daddy's lucky chance. Because I had followed him in racing all those years, I decided I'd rather be at the race than march with my class that day." Though she was a good mechanic, she would work, as usual, in the scoring stand. NASCAR did not yet allow women in the pits.

In his office at the nation's fastest speedway, Bill France Sr. argued with one of his executives, publicist N. Linn Hendershot, over how many cars should run the race. Although France had turned over NASCAR's presidency to his son, he remained the boss on Talladega matters, and he felt strongly that his crowd deserved the largest starting field ever — sixty cars, ten more than in past years. "That will make a tremendous show," said France.

Hendershot objected strongly, warning of "a real disastrous outcome." Drivers also had spoken out against a sixty-car field. "That's about 20 or 25 more than they should start . . . ," Richard Petty told reporters. "Anything can happen at these speeds, and that's just too many cars." But France brushed aside the warnings. "Bill France understood what business he was in," Hendershot said. "He wasn't just in the racing business — he was in the entertainment business. That was what got us in trouble."

Scott drove the Mercury for the first time in his qualifying session. The car ran poorly. He qualified at 163 miles an hour, 30 miles an hour slower than the pole winner, Buddy Baker. The problem turned out to be his unfamiliarity with the 429 engine — he'd adjusted the timing and valves incorrectly. He wound up fifty-eighth on the starting grid. This was hardly the way he'd hoped to begin rejuvenating his career.

However, the team that raced one of NASCAR's fastest Mercurys quickly came to Scott's aid. Leonard and Glen Wood and their driver, David Pearson, saw that Scott needed help. They gave his engine a complete tune-up, readjusting the valves and timing.

France had chosen Governor George Wallace as the event's grand marshal. Wallace's wife, Cornelia, would drive the Winston Cup pace car. At the governor's mansion that weekend, Wallace had thrown a party for the France family, NASCAR's top officials, and executives of corporate sponsors. France, in a white suit, sang for the crowd while Union Oil's president, Fred Hartley, played the piano and Wallace sat alongside in his wheelchair, chewing his ubiquitous cigar and clapping to the music.

On race day, about eighty thousand spectators packed the speedway. The governor wore a white suit, red shirt, and a white tie with red polka dots as he rode through the pit area in the pace car before the race. This was his opportunity, as at so many NASCAR races in the past, for handshaking, politicking, and getting his picture taken.

The pace car pulled up beside Scott as he was about to strap himself into the Mercury. He'd just stuffed cotton into his ears. Racing had cost him some of his hearing, and he was trying to preserve the rest.

Wallace stuck his right hand out of the maroon convertible. Scott stared for a moment at the politician who had blocked the schoolhouse door a decade ago in a symbolic protest against integration. Then Scott reached out and shook hands with Wallace. A track photographer captured the moment. Scott's expression was inscrutable.

As Scott drove the pace laps at the tail end of the huge field, he thought his engine sounded stronger. When the green flag dropped and he hit the gas, the Mercury's fierce acceleration gave him a rush of elation. At last, after twelve years on the circuit in inferior cars, this felt like the race car he'd always wanted. "That thing felt like somebody shot me out of a shotgun! Oh, man! Them cars that had outqualified me, I was walking by them like they weren't there. I was on my way to the front!"

Scott's sons watched excitedly as their father passed car after car. "The first lap of the race, I had my stopwatch and my chart," Frank Scott said. "When my father came by, I timed him at 184.5." Already Scott was twenty-one miles an hour faster than his qualifying speed and still gaining momentum. He passed about eighteen cars on the first lap.

Ten laps into the race, Ramo Stott's car blew its engine coming off turn two, bounced off the wall, and coated the backstretch with oil. Cars began crashing. Some skidded into the infield, sending up a huge, blinding cloud of red dust. Suddenly the oncoming drivers, racing into the cloud at 180 miles an hour or more, couldn't see the track or the cars stopped in front of them. That touched off one of the multicar pileups for which Talladega remains notorious today. As twenty-one racers crashed in the melee, cars flew through the air, wreckage jammed the backstretch, and in the next few seconds Scott's life would change irreparably.

A car hit Scott from behind, sending him on a long slide into the infield, far from the pileup, and he had a moment to think that perhaps he'd gotten off easy. Then he saw Slick Gardner's car leave the track at high speed and come skidding across the infield — right at him. "I saw him coming. Wasn't nothing I could do but just say 'Oh, Lord' and grip that wheel."

Gardner's car struck with a devastating impact, totaling the Mercury, mangling Scott's body. The crash fractured Scott's left leg and his pelvis in several places, broke three ribs and his right knee, ripped much of the skin off his left forearm, and seriously injured his right kidney. "I never hurt as bad in all my life," Scott said. "I didn't see no way I could live, I was hurting so bad."

Gardner, Earl Brooks, and Joe Frasson also sustained injuries, but Scott's were the worst. Frasson was furious as he left the track's field hospital in his bloodstained driver suit. "I hope to hell France is happy. . . ," he said loudly. "NASCAR had no business starting sixty cars."

From the pits, Scott's sons couldn't see what had happened. Wendell Jr. ran off toward the scene of the wreck, and Frank stayed on pit road, hoping to see his father pull in. Another driver stopped nearby, his car torn up. "I ran down and I said, 'Did you see my dad? Was he in that wreck?'

"He said, 'Frankie, your dad is dead.'"

The driver seemed dazed, however, and Frank wasn't sure he knew what he was talking about. He ran to the field hospital and pushed through the crowd outside the door. He found the room where his father lay on a padded table as doctors and nurses worked on him.

"His whole body was covered with blood, from the top of his head all the way to the bottom of his legs. It was like somebody had taken a spray gun and sprayed his whole body in red. They had his left arm up in the air, and all this flesh from his lower arm was laying back there on his shoulder. The skin was only connected on the back side of his arm."

Frank could see part of his father's arm bone. Their eyes met. "I said, 'Oh, my God!'" He wondered if his father would live.

# 33

## "What's the purpose?"

One glance at the Mercury told Wendell Scott Jr. the car could never race again. The chassis was bent, the suspension torn up, the whole left side of the body ripped away. Then he looked inside. He saw bloody chunks of flesh from his father's arm on the roll-cage bars next to the driver's seat.

At the track's field hospital, Wendell Sr. sank deeper into shock. He had to be rushed to Citizens Hospital in Talladega. The brothers conferred quickly — Frank would go with their father; Wendell Jr. would cope with the wrecked car and their gear and with gathering the family. Frank jumped into the ambulance with the attendants — "the longest ride of my life." His father had tried to prepare him for this kind of day. "He'd always said to me, 'Don't worry about me — whatever happens to me, I been doin' what I loved.' I always kept that in my mind."

As they arrived at the emergency room, Scott, groggy and racked with pain, gave Frank a surprising command. Pointing at his broken leg, he told Frank not to let the doctors put it in a cast. He didn't want the loss of muscle strength that would result from the limb being immobilized. "Already, he was thinking about how soon he could get back in the race car," Frank said. "This was only about an hour after the crash." Frank began to feel a little more optimistic about his father's survival. The doctors agreed not to use a hard cast.

Despite several shots, Scott remained conscious while the medical team worked on his mangled arm. As they stitched him up, Frank said, "Daddy told the doctor, 'You left something in my arm.'" At first the doctors were skeptical, but Scott was adamant: something was still inside his arm. "Take another look," he insisted.

"They decided to take another look, and they took a long pair of tweezers, reached down between the muscle and the bone, and took out a piece of something, and dropped it in the pan. There was blood all over it." It was a shard of metal, twisted at the end. One of the doctors, Richard Bliss, complimented Scott's fortitude. "Dr. Bliss said to my father, 'I've heard a lot about you, and I have to say you're a hell of a man.'"

From a VIP suite at the speedway, Bill France Sr. watched the cleanup of the accident that Linn Hendershot and others had predicted. "Bill came up to me and handed me his checkbook," Hendershot recalled. "He said, 'We got to go down and talk to these boys and see what we can do to make this right.'"

Then, he said, France "put his hand on my shoulder and added, 'Just do me a favor.'

"I said, 'What's that, sir?'

"He said, 'Just don't ever say I told you so.'

"He grinned, and I said, 'You got a deal.'"

France went through the garage and talked to the owners of every car involved in the wreck, except for Scott, who was already in the hospital. "Bill was coming with an olive branch," Hendershot said. "He was saying, *I screwed up, boys,* without actually saying it. It was, 'What can I do to make this right so we can race next week?'. . . He felt he needed to make some amends."

France looked over each car's damage and suggested a sum as compensation. Henderson would write the check and France would sign it. Typical payments, he said, were three thousand, five thousand, or ten thousand dollars. France "would say, 'Would that help you get back on your feet?' And they would say, 'We really appreciate your help.'" Hendershot said France was "terribly upset" by Scott's injuries, but that the subject of compensation for him didn't come up.

At the hospital, groggy from drugs but still in pain, Scott slipped into a delirium. Sitting with him as he drifted in and out of consciousness, Frank and Deborah realized just how deeply entwined in their father's psyche were the connections between his own identity and the race car that he had hoped would let him prove his ability. Scott hallucinated that he, himself, was the Mercury, and that his injuries were the Mercury's damaged parts. In this altered state, Frank said, his father pointed to his broken left leg, and "he would tell me to change the left front tire." Deborah said Scott "was moaning and groaning in pain and associating his body with parts of the car. He would say things like, 'Oh, my crankshaft hurts,' and 'my cam hurts,' talking out of his head."

Mary Scott got to the hospital from Danville the next morning. She walked into the room where her husband lay with both legs and his left arm suspended in the air. "He just looked like a dead man," she said. The family, Deborah said, hoped that Scott would quit racing. "We didn't want him to take a chance anymore." But as soon as his delirium passed, Scott told the family the same thing he'd said shortly after the crash — he planned to race again.

George Smith, sports editor and columnist for the *Anniston Star* in Alabama, visited Scott at the hospital a week after the crash. The experience left Smith shaken and puzzled. His stomach churned when he saw the ugly patchwork of bruises — yellow, purple, and green — covering Scott's left side from shoulder to hip, and he was astounded to hear Scott talk about racing again.

"On top of the sickness and nausea in the stomach as you stood there and smelled hospital smells and looked at a broken body," Smith wrote in his column, "there was a lot of wondering. Wondering what, just what, drives these men to put life itself out there in the name of sport.

"What's the purpose? Why take the risk? What are the goals, the reasons?

"I have no idea. None. I'm not even sure Wendell Scott can put it in words. But he can lay there and hurt and ache and vow he'll be back racing."

Wendell Jr. told Smith how much the Mercury had meant to the family's hopes. "We had everything in it we have . . . Anybody'll tell you he's one of the best drivers around. All he's ever needed is a top car, and we thought we might just have one . . . We had all our eggs in one basket, everything." Now, if his father raced again, it would have to be in "junk." There was no other way. "'We just don't have another $20,000,' says Wendell Jr., quietly. And sadly."

At Danville's airport on May 19, several hundred well-wishers kept a daylong vigil, waiting for a medical plane to bring Scott home after thirteen days in the Alabama hospital. Attendants carried him on a stretcher from the plane, whose departure had been delayed nearly eight hours by bad weather. Two city council members made welcoming remarks, and the local Crane Tire Co. gave him a five-hundred-dollar check. A fund drive was launched, and the wrecked Mercury, looking like a vehicle ripped open by a land mine, went on display at the tire company, right across Riverside Drive from the site of the old fairgrounds where Scott had driven the first race of his career.

Scott waved to the crowd with the one arm he could move, but he couldn't make any remarks or even raise his head. "He was just frail," his daughter Sybil said. "He was trying to smile." He had to be taken quickly to the Danville hospital, where he would spend another nineteen days.

Besides the tire company's donation, the fund drive raised several hundred dollars from local fans and friends whose contributions ranged from fifty cents to a hundred dollars. Richard Petty sent a check. "No other driver gave me a cent," Scott said. "Richard sent me $500. I cried." The France family gave fifteen hundred dollars, according to family records.

On June 25, Bill France sent Scott a two-sentence letter and a gift — the photo of Scott shaking hands with George Wallace. "Thought you would like to have the enclosed picture taken at the race at Talladega on May 6," France wrote. "Hope you are about well."

One day while Scott was still in the Danville hospital, Wendell Jr. said, his father surprised him with a question.

"He says, 'You ready to go racing?'

"I said, 'No, sir — what are you talking about?'"

Typically, his father wasn't really asking for an opinion — he was telling Wendell Jr. what was going to happen next. He had called promoters on the minor-league Grand National East and ARCA circuits. He'd told them Wendell Jr. would be driving in some of their upcoming races, and he negotiated for some appearance money. Wendell Jr. would drive his father's old Ford Torino with the crooked chassis. Bring the car back in one piece and bring back the appearance money, his father told him. Any prize money he won, he could keep.

This wasn't a promising debut for Wendell Jr.'s racing career, but it was his only chance to live up to his father's example, and the family badly needed money. They had no health insurance; Scott was still months away from being able to work as a mechanic; and another payment on the Mercury was coming due.

Still on crutches in July, Scott resolved to show up at a tribute banquet for David Pearson, and he made it to Spartanburg with Sybil's help. As drivers were introduced at the event, Scott got an ovation almost as loud as those for Pearson and Petty. "Everyone was truly happy to see the Jackie Robinson of stock car racing," journalist Gene Granger reported. Otherwise, there weren't many happy days for Scott that summer. Journalist Morris Stephenson visited him at home and found his old friend deeply discouraged. Scott's spirits, he said, were "like a balloon with the air let out. It was like the world had ended for him. He was still on crutches, and he had a long way to go to heal from those injuries, and he was down and out, depressed. The mortgage and everything was just heaped upon his shoulders. The debt was weighing heavy on him. His car was gone. His shot at making a name for himself, for being successful, that was gone. Everything was gone."

In August, NASCAR invited Scott as a guest to watch the Talladega 500 from the press box. After thirteen laps, a personable young driver whom Scott liked, Larry Smith, hit the wall with the right side of his car. To the crowd, the crash looked at first like a routine one-car accident, nothing serious. Everything in Smith's racing career had seemed to be falling into place. He'd won last season's Rookie of the Year award and landed a big sponsor.

The minutes passed, however, and Smith didn't climb out of the car. Eventually the announcement came. He had died instantly of head injuries. Smith was the eighteenth driver killed in the twenty-five-year history of NASCAR's top series, the eleventh since Scott had joined the circuit. This would be another day when people wondered about motor racing, about why drivers felt the need to be drivers, about whether that passion justified the deaths. Racing journalist Gary McCredie glanced around the press box a few minutes after the news that Smith had been killed. "I happened to look over, and there was old Wendell, over by himself in a corner, crying."

## 34

### "Business is business."

After he could walk without crutches, Scott drove in three more races during 1973. Two were Grand National East events, and even at that minor-league level, his crooked old Ford ran far off the pace. He finished poorly both times, winning a total of only $465. But he proved something important for any racer — that he still had the nerve to compete in the sport that had nearly killed him.

Scott returned to the Winston Cup circuit on October 7 at the Charlotte superspeedway. He got a ride in a faster car from an unexpected benefactor: Richard Howard. The Charlotte promoter rented Doc Faustina's 1973 Dodge for Scott. Neil Castles helped Howard to arrange this ride, just as Castles had done the previous season with the bogus Junior Johnson car. Howard and Castles may have done this favor for Scott, Faustina said, "because they had guilt feelings about that other deal, where Scott was supposed to get a Junior Johnson car and it really wasn't. That could very well have had something to do with it." Unlike the previous year, Howard didn't publicize what he'd done for Scott.

After mechanical woes during qualifying, Scott gave one of his trademark performances in the five-hundred-mile race, advancing steadily from the bottom of the grid to a respectable finish. Starting thirty-eighth, he got the Dodge into the top ten near the end of the race before a failing battery dropped him back to twelfth. Still in pain from his injuries, he ran the event without a relief driver. The fans didn't realize they were seeing the last race of Scott's career, and Scott himself didn't know it, or preferred not to. He still talked about hopes for sponsorship, but nothing came about, and 1973 turned out to be his last season. He never announced his retirement; he just stopped showing up for races.

For many years afterward, Scott would say he was simply taking a break from racing because his auto-repair business kept him too busy. At times, he'd talk about making a comeback, someday, somehow. His career had been one of the more memorable and gutsy chapters in American motorsports and in the broader struggle of black athletes to overcome segregation and prove their merits. But for Scott, it had also been sadly inconclusive.

He had accomplished things few people achieve. He had established his niche in history as the racial pioneer who broke a tough sport's color barrier in a hostile time. He had become a favorite of many thousands of fans. He had won respect and affection from colleagues who included some of the world's best racers. He remains the only black driver ever to win at NASCAR's top level. And while he didn't go into racing for political or racial reasons, the bravery, hard work, and uncomplaining grit he displayed over twenty-one years as a racer certainly helped to soften many people's prejudices in an era when American values stood at a decisive turning point.

Financially, he might have done better in a conventional job. During his thirteen Grand National and Winston Cup seasons, Scott won $180,814, an average of $13,909 a season. He spent a considerable share of those earnings on travel costs and maintaining his race cars and trucks. He refinanced his home seven times during those years. Like all NASCAR racers, he worked as an independent contractor without a pension or other benefits. To put his winnings into context for his era, factory-sponsored drivers who won championships typically collected enough prize money in that one season to equal Scott's earnings for about ten years. David Pearson, for instance, won $133,064 during his 1968 championship season. Richard Petty won $150,196 in 1967.

Scott's on-track statistics in NASCAR's top circuit demonstrate his consistency and tenacity. The numbers are especially noteworthy when one recalls that his only competitive ride lasted for just eight laps before his wreck at Talladega. He competed in 495 Grand National and Winston Cup races, driving more than seventy-two thousand miles in competition (about 2.9 times around the earth). He finished 324 of those races, or 65.4 percent. Besides his win at Jacksonville, he finished third three times by NASCAR's count, or five times by his own. He finished fourth ten times by NASCAR's figures, or eight times by his count. In six races he came in fifth, giving him a total of twenty top-five finishes. He finished sixth through tenth in 127 races. His overall top-ten finishing record: 29.69 percent.

Despite his accomplishments, Scott looked back on his NASCAR career with some deep dissatisfaction, convinced that the sport had never given him a fair chance to show what he could do. If he could have gotten a tryout for one of the auto manufacturers' teams, he said, things would have turned out quite differently. For the rest of his life, Scott would believe without reservation that he could have been a consistent winner — and that prejudice had cost him the opportunity to prove it. He was particularly rankled by Ford Motor Co.'s unwillingness to give him a chance, despite Ned Jarrett's endorsement in his meeting with Lee Iacocca. "I was a black man. They wasn't going to help a black man. That was all there was to it."

The fact that all of his courage and effort did not ultimately produce an unarguable answer to the fundamental question of any racer's career — was he really a driver of the first rank? — remained for Scott a painful hole in his life. Few epitaphs hurt worse than "I could have been a contender." The gap between his high expectations and the things he never accomplished — multiple Grand National wins, a superspeedway victory, a Grand National championship — would always stand between him and a solid feeling of satisfaction.

Sometimes Scott felt aggrieved that nobody in the racing establishment ever directly acknowledged to him one simple fact — that his career had been harmed by a pattern of injustices and prejudice. Even a belated apology from somebody in power, Wendell Scott Jr. said, would have allowed his father to look back on his struggles with more satisfaction and less bitterness. "All somebody would have had to do is tell him, 'We realize that we didn't do you right.'"

Could different choices on Scott's part have brought better results? Possibly. He didn't start racing until he was thirty, so perhaps he should have tried to move up to Grand National sooner, rather than driving sportsman and modified cars for nine years. Clearly he should have had ulcer surgery years before he did; many people of modest means postpone costly medical procedures, but few of them drive in five- and six-hundred-mile races.

Probably he should have put more emphasis on making his race cars look sharper. For some racing people, Scott's rough-looking cars evoked racial stereotypes, providing an excuse to dismiss him as a serious racer.

The appearance of his cars was part of the broader trade-off he made for the rewards of having so many children. Scott had constant financial pressure to run as many races as possible; often he had to cut corners on the appearance and mechanical preparation of his cars and drive conservatively to make sure he finished.

When asked if he had any regrets about how he'd approached his career, Scott said yes. "If I had it to do over again, I wouldn't try to run all the races. I would be more prepared when I went to the races and, I think, more determined to win than just to finish and make some money. But I probably did it the best way I could, because I had six kids — I had to keep running."

At times, Scott wondered if he'd been too restrained in his role as a racial pioneer, too willing to hide his real feelings, too reluctant to confront the power structure of his sport. Sometimes he thought he should have tried to pressure the auto companies by speaking out and criticizing their lack of support.

Some racing insiders, however, doubted whether that would have accomplished anything. Driver Tim Flock, a two-time Grand National champion, said auto manufacturers didn't sponsor Scott during the 1960s because they feared — realistically — that a racial backlash would cost them business. "Would you have sponsored him, if you was a big company? It would have ruined you, probably . . . I would say they were scared. It was tough back then in the South." Racing journalist Bob Myers said: "I don't believe it was the time for a black person to get a factory deal."

Still, the question of what might have happened had Scott decided to be less guarded in his approach, more willing to be provoke, invites some intriguing speculations. His cautious approach may have cost him some opportunities. If he'd been willing to bump Gip Gibson out of his way at South Boston Speedway in 1959, car owner Monroe Shook might have put him into a competitive Grand National ride. If he'd privately confronted Richard Howard before the 1972 World 600 about the phony

Junior Johnson car and raised the possibility that he'd withdraw from the race and talk to the press, Howard might at least have gotten a competitive engine into the car. The millionaire promoter could have made that happen overnight.

Of course, any discussion of what might have given Scott a greater chance for success leads directly to the role of Bill France Sr. As the czar of NASCAR, France wielded enormous influence over the destiny of Scott's career. The record of Scott's treatment clearly raises questions about France's views of how much and what kind of fair play the sport's only black driver should be given. He had to balance that question against his business interests and the influences of those promoters, fans, politicians, drivers, and NASCAR officials whose actions sometimes suggested they would have preferred that the sport had remained all-white. In looking at how France juggled those priorities, it's useful to consider three periods: Scott's earliest experiences in racing, his years in NASCAR's minor leagues, and his career on NASCAR's top circuit.

When Scott first crossed the color barrier in southern stock car racing, NASCAR had nothing to do with it. A rival sanctioning body, the Dixie Circuit, now defunct and forgotten, invited Scott into the sport in 1952. The day after his first Dixie Circuit race in Danville, Scott began trying to compete in NASCAR. He towed his race car to Bowman Gray Stadium in Winston-Salem, North Carolina, a speedway operated by France and a partner. Officials turned Scott away because of his race. The historic record hasn't yet answered the question of whether France played a part in ordering Scott's exclusion, but it's highly unlikely that he didn't promptly learn about it. Nobody called Scott to say that a mistake had been made and he should come back next week. A few days later, a second NASCAR track refused to let Scott race. He decided, for the time being, to race only at non-NASCAR tracks.

Eventually, a sympathetic local NASCAR steward at a Richmond speedway exercised his own authority and licensed Scott as a NASCAR driver. A NASCAR spokesman said that apparently happened in 1953, though the exact date isn't known. Later, that steward, Mike Poston, confided to Scott that officials at NASCAR's headquarters had "raised hell with him" over his decision. The available evidence about France's position on Scott during this early period, while not ironclad, points toward the conclusion that France simply didn't want a black driver in NASCAR.

The contrast with baseball is striking. Facing the controversial question of integration back in 1947, top officials of major-league baseball grappled with the moral issues and practical problems and decided the time had come to do the right thing and admit Jackie Robinson. For NASCAR, however, Wendell Scott evidently arrived as an unwelcome surprise, a party crasher. Although NASCAR apparently hadn't decided to let down its color barrier, Scott found a way to slip around it.

Nevertheless, France deserves credit for his handling of the situation during the second period of Scott's career, his years in NASCAR's minor leagues. France shook Scott's hand when they first met in 1954, welcomed him to NASCAR, and told him he'd be treated like any other driver. He did so in a decade when segregation still flourished. Some sports had admitted black athletes, but in others, exclusionary policies would persist for years. For example, Charlie Sifford, the Wendell Scott of golf, wasn't allowed on the PGA Tour until 1961. Black figure-skating pioneers Atoy Wilson and Richard Ewell III were blocked from Olympic eligibility until 1965.

During the rest of the 1950s, Scott raced at numerous local NASCAR tracks without having to worry about being turned away. During his first appearance at Bowman Gray Stadium, the track announcer introduced him cordially to the crowd and praised his driving. When a vengeful competitor rammed Scott's car after a race at Lynchburg, where Scott was popular with fans, France warned drivers that such conduct would result in suspensions.

To be sure, it quickly became evident that Scott's participation in NASCAR's minor leagues didn't threaten to harm France's business interests or to draw NASCAR into racial controversy. Scott competed mostly in Virginia and North Carolina during the 1950s. He'd already won acceptance and fans at many tracks before he got his NASCAR license. He rarely raced in the Deep South. His example brought no other black drivers into the sport. And France welcomed Scott to NASCAR only in a private conversation, not in any public statements supporting integration as a matter of principle. Still, France could have resisted Scott's involvement in many ways during those years, and clearly he decided not to. France's acceptance of Scott at this regional level of the sport paved the way for Scott to become NASCAR's first black state-level champion in 1959.

When Scott moved up to NASCAR's national-level circuit in 1961, however, France faced a new set of moral and financial choices. By the early 1960s, both the nation's political climate and France's business ambitions were changing dramatically. Civil rights conflicts had polarized the country, and rioting in some cities further inflamed racial antagonisms. NASCAR racing was flourishing, and France had already envisioned his sport's growth into the modern superspeedway era. He had opened his Daytona facility and was cultivating the political support he would need for his second superspeedway project, which would become the Talladega venture. Soon France would launch his long friendship and political collaboration with the era's most prominent segregationist politician, George Wallace.

On the Grand National circuit, where competitive results required big-money sponsorship and where Scott faced intense racial hostility at some southern tracks, his chances for success came to depend on France's willingness to exert influence on his behalf. Repeatedly, the record suggests, France decided not to do that. Darlington Raceway's refusal to allow Scott to compete became a litmus test for France's promise that NASCAR would treat Scott fairly.

If Scott had ever had any chance for a factory-team ride, his exclusion from Darlington put those prospects on hold. No auto manufacturer would consider a driver who couldn't race at one of NASCAR's top tracks and whose presence on the team would embroil the company in racial controversy. Clearly, France was unwilling to confront the speedway's racist president, Bob Colvin, and to disturb Darlington's Confederacy-boosting, proud-to-be-a-redneck atmosphere, which helped draw huge crowds to the South Carolina track. Season after season went by with no sign of support for Scott by France.

Scott recalled that when he finally approached France about Curtis Turner's suggestion that he sue Colvin for harming his livelihood, France begged him not to do it, describing Colvin as his "old friend" and talking about Darlington's importance to NASCAR. It was the passage of the Civil Rights Act — not any action by NASCAR — that eventually allowed Scott to race at Darlington.

Besides NASCAR's complicity in Darlington's discrimination, Scott repeatedly faced other forms of unfair treatment during his Grand National years. The pattern suggests strongly that France consciously reneged on his promise to Scott, sometimes through direct choices but more often by simply standing back and allowing the racism of the era to take its predictable course. During Scott's first Grand National season, he scored more points than any other rookie, but France picked another driver as Rookie of the Year. Competitors who sought to wreck Scott presented France with another choice. Although France had once warned minor-league drivers against deliberately wrecking Scott, he was silent after Scott reached NASCAR's national circuit, and the popular, Pontiac-sponsored driver Jack Smith became the aggressor.

Scott repeatedly experienced more problems at Grand National events run by NASCAR's top level of officialdom than he'd encountered while breaking the color barrier at dozens of local speedways a decade earlier. NASCAR's shabby treatment of his Jacksonville victory isn't an isolated example. France had promised him that he'd be treated like any other driver, but that promise wasn't kept. Besides Scott's years of troubles at Darlington, he was also excluded at various times from Grand Nationals at Charlotte, Daytona, Riverside, and Martinsville. Fellow racers verify Scott's accounts of repeated harassment by NASCAR officials over issues ranging from paint blemishes on his race car to his sons wearing beards. The underlying message was clear: Scott couldn't count on any real support from NASCAR's front office. Given the racial climate in the 1960s, Scott needed France's active help to have a fair chance at success. He didn't get it, and that served to keep him a marginal competitor and to shield NASCAR from the backlash that a front-running black driver could have provoked.

As Scott's popularity grew and he repeatedly scored top-ten finishes in mediocre cars, France easily could have arranged a few competitive rides for him, some insiders said. France had done that on occasion for others

— making possible, for example, a Talladega win for driver Bill Ward, whose support among fans was minuscule compared with Scott's. France's influence, his persuasive skills, and a few phone calls could have let fans find out if Scott really had the talent to challenge NASCAR's stars.

Some knowledgeable observers, however, felt that putting Scott in a position to win would have been an unwise business decision for NASCAR. "I have a feeling that the audience would not have accepted it," said William Neely, who headed public relations for Goodyear's NASCAR program in the 1960s. "The Richard Petty fans, the David Pearson fans, the Freddy Lorenzen fans — if there was a black driver beating their guy, I just don't think it would have set too well, I'm sorry to say."

Driver Frank Warren was among those who felt that Scott suited NASCAR's purposes only as long as he remained uncompetitive. "They tolerated him. In some areas, it might be good publicity to have a black man racing. At the same time, they knew he didn't have real good stuff [to drive]." NASCAR officials' view of Scott's role, Warren said, "was like a lot of those guys when it came to women: barefoot and pregnant. And I guess they figured if they just kept him down enough, and let him play, he'd never be a factor." NASCAR valued Scott, Warren said, only as one more driver to fill out the field — "just another number."

It's important to record Scott's own comments about France. In their personal contacts, Scott said, France dealt with him in a friendly, respectful way. Scott expressed positive feelings toward France. "Bill France Sr. and I, we had a real good relationship," he said. If Scott were alive to read this book, it's likely that he'd disagree with some of its criticism of France. "I had a lot of bad incidents in NASCAR," Scott said, "but I don't fault Bill France for it."

Why wouldn't Scott hold NASCAR's chief executive responsible for the way NASCAR treated him? His personal history suggests one possible answer. For Scott, a major priority since boyhood had been to avoid a life spent under the control of a boss. As a proud individual, Scott may well have found it hard to accept how closely the path of his career wound up coinciding with the business interests of the boss of NASCAR. To look at his racing accomplishments from that perspective would point toward a conclusion he would have found repugnant — that he had wound up doing exactly what he'd wanted to avoid: working for The Man.

Motorsports author Ken Vose, who spent time with Scott on the circuit and co-wrote a movie loosely based on his career, *Greased Lightning*, summed up Scott's dilemma this way: "I think he never got any backing for the obvious reason — it was a southern sport, and he was black. While it was good for business to have him there, because it kept black people coming to the races, it wasn't good business to have him win. Business is business. If he started winning on any regular basis, I think it would have cost them money. And I think everybody knew that, including Wendell."

NASCAR, however, maintains that it always treated Scott fairly and without regard to his race. "Bill France Sr. worked very hard to have Wendell treated just like every other driver . . . ," said Jim Hunter, NASCAR's vice president for corporate communications. "He always said if a man or woman, regardless of color, presents a car that meets the rules requirements of NASCAR, that person should be afforded the opportunity to participate . . . To my knowledge, NASCAR never held any discussions regarding the pros and cons of a black driver winning a race." Asked about specific incidents when Scott was banned from tracks or had other problems with NASCAR officials, Hunter said the organization has no record of such incidents.

Bill France Jr., who died in 2007, insisted in an interview before his death that NASCAR has nothing to apologize for concerning Scott. "From NASCAR's standpoint, we were always supportive of Wendell . . . I would assume in those days, if a guy was white, he'd have had a better shot at getting some funding from somewhere. I wouldn't dispute that. But from the sport's standpoint of a competitor coming in through the gate with his car, I can categorically say he was treated like everybody else."

Speaking heatedly, France said he was "disappointed in Wendell" and questioned his credibility for voicing some public criticisms during his retirement years, after making no such statements during his racing career. "What happens to him after he got hurt in Talladega and he quit driving, and the civil rights movement really began moving, and it was kind of the thing to do, and other people got ahold of you, and then all of a sudden the only reason he didn't go anywhere is because he was black, and that's simply not true."

During the first half of the 1960s, when Scott was banned from Darlington, Bill France Jr. worked under his father as a senior member of NASCAR management and played an executive role in running such events as Darlington's Southern 500. He said he knew nothing, however, about Scott ever being banned at Darlington. "I cannot recall any time anybody tried to keep Wendell from racing." He maintained that no NASCAR official ever treated Scott unfairly. "I feel that he was always treated fairly by NASCAR. That's a flat statement."

## 35

### "I couldn't drive like he drove."

Wendell Scott Jr. had been going to speedways with his father since he was a boy, and they'd talked many times about how he, too, would become a driver someday. But at the age of twenty-six, he still had only negligible racing experience when the Talladega wreck abruptly thrust him into his new role of driving the family race car. By his own account, he brought little more than a young man's daring to this assignment of driving against seasoned professionals. He'd never run even a partial season of local competition. In hindsight, he said, "I wasn't ready."

He was not a complete neophyte. He'd driven the Ford in one race, before his father's Talladega injuries. They were at Columbia, South Carolina's half-mile speedway for a minor-league Grand National East event on April 20, 1973, he recalled, when his father surprised him. Wendell Sr. had qualified the car, and they were hurrying to prepare it for the race. "He suddenly asked me if I thought his racing uniform would fit me.

"I said, 'I don't know, Dad — this is a hell of a time to talk about that.'

"He said, 'Get in the truck and try it on.'

At that point, he realized his father was telling him to drive in the race.

"He said, 'Go on out there, boy. You gotta start sometime.'"

Exactly where Wendell Scott Jr. placed in the lower ranks of the finishing order has been lost to history, but he did manage to bring the car back undamaged.

Now, with Wendell Sr. lying in a Danville hospital bed, there was no chance for any father–son driving instruction before Wendell Jr. began racing on his own. At one point, he said, he asked about adding two letters to the driver's name on the car, making it "Wendell Scott Jr." His father, he said, told him no — emphatically.

Wendell Sr. had entered him in Grand National East events at two half-mile dirt tracks in Pennsylvania, Selinsgrove and New Oxford. Wendell Jr.

traveled with one volunteer crewman, a family friend who knew little about working on cars. At Selinsgrove on May 30, he struggled to drive even adequately. The night before the June 2 race at New Oxford, Tiny Lund walked up to Wendell Jr.'s table at a restaurant. Lund had won at Selinsgrove and would finish this season as the Grand National East champion for 1973.

"Tiny said, 'Wendell, what are you doing early in the morning?'

"I said, 'Sleeping.'

"He said, 'No, you're gonna have your ass out at that racetrack.'"

His driving at Selinsgrove, Lund told him, had looked like a monkey attempting intimate relations with a football. At the track the next day, Lund put Wendell Jr. beside him in the race car. They ran many laps as the always ebullient Lund held forth on the techniques of power-sliding.

"He said, 'First of all, stop trying to protect the car. Your daddy sent you up here to race. Don't worry about tearing this car up. The most you're going to tear her up, on these short tracks, is just some sheet metal.'"

Lund told him he had to do exactly what his instincts told him was wrong. "He showed me how I was binding the car up in the corners." His mistake, Lund explained, was backing off and turning the steering wheel left to enter a turn. Instead, he had to mash the gas pedal to the floor, throw the car into a slide, and manage the slide by steering to the right.

"That was the hardest thing, just seemed ridiculous at first. But he would do it like that, and the car would do just the right thing. He worked with me for four or five hours that day. I was real grateful to him."

Using what he'd learned, Wendell Jr. drove considerably faster in that night's race. "Somebody in Bobby Fleming's pit signaled that I was running ninth. I'm thrilled to death. Then my oil pressure started dropping, and I said, 'Oh my God.'"

He pulled into the pits. His crewman was nowhere to be seen. He unbuckled, got out, raised the hood. Oil had spewed all over from a pinhole leak in an oil line. He ran to the truck, found some oil. He overfilled the engine, hoping to compensate for the leak, and finished the race, now well out of the top ten.

Lund praised his driving, and *Stock Car Racing* magazine gave his performance a positive mention, calling him "quite impressive for a rookie, despite suffering from his father's age-old problems of trying to finance a race car on a limited budget."

The next weekend, however, he would run a speedway completely different from those Pennsylvania short tracks — and far more daunting. Wendell Sr. had entered him in a 300-mile race on the paved 1-mile oval at Rockingham, North Carolina, where competitive cars turned lap speeds well over 130 miles an hour, more than twice as fast as Selinsgrove. Lund's dirt-driving lessons wouldn't help him at Rockingham.

Wendell Jr. worried, too, that the brief drop-off in oil pressure had scorched the engine bearings. "I knew there was no way I was going to finish no superspeedway race with that engine. There was no spare engine. I knew how to build engines, but I hadn't built no racing engines, so I had to go with what I had." His crew for the race comprised his brother and a couple of neighborhood kids.

He got no practice time because of rainstorms. "That was my first superspeedway, and the first lap I took was the caution-flag lap before they started the race. Daddy was home in the hospital, and I got the family's only bread and butter in my hands, and I ain't never been out there before. Whew! That was a mental whupping I took that day."

The forty-car field combined some Winston Cup competitors with lesser-known drivers from ARCA, the minor-league circuit sanctioning the race. Quickly Wendell Jr. discovered that turn one would throw his car up close to the wall, much like what he'd seen at Darlington's turn four. "Man, that was an awesome feeling." As his driving settled into a rhythm, "I learned there were some guys I could outrun, and that was thrilling."

But the Ford still had the same balky handling that had so frustrated his father. Early in the race he felt his fingers going numb from his constant tussle with the steering wheel. "That car — after ten or fifteen laps, I started wishing for a better car. I knew Daddy's feelings, because I had driven that car as fast as it would go, and I was wanting something else." NASCAR driver Charlie Glotzbach, on his way to winning, began lapping Wendell Jr. and other slower cars in his dominant Monte Carlo. "When he'd come by me, it'd shake my whole car, he was running so fast."

As Wendell Jr. had feared, the Ford's engine blew, throwing a connecting rod through the oil pan. He was one of the first drivers out of the race. The wish for a better car, he understood, was unrealistic — there was no money. He'd been sent out to race, after all, because of the family's debt for the wrecked Mercury.

Except for a few exhilarating moments, the prospects for a racing career looked discouraging. He revealed his mixed feelings that summer to journalist Bob Myers: "I'd dearly love to be a race driver. I've learned a lot following daddy around for many years. But I don't want to suffer as he has. I'm smart enough to know I'd be a fool to try under similar circumstances."

Later in the season, when his father had recovered enough from his injuries to do some driving, they went together to a few Grand National East events. They shared the driving, with Wendell Sr. qualifying and starting the race and Wendell Jr. taking over as relief driver. Wendell Jr. wound up twenty-fourth in season points, two spots ahead of his father. Neither had any finishes in the top ten. The season's final race at North Carolina's Hickory Speedway on November 11 seemed like a preview of what Wendell Jr. could expect if he continued racing. As the last driver whose car was still running at the finish, he placed thirteenth — sixteen laps behind the twelfth-place car and thirty-five laps behind the winner, Tiny Lund.

When people asked about his plans, Wendell Scott Jr. maintained that he'd be racing in 1974. His goal, he said, was to win the Winston Cup Rookie of the Year award to honor his father, who had deserved to win it back in 1961. Privately, though, he was full of doubts. At a couple of the faster tracks, he'd experienced moments of fear in situations he didn't believe would have scared his father. As he sped toward the turns, he knew he was slowing down sooner than his father would have. "When I got the opportunity to drive those tracks and you want to let up at the flagman's stand, that's when my respect really grew. I said, 'I ain't staying on this [gas pedal].'"

Looking back on his season, he felt that "I had enough talent, for the speed the car would go, to finish close to where Daddy would have finished, except I didn't have the talent Daddy did . . . I can drive, you know, probably better than the average citizen, but I couldn't drive like he drove."

Since childhood he'd measured himself against his father, and now, as he saw it, he'd fallen short. By November 1973, according to one of the many court documents that tracked his crimes over the next two years, he had "started back seriously on drugs."

They sat in the food store's parking lot with a sawed-off shotgun, four young men in a red Volkswagen, their troubled lives about to become more troubled. In the darkness of a winter night, they debated their plan to rob the Hop-In Market in Martinsville, Virginia, trying to get up their nerve.

The stickup would be easy, one of them said. At first Wendell Scott Jr. told his companions he didn't like the idea. "This ain't gonna be hard," another insisted, according to a document from the criminal proceedings that would prove him wrong.

Wendell Jr., unemployed, had gone back to using heroin regularly only a few months earlier, but already the cost was approaching sixty dollars a day. His daily hunt for money and drugs dominated his existence.

Eventually, at 8:30 PM on January 17, 1974, he took the shotgun and walked into the market. He told the woman at the cash register to hand over the money. He got about a hundred dollars. They split it four ways and sold the shotgun for thirty dollars and some cocaine.

Apparently, local detectives had an informant. A week later Wendell Jr. was in jail, charged with armed robbery. His arrest made page one of the *Martinsville Bulletin*, which noted that he was the son of the former NASCAR driver. He admitted that he'd robbed the market. He identified his companions. "Scott stated that he was sick doing drugs, that he tried to get someone to take him to the drug [treatment] center" before the stickup, a sheriff's report said. His parents put up their home as security for ten-thousand-dollar bail. After police arrested his accomplices, one of them began informing on Wendell Jr., alleging that he'd taken part in some burglaries in Danville. Within a month, he faced new felony charges for two break-ins.

He was living with friends and in rented rooms and motels — trying in particular, he said, to avoid his father. "I didn't want to be around him when

I was using." Wendell Sr. tried to intervene. "Every morning he got up, the first thing Daddy would do was find out where I was. He would do detective work. He followed me everywhere. The man was scared to death." The former moonshine runner, however, knew little about the world of drugs. At one point he got into his son's living quarters, found what he believed to be a stash of dope, and took it home to show Mary. The substance turned out to be incense.

The Danville police began looking for Wendell Jr. as a suspect in another burglary. He avoided arrest by entering inpatient drug treatment at Richmond's veterans' hospital. "He stated that he had been strung out on drugs off and on since 1971 . . . ," a report said. "He indicated he wants to get off drugs but seems to keep falling back into his drug habit."

By this time, he understood that just enduring another cold-turkey withdrawal wasn't enough. The hospital put him into a therapeutic community, a program in which addicts are immersed for a year or more in a highly disciplined, confrontational, hierarchal environment that seeks to compel positive changes in their thinking, feelings, and behavior. This approach has produced many success stories, but some addiction professionals criticize it as excessively rigid and punitive.

For several weeks, he "made much progress in therapy," a hospital official wrote. He earned a leadership position and weekend passes. Nevertheless, Wendell Jr. said, ultimately he wasn't able to accept the system of humiliating punishments for rules infractions or expressing unacceptable attitudes.

"This [program] entailed, 'Okay, you want to be in this drug program, you want to help yourself — first thing we do is cut off all your hair. Then we send you in that little room where we got a female counselor to trim the hair on your balls. We cut your eyebrows off, and we put you in a diaper. The first time you show rebellion, you have to wear boxing gloves for a month. Then you had to stand in a corner for a month the next time you show rebellion.'" He went through those punishments, he said, but found he still had the desire to get high.

His troubles escalated drastically in September 1974. He was convicted of a Danville burglary and arrested for grand larceny in another. Again his parents put up their home as bail collateral. At the hospital, a urine test revealed he'd recently used heroin. He "left the program because he was afraid of the punishment that may be imposed on him by the therapeutic community," a court document said, and entered a different drug-treatment program in Richmond.

At his burglary sentencing, he avoided prison, at least temporarily, after his probation officer and a hospital official emphasized in reports to the judge that he'd tried hard to overcome addiction. The hospital official said his "condition at the time of his offenses could be termed as an illness." The probation officer noted Wendell Jr.'s army service and teaching work. "The subject has potential for doing all right if he can control his drug habit," he wrote. He reported that the family "wants to help him in any way they can." Wendell Sr., like Mary, was "quite disturbed over his son's drug problem and is extremely concerned over seeing that he gets the best help available for his drug addiction."

Judge Stuart Craig put Wendell Jr. on probation, leaving open the possibility of prison time if he used drugs or failed to complete the new treatment program. Two months later a jury convicted him of petty larceny in another pending burglary case, and again Craig gave him a break: probation with the same conditions. Despite these second chances, he found his his way back to heroin, crime, and the street life. Already he'd broken into a house near Petersburg, pawned some of the loot, and forged some of the homeowner's checks. Desperate for drugs, he endorsed them with his own signature and driver's license number.

He slept on park benches and in the backseats of cars in auto junkyards. In supermarkets he'd open up some baloney, bread, and mayonnaise and stand in the aisle eating his free sandwich. He avoided his family and almost everyone from his years of involvement in racing. On one bad night, however, he sought out racer Tom Pistone — who, he said, may have saved his life.

"When I was strung out on dope, I was staying in Charlotte one night, and I was feeling suicidal. I couldn't think of nobody to talk to, and I went out to his shop, and we talked and talked, and he didn't condemn me." Pistone told him about someone who had committed suicide while using drugs. He talked about the pain that loved ones had suffered. "He's somebody you can talk to when you want someone to tell you the truth. I will never forget that night. Tom cried, and he gave me $150, every dime he had in his pocket. He said, 'You need to eat.'"

Nevertheless, Wendell Jr.'s life continued to plummet. On January 10, 1975, he was arrested on new burglary charges, this time while driving to a Richmond hospital to seek help again for his drug addiction. By now, the legal system was becoming skeptical of pleas for another chance and more attempts at drug rehabilitation. The probation officer who had written hopefully of his prospects five months earlier gave Judge Craig a far more pessimistic report in February. Wendell Jr. had now dropped out of two drug programs, he wrote, and apparently remained an active burglar. The charges against him now included grand larceny, forgery, four home burglaries, and the Martinsville armed robbery.

The Martinsville judge revoked his bond, putting him back in jail, and over the next several months he pled guilty or was convicted in all the pending cases. The sentences that resulted made it clear he would spend a long time in prison, longer than some criminals who did violent harm to their victims. He got four years for the burglary near Petersburg. The hundred-dollar stickup in Martinsville brought a five-year sentence. The Danville judge who earlier had granted him probation in two burglary cases, conditional on drug rehabilitation and good behavior, revoked the probation and gave him twelve years for receiving stolen property, worth about seven hundred dollars. So far he was facing twenty-one years from three cases.

The most devastating sentence, however, came for a burglary he still maintains that he didn't commit. This was the case that had led to his arrest as he drove to the Richmond hospital. He was charged with breaking into a house the previous day about twenty minutes west of Danville, on an afternoon when nobody was home, and taking items worth about thirteen hundred dollars. A relative of the homeowners, who lived nearby, said she'd seen Wendell Jr. leave the house with the loot. Another relative said she'd seen him in the neighborhood a few minutes earlier.

Wendell Jr. insisted that he'd been in Danville at the time, with his car broken down. His father and other family members believed that, in this case, he was telling the truth. His first trial ended with a hung jury. At the second trial on November 3, 1975, the prosecution again presented the two women who said they'd seen him. A deputy sheriff testified that tire tracks at the scene matched the tires on his car.

Wendell Scott Jr.'s court-appointed lawyer presented three alibi witnesses who said he'd been in Danville on the afternoon of the burglary. His half brother, Michael, testified that they'd been dealing with his car problems. A cabdriver said he'd driven Wendell Jr. to meet Michael. An acquaintance testified that Wendell Jr. spent the rest of the afternoon watching TV at her house. Wendell Scott Sr. testified that his son's car did have a bad ignition problem. But the defense case left some loose ends and contradictions, and the defense lawyer's decision to let Wendell Scott Jr. testify allowed the prosecution to inform the jury that he was a convicted felon and heroin addict.

The jurors found him guilty of burglary and grand larceny. He was sentenced to twenty years on each count, and the judge ordered that he would serve the sentences consecutively. He asked if Wendell Jr. wanted to say anything. He didn't.

The deputies escorted him out of the courthouse, where a statue honors Confederate soldiers "who died for truth and right," and took him back to jail to await his transfer to the state prison system. He would wonder, of course, whether any white defendant would have gotten forty years for a burglary.

As a boy, Wendell Jr. had imagined a future in which he'd be a racing driver and make his father proud. Now, at twenty-nine, he had lost that dream, along with his freedom and self-respect, and he was facing sixty-one years in prison.

# 36

## "I saw a different Wendell."

During his late fifties and into his sixties, Scott continued working long days, many of them following the same pattern. He woke up with Mary in the small house where they'd lived for many years at 243 Keens Mill Road. He got dressed in worn coveralls. Mary, who worked in a nursing home, served breakfast at the kitchen table; their house had no dining room. She washed the dishes in the sink with its patina of rust; they had no dishwasher. Then, still limping a bit from Talladega injuries, he'd climb into his aging pickup and drive down the street to 120 Keens Mill Road.

This was where he'd built his racing garage and the family's other modest house years ago, when he'd needed extra space for his mother and all the children. Now the garage served as the shop where Scott repaired customers' autos. Outside in the weeds sat old, rusting race cars and faded trucks, worn out from hauls to speedways all over the country. The weather-beaten garage had no sign. Scott's business had no name, no phone. Neither was needed. People in Danville knew he could fix anything on a car, and they knew where to find him.

Some days he'd travel to the prison to visit his son. Some days he'd meet with lawyers working on appeals, or with friends writing letters to state officials and to others with influence, asking for some relief of Wendell Jr.'s lengthy sentences. Mostly, he worked at the shop, often putting in twelve hours or more. Relaxation had never figured much in his life, and he still owed more than eleven thousand dollars on the mangled Mercury.

No stranger who met this graying, unpretentious mechanic in his scruffy workplace would have picked him as somebody who had inspired a Hollywood movie. But in 1976, at several speedways and other sites in Georgia, the filming began for *Greased Lightning*, a comic melodrama based loosely on Scott's life — quite loosely. The film offered a sympathetic but carefully shallow portrayal of what he'd faced as southern stock car racing's first black driver.

The movie's upbeat story line went like this: At first, a few rednecks harassed him with some fender-banging, hostile remarks and threatening glares. A couple of times, early on, officials also gave him a hard time. However, none of these problems persisted for very long. The Scott character persevered and was rewarded by winning the Grand National championship. "This film is based on the true life story of Wendell Scott," viewers were assured in the credits.

Released by Warner Bros., produced by Third World Cinema, *Greased Lightning* starred Richard Pryor, with Pam Grier as Mary Scott. Beau Bridges, Cleavon Little, Vincent Gardenia, and Richie Havens also played major roles. Scott served as the movie's "technical adviser," but he said he had little influence over its accuracy. "They didn't really ask my advice. If I saw 'em getting too far off, I would tell them about it. Some things they'd change, some they wouldn't. They would tell me, 'This is the way we want it.' They had to please the public." The movie, which opened in July 1977, fudged or ignored some of Scott's most basic problems. The script didn't address the auto companies' failure to give him a chance for a competitive ride. There was nothing about NASCAR's failure to give him the equal treatment its founder had promised. In fact, NASCAR wasn't mentioned in the movie. There was no Bill France character, no Lee Iacocca character. Darlington's logo appeared momentarily, just to show Scott competing there. To the millions of viewers who knew little or nothing about Scott's career, the story told in *Greased Lightning* suggested that he'd faced more resistance to his racing ambitions from his wife than from any establishment figures in his sport.

The movie ends with the Scott character capturing the championship — which the movie presented as determined by a single race, not by the season's points — under the most improbable circumstances. He wins the race in a backyard-built car with a loose, wobbling wheel. In the final freeze-frame he beams at the camera, a checkered flag waving, all his efforts rewarded, his big dream come true.

One of the screenplay's co-authors, Ken Vose, acknowledged wryly that a happy ending had been mandatory. "Obviously, in the movie, Scott was going to have to win," Vose said. "That was going to be the ending, or there was going to be no movie." The *Washington Post*'s review noted the contrived superficiality: "The film seems to grow out of a conception so carefully lightweight and inoffensive that it borders on the ephemeral."

In any case, historical authenticity wasn't Scott's biggest priority, as he would candidly explain. "I want to get rich from this movie," he told a reporter. "I hope this is all nice for my bank account. I'm more interested in that than anything else."

The project had started in 1971 when Vose approached Scott on a racing weekend at Texas World Speedway. Scott signed a contract providing for an upfront payment, which he remembered as twenty-five thousand dollars, plus a percentage of the profits. Later, Scott went to Washington for a meeting with "some high official" of the project, Wendell Scott Jr. recalled, and returned confident that he'd assured his family's financial security.

"Daddy was under the impression that he had a $350,000 handshake from this guy," Wendell Jr. said. "When Daddy came back home, he was satisfied. He's saying, 'That's over a quarter million dollars.' It sounded like the man had quoted that sum to him.

"I said, 'Daddy, where is it in writing?'

"He said, 'Well, everything doesn't have to be in writing.'"

Scott helped the filmmakers with some of the racing scenes as they shot the movie in Georgia. He worked with Neil Castles, whom the producers had hired as a stunt driver and "designer of race sequences." Castles, Scott said, "would ask me how I wanted to do some of the scenes. I don't think he ever liked me, so I told him to do it the way he did me in real life."

Scott enjoyed some months of celebrity during the summer of 1977. He socialized with famous people and wore a tuxedo to glitzy banquets. A few weeks before *Greased Lightning*'s release, the Black Athletes Hall of Fame inducted him at the New York Hilton. Bill Cosby hosted the evening for Scott and the other new members: Wilt Chamberlain, O.J. Simpson, Dick "Night Train" Lane, Larry Doby, Ed Temple, Ike Williams, and Nell Jackson. On the movie's opening day, Danville's mayor proclaimed a Wendell Scott Day and gave him a key to the city. Journalists wrote profiles. Strangers would show up at his house clutching autograph books.

Soon, though, life returned to its old rhythm of long days at the garage and the struggle to meet his bills. In late September, *Variety* still listed *Greased Lightning*'s gross receipts among the top fifty for current movies, but the Scotts heard nothing about any money from the profits. The movie experience had been exciting, Mary Scott said, "but it hasn't taken us out of debt." Scott sought advice from Paul Jones, manager of Danville's Riverside Theater, where *Greased Lightning* had run. Jones explained some common knowledge about the movie industry: that under the studios' accounting methods, even highly popular movies often don't show a profit on paper. As the *New York Times* once put it, Hollywood "creates its own version of reality in its financial accounting just as on the big screen," using inflated cost figures and large payments by studios to their own subsidiaries to wipe out any "profits" that otherwise would have to be shared with outsiders. Jones recalled their conversation: "I said, 'What kind of deal did you make?'

"He said, 'I signed a contract for that down payment and a percentage of the profits.'

"I said, 'Wendell, that's where you made your mistake. It should have been a percentage of the gross, not the profits.'

"He asked me, 'What can I do?'

"I said, 'The only thing I can tell you is get the best lawyer you can find. But I'm afraid you're trying to lock the door after the horse has been stolen.'

"He said it looked that way to him, too."

Three years later, still seven thousand dollars in debt for the Mercury, Scott told a racing newspaper, *Southern MotorSports Journal*, that he'd given up hoping for any share in the profits. "I thought it was going to be the turning point of my life. I was supposed to get some royalties but Warner Bros. tells me the movie is still $4.6 million in the red. I just don't believe it." A man who'd grown up in Danville came back on a vacation from California and brought his little boy to Scott's house. "My wife was showing the boy my trophies," Scott said, "and he looked up and said to his daddy, 'I thought he would be living in a mansion.'"

The movie experience, Scott told his friend Leonard Miller, felt like part of a pattern. "Wendell said, 'Leonard, don't you ever go through this type of thing that I'm going through. No matter what, the white community takes advantage of me. I'm not highly educated, I don't have money to get a lawyer, I don't have anyone to help me, and I'm of the old school — I trust people on their word.' He was really hurt." Scott finished paying off his debt for the Mercury in April 1983, a decade after he had bought the car that was supposed to prove he could run with NASCAR's best. The car, which still sat rusting in his backyard, had wound up costing him nearly $2,750 for each of the eight laps he'd raced it at Talladega.

During his post-NASCAR years, Scott became active with his church, the North New Hope Baptist Church, something he hadn't had the time or interest to do while he was racing. In his dark blue pin-striped suit, he would listen intently to Pastor Willard D. Smith during services that typically lasted more than two hours. Scott had hoped, he said, to use some money from movie profits to help pay off the church's mortgage. "I'm trying to be a good Christian," he said. "I haven't always been one."

Scott's admiration for the pastor grew over the years. "He really teaches." He appreciated that Smith thought out and composed his sermons before the services, rather than "whooping and hollering" in an improvisational style. Scott's involvement with the church, family members said, gave him a new calmness. He finally understood, he would say, why his wife had been such a devout churchgoer. He seemed, according to Sybil Scott, "so much more at peace."

Morris Stephenson, Scott's journalist friend, had gotten involved in publicizing races at Virginia's Franklin County Speedway. He arranged in June 1984 for Scott to race a late-model car there as a promotional gimmick. Stephenson hadn't seen Scott in some years. "I could tell he was a changed person from the man I used to know," Stephenson said.

He remembered Scott's total, near-obsessive absorption with racing. "It was from week to week, and he was dealing with all these problems every week, lack of money being the main one, and how to get what he needed to race the next week, calling everybody trying to get parts — 'You got a spare one of these, an old one of those?'"

Now Stephenson could see that his friend had come to terms with being a retired racer, though Scott would never say so. "I saw that he realized he was through racing." Scott considered the Franklin County event just an enjoyable diversion, Stephenson said. "I saw a different Wendell. The desire and the drive, the way that racing was pushing and pushing at him, like that was all there was — he wasn't centered on that anymore. He talked about family. He talked about Frankie. He talked about the girls. He talked about Wendell Jr. — he'd never given up on him. It gave us a chance to catch up on what had been happening in each other's lives. His life was focused in a different direction."

There were still occasional moments in the spotlight. Admirers and family arranged a large tribute dinner for Scott in Atlanta in August 1986 in honor of his sixty-fifth birthday. Georgia state senator Julian Bond, the civil rights activist who would later become national chairman of the NAACP, gave the eloquent keynote address. "In a field where few black people have competed," Bond told the crowd, Scott "achieved and excelled. In a field where few men or women had a real chance of success, he fought and struggled and struggled again and struggled again and succeeded.

"How different things might have been if there had not been a Wendell Scott. How different things might have been if there had not been a Rosa Parks. How different things might have been if there had not been a Martin Luther King. For each of these people, each in their own way, has made an indelible contribution to the ongoing struggle for human improvement and human decency, a struggle that will be recorded in history for years and years to come."

Most of Scott's days in his later years, however, came and went as those of a small-town mechanic, far removed from any talk about history. On a typical day, the only social issue that came up in his life was the city's effort to make him get rid of the old cars and trucks on his property. When business got slow at the shop, he'd make a few dollars scavenging radiators and batteries from those vehicles to sell to the junkyard. At stores, he'd ask the clerk if senior citizens got a discount. Every evening he bought a state lottery ticket. Often he played 243, his house number.

One chilly afternoon in 1989, the sixty-eight-year-old Scott labored over a customer's ragged Mustang II in the oil-soaked gravel driveway outside his garage. The distributor shaft had frozen. He wasn't sure whether the car's owner, a young woman with no front teeth, had any money to pay him. Nearby, his wrecked Talladega Mercury was mostly covered by vines and bushes. A sharp wind blew dust around the yard.

Scott had been limping more than usual recently. "My bones been hurting me today, right much," he said. One of his feet felt a little floppy. So far, the doctors didn't have an explanation. They didn't yet realize that a cancerous tumor had begun wrapping itself around his spinal cord.

A visiting reporter mentioned that day's biggest news development in auto racing: A black driver named Willy T. Ribbs, thirty-two years old, had just landed the multimillion-dollar sponsorship that would make it possible for him to become the first African American ever to qualify for the Indianapolis 500.

Scott's reply, as he hunched over the Mustang's engine in his greasy corduroy coat, could barely be heard. A tiny distributor part slipped past his cold fingers and fell into the dirt.

"I come along too soon," the most famous man in Danville muttered. "Too soon."

## 37

### "Hope for the best."

As Scott moved into his late sixties and his health declined, two men who admired him worked on a project they hoped would bring him a career-celebrating tribute. Although Scott knew them only slightly, Kim Haynes and Tom Cotter were well connected in NASCAR racing.

Haynes, owner of a North Carolina company that restores historic stock cars, and Cotter, then the public relations director for Charlotte Motor Speedway, were trying to get Scott inducted into one of stock car racing's more prestigious halls of fame. They lobbied influential racing people and collected petition signatures. They found a good deal of support for their position that Scott's record of numerous top-ten finishes, his victory at Jacksonville, and his overall contribution to the sport made him a worthy candidate even though he hadn't won multiple races or a championship at the Grand National level. "Given the fact that this record was accomplished without factory backing, we feel this honor is overdue," declared the petition calling for Scott's induction into the National Motorsports Press Association Hall of Fame, which is based at Darlington Raceway.

Cotter, an amateur racing driver who later founded a major sports-marketing firm, would argue passionately that Scott's unique situation in NASCAR supported a new way of looking at hall-of-fame eligibility. "This guy was asked to run a marathon, but he had to carry an extra fifty pounds," he said. "Scott prepared his own cars, drove the truck, sometimes had to do his own pit stops — he had the weight of the world on his shoulders. He just overcame adversity by saying, 'Well, if that's the way it is, that's the way it is.' Still, he wound up doing darn well for the resources he had. That needed to be recognized. I don't think that hall of fame is just for champions, big names, big winners. A hall of fame has to honor effort as much as success." They didn't tell Scott about the petition.

Some prominent NASCAR figures agreed that Scott should be inducted. They included three drivers who already were members of the NMPA Hall of Fame: Tim Flock, Ned Jarrett, and Fred Lorenzen. Other well-known racing people who signed the petition were Skip Barber, Bill Elliot, Jeff Hammond, Dick Hutcherson, Alan Kulwicki, Ralph Moody, Bruton Smith, Darrell Waltrip, Humpy Wheeler, and Smokey Yunick. Prominent motorsports journalists who signed included Dick Berggren, Chris Economaki, Allan Girdler, Ken Squier, and Deb Williams.

Others, though, opposed the selection of Scott. Jack Smith, a hall-of-fame member, refused to sign the petition, according to Haynes: "He said you ought to have won at least four races to qualify." Some members of the press association, which selects the hall of fame's members, felt that only the sport's top achievers should be inducted and that to depart from that standard would devalue the honor.

Jarrett said he sat in on the NMPA committee meeting where the idea of inducting Scott was discussed. "In fact, I think I brought his name up as a possibility." Some committee members considered Scott's accomplishments insufficient. "That was part of the discussion when his name was brought up — that there were others with much better statistics . . . He didn't make the final ballot." As it turned out, this rejection would be the last official action toward Scott during his lifetime by any organization connected with the NASCAR establishment. The fact that the situation involved Darlington Raceway gave a whiff of déjà vu, of course, to the press association's unpublicized decision against admitting Scott. One result of that decision was that it averted the possibility of any public commentary about Darlington's discrimination against Scott, NASCAR's role in the issue, or why the press corps hadn't pursued the story.

Every Wednesday night, a group of recovering drug addicts in Danville met to work on keeping their lives sane and productive. The group was affiliated with an international drug-recovery organization that had adapted the twelve-step program of Alcoholics Anonymous. The members listened to speakers tell of struggles, setbacks, and victories. They discussed their own aggravations and achievements. They helped one another to follow the recommended steps toward abstinence and personal renewal. They talked about spirituality. They worked with newcomers and those who'd relapsed, regarding such service as crucial to keeping themselves drug-free.

On November 28, 1990, they celebrated their group's fifth anniversary. As the evening's main speaker, they chose the group's founder. A forty-four-year-old ex-convict, he looked buoyant as he stepped to the podium. Some of his family members sat in the folding chairs. They remembered how, years ago, his face often showed nothing but angry desperation.

He grinned. "My name's Wendell, and I'm an addict," Wendell Scott Jr. said, and he began talking about how he had wrecked his life and used this program to create a new one. He spoke of "the real miracle that I don't have to use today, that I have a choice."

Behind bars, he began to learn that helping others gave him some relief from the fear, rage, and boredom of prison life. For illiterate prisoners, he ghost-wrote letters to family and friends. He taught classes for inmates who had dropped out of school. He coached sports teams, organized birthday celebrations. He taught craft courses so that prisoners could create leatherwork and stained-glass gifts for their families on visiting day. "The respect Mr. Scott earned among his fellow inmates was obvious . . . ," Evalyn Chapman, a community activist and teacher, wrote to the parole board. "He served as a counselor and listener to literally hundreds of men who needed help with their problems."

He received prison awards for his service. He graduated cum laude from Virginia's community-college system, winning membership in a national honor society. His deputy warden described him as "a model prisoner." Year after year, though, he watched other inmates who had committed violent crimes go free on parole after only a few years. After nine years and many letters from supporters to state officials, he finally won release on parole in 1984.

Despite his positive accomplishments in prison, drugs still remained a temptation. The next year, while working as a janitor in Richmond, he went back to using heroin for about three months and was charged with forging checks and shoplifting. He remained free while the courts and parole officials considered his future, and during this period, he made what he described as a life-changing decision.

He got himself admitted for inpatient treatment at Richmond's veterans' hospital, the same facility where he'd dropped out of a drug program in 1974, finding it too punitive and humiliating. But this time, a different treatment philosophy at the hospital inspired the beginnings of a deep change in him. The hospital's program emphasized participation in a 12-step drug-recovery group. (The organization's name is not being used here because of its practice of anonymous membership.) He listened to counselors and fellow addicts discuss the steps that could bring about a daily reprieve from drug use. They included admitting the problem, seeking help, engaging in a thorough self-examination, disclosing one's flaws to another, making amends for harm done, helping other addicts.

Wendell Jr. felt the spark, he said, of "a spiritual awakening and a desire for a better way of life." The staff chose him to lead the program's twice-daily meetings of fifty patients. Discharged as "capable and responsible," he moved to Danville and founded the recovery organization's first group in his hometown. He sought out local addicts and spoke at recovery meetings in nearby communities. "Many people and powers told Mr. Scott a group could not be started for poor, needy addicts in Danville," a group member later wrote to parole officials. "Many turned their backs and closed their doors. But he would not give up. He kept asking, seeking, knocking . . . He found those who wanted and needed help but had nowhere to turn, those who could not afford weeks or months at expensive treatment centers."

Despite such appeals from supporters, however, Wendell Scott Jr. was locked up again in January 1986. The state revoked his parole, and his crimes during his relapse added six more years to his prison term. His father and others appealed to parole officials to give him another chance. "Subject's father was very supporting of his son and is quite concerned about his future," an official wrote. Those urging his release included an officer of the American Legion post where the Danville recovery group held its meetings. "Through Mr. Scott's efforts, the city of Danville has a place where people suffering from drug and substance abuse can come and seek help," he wrote. Nevertheless, Wendell Scott Jr. would serve almost three more years before he was granted parole again.

Looking for some way to support his son, Wendell Scott said he decided to make a commitment to do all he could to keep the drug-recovery group going. "We ran that meeting while he was doing his time. We never did miss a week, Sybil and I and another girl." They made sure the members had sandwiches, cake, and coffee.

When Wendell Scott Jr. was released and moved back to Danville, he opened a neighborhood grocery store. His father spoke of the pride he felt in his son's store, which evoked memories of his own mother supporting the family with a similar grocery. "He's got that place looking so good." He enjoyed bragging to visitors about his son's frequent invitations to speak at drug-recovery meetings around the state.

At the fifth-anniversary meeting of the group Wendell Scott Jr. had founded in Danville, he spoke of his sense of wonder at being part of "a worldwide fellowship of men and women who came to believe that a greater power than themselves can restore them to sanity." The meat truck had come to his store that day. The driver noticed a ring he was wearing with the emblem of his recovery group. "What's that ring mean?" the driver asked.

The question, Wendell Jr. said, prompted a surprising realization: He hadn't had even a passing thought about how to steal some meat from the truck or cheat the driver out of money. Today, he said, "being clean is giving me the opportunity to be able to say, 'Hey, mister, you dropped your wallet,' or 'Miss, you gave me too much money.'"

His father had hoped to hear him speak, but he'd been too ill to attend the meeting. From his bed the next day, unable to move, speaking with difficulty, Scott wanted to make sure a visitor knew of his pride in his son. He could get out only a few words: "He's been doin' good. Real good."

When this writer first came to Danville to begin work on a biography, Scott displayed his confidence in his son by asking him to work extensively on the project — to serve, in some significant ways, as his father's voice. He got this assignment partly because he had been so deeply immersed in his father's racing life, he said, and partly "to say some of the things he didn't want to say himself."

Wendell Jr. welcomed the warming of their relationship, but it didn't mean that each day brought a glow of serenity. Running his store had its satisfactions, but it was not a calling. He brooded about the time he had lost to drugs, and about never succeeding as a racing driver: "Every day of my life I'm thinking of what I didn't do." At his recovery meetings, people often talked about striving for progress, not perfection, and he tried, with mixed success, to keep that in mind.

Throughout 1990, his father's condition deteriorated. Doctors finally found the cancerous tumor wrapped around Scott's spine, and he underwent surgery. They told him he'd narrowly escaped permanent paralysis. The family waited for test results that would reveal whether the cancer had spread. "But I'm not worried," Scott said. "I got a lot of faith."

The tests showed he had advanced prostate cancer. The doctor told him, Scott said, that this operation "would take all my nature away from me. I told him it didn't matter. I just got to tough it out and hope for the best." In August he was back in intensive care with pneumonia, high blood pressure, and kidney problems.

Old racing friends like Bobby Fleming, Mike Sykes, and Jimmy Lewallen came to his bedside to wish him good-bye, without saying those words. Carl Simpson realized he'd left something unsaid during their long friendship. "You think a lot of a person," he said, "and you take it for granted that he knows." He went to see Scott in the intensive-care ward. Scott lay unconscious, but he woke up as Simpson sat beside him. "I said I had something to tell him — that I loved him, like a brother. And Mary said, 'Well, I believe you do.'"

On a sunny November morning with a flawless blue sky, the doctor came to Scott's hospital room with more bad news. His wife and his pastor sat with him. His face pained and puffy, Scott faded in and out of consciousness. The cancer had spread to his liver, the doctor said. Nothing could be done. Mary Scott told Pastor Smith they were happy that Scott had reconciled his relationship with God before he got sick. "Whatever happens, he is in Jesus again," she said.

Later, Scott sent word that he wanted the pastor to visit him again. "He couldn't talk — he just whispered," Pastor Smith said.

He leaned over to hear Scott's words, which Scott uttered with great difficulty. "He said, 'Reverend, I have something to say to you.'

"I said, 'Talk on, brother. I'm listening.'

"He told me, 'Reverend, I've got my life together.'"

After workdays at the store, Wendell Jr. often spent nights at the hospital, sitting with his father, trying to keep him comfortable while he drifted between lucidity and apparent unconsciousness. Occasionally his father would get bossy and demanding about some detail of his care. Usually Wendell Jr. found he could shrug off his annoyance.

Mostly, they just spent time together, two men with large disappointments about their lives who, each in his way, had found some comfort in spiritual pursuits. Many hours passed in silence, except for the muted sounds of a hospital after midnight.

As things turned out, they never had the climactic conversation that a scriptwriter would consider obligatory — the airing of grievances, the offering of apologies, the explicit exchange of forgiveness. Perhaps that was just as well. Each of them had made it clear that things had changed. Their pride was mutual now, their conflicts receding into the past.

During those hospital nights, Wendell Jr. began to suspect that his father might have more awareness than he could express. He felt that even when his father seemed completely comatose, he somehow understood when someone he loved was with him.

Wendell Jr. began testing his theory. He would pick up Wendell Sr.'s limp hand. "Squeeze my hand, Daddy," he would say.

Sure enough, almost every time, his father squeezed his hand.

After all of the years of smoldering anger between them, Wendell Jr. sat in the darkened room feeling gratitude and satisfaction. They were, it seemed, finally at peace with each other.

## Epilogue

Scott died on December 23, 1990, at the age of sixty-nine. During the funeral at his church, speakers talked about how his public example of dedication and quiet dignity helped to change the way that many thousands of people looked upon African Americans.

Scott's influence, Ned Jarrett told the mourners, extended beyond stock car racing. "I don't know of any man in the sport that worked any harder than he did or accomplished more than he did with what he had," the former NASCAR champion said. "He built a lot of respect . . . More important, he helped to open many minds and hearts . . . He was not as fortunate as some of us as to the type of equipment he had to drive. But he went out there and toiled and made it work and won — not only won races but won the hearts of people around the world."

Another speaker, the Reverend Jasper Watkins, said: "God gives every generation a few great men. These men are builders of bridges. While others are builders of walls that separate people, men like W.O. Scott are builders of bridges that bring people together . . . He was a positive force in the field of racing and a positive force in the human race."

Speaking years later at a ceremony honoring Scott, his friend Carl Simpson described himself as typical of the many white southerners during the civil rights era whose racial stereotypes were undercut by Scott's display of determination. Simpson grew up in a prejudiced atmosphere, he said, in which "the white people, they just thought they was better. The bottom line is, knowing Wendell Scott made me a better person toward my fellow man, as far as what I felt about the black people."

Scott would have enjoyed the lead sentence of his obituary in the *Charlotte Observer*. "If courage could be measured truly, it probably took more for Wendell Scott to break the racial barrier in NASCAR stock car racing than it did for Jackie Robinson to bring down those of major league baseball," racing reporter Tom Higgins wrote.

The years after Scott's death brought an abundance of public recognition, far beyond what he'd attained in his lifetime. The Virginia State Legislature passed a resolution honoring him. The street in Danville where he'd lived with his family got a new name: Wendell Scott Drive. He was inducted in 1999 into the prestigious International Motorsports Hall of Fame, the state-operated facility that former Alabama governor George Wallace had approved for Bill France Sr. at the Talladega speedway.

The next year, in ceremonies at another improbable setting, the Darlington Country Club in South Carolina, Scott was inducted into the National Motorsports Press Association Hall of Fame, where he'd been rejected while he was still alive. He has also been inducted into several state and regional halls of fame. The History Channel broadcast a documentary on his life in 2003.

Later that year, Scott's family traveled to New York City for his induction into the Black Sports and Entertainment Hall of Fame. Presenting the award was racing driver Bill Lester, who at that time had become the most successful black competitor in NASCAR since Scott's departure in 1973. Lester's career coincided with NASCAR's efforts in recent years to outgrow its past as a Dixie-bred sport for white men, but his story also shows how far NASCAR still has to go to attain that goal.

Major-league NASCAR racing has remained almost exclusively white. Since Scott's debut in 1961 on NASCAR's top circuit, only four other black drivers have competed at that level, none successfully. They were George Wiltshire (two races, 1971 and 1975), Randy Bethea (one race, 1975), Willy T. Ribbs (three races, 1986), and Lester (two races, 2006). But as NASCAR has expanded beyond its southeastern roots in recent years to become a major American sport, the organization has launched a high-profile, multifaceted diversity program.

Under chairman and CEO Brian France, Bill France Sr.'s grandson, NASCAR is seeking to broaden its fan appeal by helping blacks, Hispanics, and women to rise through the sport's ranks as drivers, car owners, and crew members. Some top teams and sponsors are involved. The effort includes Wendell Scott Scholarship Awards for minority students. Wendell Scott Jr. has served as a mentor to some participants in the diversity program.

Bill Lester, who left a lucrative career as a computer engineer to go racing, moved into the sport's diversity spotlight in 2001 when he became the only black driver in NASCAR's national Craftsman Truck Series. The truck circuit enjoys considerable prestige, although it is two tiers below NASCAR's top-level Sprint Cup series. The races are run at major speedways across the country, with well-known competitors, television coverage, and many fans. Lester drove for competitive teams, and his sponsors over the years included Dodge, Toyota, and other large companies such as Waste Management and the Checkers restaurant chain — the kind of corporate support that Scott longed for but could never get in the NASCAR of the 1960s and '70s.

Lester scored two top-five finishes, seven top-tens and three pole positions. The 2007 season, however, found him forty-six years old and still winless after 142 starts in the truck series and two in Sprint Cup. He lost his financial backing, and his NASCAR career collapsed, at least temporarily. He moved to professional sports car racing for the 2008 season, saying he'd still try to find another NASCAR sponsor. His departure left NASCAR with no black drivers in any of its three national-level series, seven years after it began trying to achieve diversity.

Although some talented black racers have been competing at lower levels of the sport with NASCAR's assistance, the organization's diversity program has received some harsh criticism. Some call it too heavy on public relations and too light on results. In any case, Lester's experience suggests one clear conclusion: If Wendell Scott were racing today, he would at least get a solid opportunity to enjoy a very different kind of career.

Meanwhile, some positive news broke on the NASCAR diversity front in March 2008: A promising black driver, eighteen-year-old Chase Austin, signed a contract to race on NASCAR's second-tier national circuit, the Nationwide series. Subsequently, however, a sponsorship cutback delayed his debut and sharply reduced his planned schedule.

Some racing insiders, such as former Charlotte promoter Humpy Wheeler, have suggested that the diversity effort could get a boost if NASCAR gave Scott some high-profile official recognition and some acknowledgment of the problems he'd faced. It's past time, Wheeler said, "to pay tribute to him."

Associated Press sportswriter Chris Jenkins wrote in 2007 about the contrast between baseball's extensive tributes to Jackie Robinson and the absence of anything similar for Scott. "Okay, NASCAR, it's your turn: When's Wendell Scott day? . . . Where's the big-stage tribute to the man who broke racing's racial boundaries? NASCAR isn't ruling it out, but it's not in the works yet." Perhaps, Jenkins suggested, "NASCAR could make Scott a major part of the new Hall of Fame," opening in 2009 in Charlotte. In any case, he wrote, the sport "needs to do a better job recognizing the pioneering efforts of the first — and only — black man to win a race in NASCAR's top series."

An intriguing idea, though not without complications. One way to honor Scott's historic Jacksonville victory would be to present his family with a proper trophy, a replacement for the small, cheap trophy he considered an insult when he finally got it four weeks after winning the race. That kind of tribute, of course, would involve NASCAR in an unflattering flashback to how it handled his victory in the first place. Another approach to recognition is suggested by Wendell Scott Jr.'s recollection of one thing his father always wanted but never got — a simple acknowledgment from anybody in the establishment of his sport that in some important ways, he really wasn't treated right. Obviously, that could be a sticky subject. What sort of unwelcome headlines might result? "NASCAR Apologizes for Founder's Lapses"? "NASCAR's Boss Faults His Grandpa"? Perhaps any sort of official tribute could stir up public relations embarrassments, with skeletons falling out of closets and so forth. And why consider apologizing to someone who's dead and wouldn't even know it happened?

Well, the question of what the dead might or might not know gets into areas of speculation and belief far beyond the scope of this book. But for what it's worth, here's a final anecdote. A few months after Scott's funeral, his son Frank had one of those curious experiences that survivors sometimes report after the loss of a family member, an incident that lead them to speculate on the nature of death.

His father's long illness had left the Scotts with a worrisome burden of unpaid medical bills. Friends and family were organizing a benefit in Danville to collect donations and sell souvenirs to help pay the debt. Frank

Scott's role included getting his father's 1962 Chevrolet stock car running and ready for display. The Chevy needed a water pump, and Frank vaguely recalled that his father had put an extra one aside.

But where was it? He searched his father's shop and every other storage place he could think of, without success. The car had a racing engine, so this wasn't a pump he could replace at the auto-parts store.

As time grew short, an unusually vivid dream jolted him awake at about two thirty one morning. It felt much more real than an ordinary dream, he said, and it went like this:

His father appeared before him suddenly. He ordered Frank to go to an old school bus that had sat for many years in a brushy thicket in their backyard. He gave no further explanation.

"Daddy, I don't want to," Frank responded. He was a busy high school teacher and basketball coach. He had too much on his schedule to waste time visiting a derelict bus.

"Do what I tell you, son," replied the dream figure, in exactly the stern tones Frank had heard so often in real life.

The next day, feeling oddly obliged to carry out what felt like a fool's errand, he drove over to the house. He hadn't been anywhere near the rusty bus in ten years. He pushed through the bushes and tugged open its rear door. His father, it turned out, had used the bus as a storage shed for auto parts. It was stuffed with them.

Frank worked his way up the aisle through the clutter. Near the front of the bus, he found the water pump.

## Acknowledgments

I am deeply grateful for the love, patience, and support I've received during this long project from my wife, Dr. Ellen B. Kanner, and our children, Rebecca Margolis and Gregg Donovan. They helped me in countless small and large ways, while giving me pride in their own accomplishments.

This book could not have been written without the cooperation and insights of Wendell Scott and his family (who had no control over the contents). My special thanks go to Wendell Scott Jr. for his generous and extensive assistance and his brave candor, and to Mary Scott, Sybil Scott, Deborah Scott Davis, Guelda Scott King, Cheryl Scott Ashley, and Frank Scott.

My deep appreciation goes to the 213 other people I interviewed for the book, many of them several times. Their names are listed at the beginning of the endnotes. Their contributions were invaluable.

I'm indebted to my persistent agent, Robert Guinsler, and to Flip Brophy, his colleague at Sterling Lord Literistic, for believing in this book and for finding it a home.

My editor at Steerforth Press, Nicola Smith, suggested many improvements in the manuscript. Her hard work, keen eye, and good questions made this a better book. So did the vigilant scrutiny of the manuscript by my copy editor, Laura Jorstad. The enthusiasm and commitment of Steerforth's Chip Fleischer, Helga Schmidt, Kristin Camp Sperber, Christa Demment González, and Doran Dal Pra have been gratifying.

I appreciate the insightful advice I got about various drafts of this book from my wife, our daughter, my friends Phil Asaph and Harris Tobias, and my father-in-law, S. Lee Kanner. Special thanks for help, encouragement, or both also go to Robert J. Axelrod, Andrea Auricchio, Jack Clemente, Mike Collins, Robert W. Conner, Dave Donovan, Gregg Donovan, Susan Donovan, Evelyn Drummond, Jim Dwyer, Robert Edelstein, David Halbfinger, Mary Jane Hodge, Amy Jorrisch, Darrien King, Eden Laikin, Tom Maier, Ben Margolis, Sandra Peddie, Bernie

Reagan, Susan Russo, Eric Sprague, Jacob Sprague, Joel Shadle, Laura Spivey, Lauren Terrazzano, Chris Tyrrel, and Andrea Wasserman.

Many dedicated, capable librarians helped me significantly, some of them many times. They include Dorothy Levin of *Newsday,* Ted Polk of The Library of Virginia, Betty Carlan of the McCaig-Wellborn Research Library at the International Motorsports Hall of Fame, Joyce Throckmorton of the State Library of North Carolina, Suzanne Wise of Appalachian State University's Belk Library, and Cory Brust and other research librarians at the Huntington, New York, public library. My thanks, as well, to Betsy Tolley at the Spartanburg, South Carolina, public library, to Naomi Nelson at the Emory University library, and to those who assisted me at the Alabama Department of Archives and History; at public libraries in New York City; Atlanta, Georgia; Danville, Virginia; and Anniston and Talladega, Alabama; as well as at the *Charlotte Observer,* the *Atlanta Journal-Constitution,* and the *Florida Times-Union.*

The work of many authors and journalists helped to shape this book. I was inspired to begin this project when I read the chapter about Wendell Scott in a wonderful book by Jerry Bledsoe, *The World's Number One, Flat-Out, All-Time Great, Stock Car Racing Book.* I'm indebted to Greg Fielden, whose historical works on NASCAR — the *Forty Years of Stock Car Racing* series and *High Speed at Low Tide* — were an invaluable resource. Derek Nelson's *Moonshiners, Bootleggers & Rumrunners* provided an entertaining education. I learned much about NASCAR's early years from *Dirt Tracks to Glory* by Sylvia Wilkinson, *Holman-Moody* by Tom Cotter and Al Pearce, *Fast as White Lightning* by Kim Chapin, and *Full Throttle* by Robert Edelstein. For civil rights history, I kept *Eyes on the Prize* by Juan Williams on my desk. Dan T. Carter's *The Politics of Rage* is a definitive and disturbing portrait of Bill France Sr.'s benefactor and friend George Wallace.

The many journalists whose articles have enriched this book include Lou Bonds, Bo Brown, Dave Burgin, Wes Cashwell, Bill Dyer, Larry Evans, John Fowler, Gene Granger, J. Michael Head, Tom Higgins, Ed Hinton, Chris Jenkins, Tom Kelly, Ed Martin, Al Milley, Bob Myers, Randall Patterson, Benny Phillips, David D. Ryan, George Smith, Mike Smith, Morris Stephenson, Dick Thompson, Steve Waid, and Brock Yates.

The reader owes much to the careful work of those who transcribed the hundreds of interview tapes: Kathy Diamond, Virginia Chepak, and especially Stan Organ, who did most of them.

Some of this material originally appeared in an article I wrote for the Atlanta Historical Society's magazine, *Atlanta History: A Journal of Georgia and the South.* Their cooperation is appreciated.

# Notes

## PROLOGUE

4 **on unpaved streets** The neighborhood of Jacksonville Speedway Park is described in Gene Odom and Frank Dorman, *Lynyrd Skynyrd: Remembering the Free Birds of Southern Rock* (Random House, 2002).

4 **"There were some real rednecks"** This quotation, like many in the book, is from an interview by the author. From here on, quotations will be mentioned in these notes only if they come from another source. All others are from author interviews. While researching this book, I interviewed the following people (in addition to the Scott family), and I'm grateful for their help: Elizabeth Adkins, Johnny Allen, Eddie Allgood, Jack Anderson, Ray Arnold, Buck Baker, Buddy Baker, Margaret Baker, Sandy Roach Baldwin, Earl Barksdale, Leo Beebe, Mike Bell, Anne Blair, Bill Blair, Jerry Bledsoe, Richard Bliss, Roy Boddie, Clyde Bolton, Harold Brasington, Bill Brodrick, Perk Brown, Raymond Burdette, Kenneth Campbell, Tommy Campbell, Alonza Carter, Dan T. Carter, Neil Castles, Frances Causey, S.W. Chaffee, Barney Clark, Joseph Coleman, Tom Cotter, Jack Cousins, Curtis Crider, Eddie Crouse, Herman Dodson, Donnie Drummond, Harold Drummond Jr., John Drummond, Clay Earles, Wanda Lund Early, Chris Economaki, Robert Edelstein, Hoss Ellington, Joe Epton, Joey Evans, Frances Dalton Farmer, Doc Faustina, Aubrey Ferrell, Greg Fielden, Susan N. Fleishman, Bobby Fleming, Tim Flock, Jim Foster, Ray Fox, Bill France Jr., Larry Frank, C.M. Franklin, Jeff Frederick, Brook Galbraith, Dennis Garrett, Bill Gazaway, Joe Gazaway, Paul Goldsmith, Peter Golenbock, Gary Gore, Al Gore, Todd Goyer, Gene Granger, Gary Grant, Dave Grayson, Bob Greenberg, Wayne Greenhaw, Ced Hailey, Pete Hamilton, P.C. Hansberger, Earl Hatcher, Kim Haynes, N. Linn Hendershot, George Henderson, Wayne Hensley, Tom Higgins, Bobby Hill, Richard Howard, Don Hunter, Jim Hunter, Bob Ingram, William Jackson, Ned Jarrett, Ray Jenkins, Cal Johnson, Junior Johnson, Anne B. Jones, Billy J. Jones, Paul M. Jones, Warren Jones, Jimmy Keen, Joe Kelly, Tom Kelly, J.C. King, Tom Kirkland, Greta Krapac, Elmo Langley, Catherine Latendresse, Bob Latford, Erskine Lessley, Leo Levine, Jimmy Lewallen, Rodney Ligon, Ed Livingston, Fred Lorenzen, Gerald Lovelace, Mary Beth Lucas, Clyde Lynn, Bill Mangum, Dave Marcis, Coo Coo Marlin, Banjo Matthews, Gary McCredie, Charlie McGee, Bob McGinnis, Buz McKim, Sam McQuagg, Morris Metcalfe, Leonard Miller, Art Mitchell, Ralph Moody, Roy Moody, Artis Moore, Little Bud Moore, Claude Moore, T.A. Mosley, Bob Myers, Bill Nalley, Bob Neal, William Neely, Ed Negre, W.L. Newkirk, Mojo Nixon, Stephen O'Neill, Cotton Owens, Slick Owens, Marvin Panch, Pal Parker, Raymond Parks, Jim Paschal, Jacques Passino, Harold Pearson, Pierre Pelham, Pete Peters Jr., Richard Petty, Tom Pistone, Don Radbruch, Butch Rader, Joie Ray, Doug Reynolds, Harlow Reynolds, Russell Riley, L. Mendel Rivers Jr., Doris Roberts, Pamela Roberts, J.P. Rotton,

David D. Ryan, Eddie Samples, Hank Schoolfield, Charles Scott, Bobby Scruggs, Royette Shepherd, Clarence Shook, Carl Simpson, David Sisco, Bruton Smith, George Smith, Jack Smith, Johnnie M. Smith, Charles Snider, Gober Sosebee, G.C. Spencer, Speedy Spiers, Buddy Steinspring, Morris Stephenson, J. Steve Strosnider, Brice Stultz III, Tim Sullivan, Dede Swartz, Mike Sykes, Don Tarr, Barbara Tennant, Jabe Thomas, Dick Thompson, Seymore Trammell Jr., Harold Tuck, Bill Turner, Rich Turner, Tom Turnipseed, Toy Russell Van Lierop, Robert Van Witzenberg, Linda Vaughn, Ken Vose, Bill Ward, Chip Warren, Frank Warren, T. Taylor Warren, Bob Welborn, Humpy Wheeler, Rex White, Deb Williams, Joe Williams, Woodie Wilson, Eddie Wood, Glen Wood, Leonard Wood, Smokey Yunick.

## CHAPTER 1

7 **his younger sister, Guelda** For clarity, I'm referring to three members of Scott's family by the names that they actually used rather than by their formal names. Scott's sister Guelda was born Martha Guelda Scott; his daughter Ann was born Willie Ann Scott; and his son Frank was born William Franklin Scott.

7 **essentially controlled Danville** Interview with former Danville city councilman Aubrey Farrell.

8 **"I'll never go work"** Interview with Scott's friend Herman Dodson.

10 **Her husband's lifestyle** Interview with Guelda Scott.

11 **"There weren't any white kids"** *Stock Car Racing* magazine, July 1973.

12 **his mother's father had been a white man** When Martha and Will Scott received their marriage license in 1919, the Danville court clerk's office simply listed both of her parents' identities as "not known," a practice that circumvented the recording of interracial relationships.

## CHAPTER 2

16 **"solved the mysterious disappearance"** *Danville Register,* March 24, 1942. The rationing system during World War II was not a factor in the case; motor oil was not a rationed product.

## CHAPTER 3

25 **"When I'd make it one week"** *Fayetteville (North Carolina) Observer,* 1977 clipping from Scott's scrapbook.

25 **"In actuality, the game"** Derek Nelson, *Moonshiners, Bootleggers & Rumrunners* (Motorbooks International, 1995), p. 143.

## CHAPTER 4

32 **"arrested Wendell O. Scott"** *Danville Register,* May 1, 1949.

32 **"As usual, the majority"** *Danville Register,* September 13, 1949.

## CHAPTER 5

36 **"The police told him"** Associated Press, August 3, 1969.

37 **"That thing was whipping"** Racing Legends panel discussion, Charlotte Motor Speedway, February 1988.

37 **"aren't bad people"** Earl Warren, *The Memoirs of Chief Justice Earl Warren* (Doubleday, 1977), p. 291.

39 **"'Respectable' people didn't think much"** Jerry Bledsoe, *The World's Number One, Flat-Out, All-Time Great, Stock Car Racing Book* (Doubleday, 1974), p. 37.

40 **"I had tears in my eyes"** *Stock Car Racing,* January 1968.

**CHAPTER 6**

43 **"eyes started changing"** Martinsville Speedway Web site, August 31, 2000.

**CHAPTER 7**

48 **One man, whose father was a driver** Interview with P.C. Hansberger.

49 **"recognized as one"** *Waynesboro News Virginian,* May 27, 1953.

49 **"has been among the top drivers"** *Staunton News Leader,* June 6, 1953.

49 **"The lady got all excited . . . damn cheap steaks"** Racing Legends panel.

51 **"I'd have had to fight"** *Circle Track* magazine, October 1986.

53 **"They walked up close"** *St. Petersburg Times,* November 2, 1969.

53 **The promoter handed him a check** *Ibid.*

**CHAPTER 8**

57 **"a force of nature"** *Stock Car Racing,* September 2002.

57 **"I told him we've never had any black drivers"** *Richmond Times-Dispatch,* June 22, 1977.

58 **"He told me that when"** Racing Legends panel.

58 **the twentieth century's first** Although Jackie Robinson is often described as the first black player in the major leagues, baseball historians say that's not technically accurate. Two black men, Moses Fleetwood Walker and his brother, Weldy, played for the major-league Toledo Blue Stockings of the American Association in 1884.

59 **a professional film crew** See www.raresportsfilms.com.

61 **They were like brothers** *Winston Cup Scene,* September 26, 1996.

62 **France's action won Scott's loyalty** Interview with Carl Simpson.

**CHAPTER 9**

64 **"Fans who witnessed"** *Petersburg Progress-Index,* June 30, 1954.

65 **"one of the best drivers . . . startling brand of driving"** *Norfolk Virginian-Pilot,* August 4 and August 11, 1954.

65 **"Scott Ranked High as Driver"** *Danville Commercial Appeal,* August 2, 1954.

66 **"Wendell Scott, popular colored driver"** *Petersburg Progress-Index,* July 23, 1954.

66 **"has been winning statewide acclaim"** *Waynesboro News Virginian,* August 30, 1954.

67 **"I spent more time duckin' wrecks"** *Stock Car Racing,* March 1968.

68 **"I remember every driver"** *Fredericksburg Free Lance-Star,* July 22, 1977.

68 **"I don't think any white driver"** *Danville Commercial Appeal,* June 30, 1958.

68 **"When I look back"** Martinsville Speedway Web site, August 31, 2000.

68 **"tells the story of how"** *Danville Commercial Appeal,* June 30, 1958.

68 **"Only way to make any money"** *Danville Commercial Appeal,* August 2, 1954.

69 **"Racing cars gets to be"** *Fredericksburg Free Lance-Star,* July 22, 1977.

## CHAPTER 10

72 **"A murderer"** *Atlanta Journal,* May 12, 1967.
73 **Augusta's Soap Box Derby** *Atlanta Journal,* June 17, 1955.
74 **"driving better and faster"** *Danville Commercial Appeal,* July 1, 1957.
75 **"to settle the fracas"** *Lynchburg News,* June 22, 1952.
78 **"Wendell Scott, who once said"** *Danville Commercial Appeal,* August 11, 1958.

## CHAPTER 11

81 **Scott's share of the prize money** No records exist to determine how much the team won.
84 **For years, France had aspired** *Sports Illustrated,* June 26, 1978.
85 **lucrative package of governmental benefits** *Winston Cup Scene,* October 2, 2003.
85 **"Murchison's financial clout"** *Stock Car Racing,* 1993.
86 **"There wasn't a man there"** Greg Fielden, *Forty Years of Stock Car Racing,* vol. 2 (Galfield Press, 1988), p. 11.

## CHAPTER 12

90 **a mental count of his wins** Unfortunately for racing history, Scott kept no written record of his minor-league victories, and local tracks and regional sanctioning bodies often did little record keeping.

## CHAPTER 13

93 **first black driver to become a regular** Although Scott was the first African American to establish a career on the Grand National circuit, he was not the first black driver to race in that series. Another black driver already had competed in one Grand National race. On July 31, 1955, Elias Bowie drove in the Grand National at the one-mile dirt track in San Mateo, California. Bowie never returned to the circuit, so that first episode of integration in NASCAR's top series lasted only for one event.
95 **"like wooden Indians"** *Spartanburg Herald,* March 5, 1961.
95 **"There's not enough troops"** This quotation has often been published with the words "Negro race," but the audiotape of Strom Thurmond's speech on July 17, 1948, shows he said "nigger race."
96 **a white-collar alternative to the Klan** Mendel Rivers's speeches to the White Citizens' Council were described in Stephen O'Neill, *From the Shadow of Slavery: The Civil Rights Years in Charleston,* doctoral dissertation, Department of History, University of Virginia, 1994.
96 **He called the NAACP a communist group** *Charleston News and Courier,* November 29, 1955.
96 **"was a racist by any definition"** Margaret Middleton Rivers, Margaret Middleton Rivers Eastman, and Lucius Mendel Rivers Jr., *Mendel, Slices of Life with an American Statesman* (Quin Press, 2000), p. 138.

## CHAPTER 14

101 **"no one would come"** *Charlotte Observer*, January 24, 1967.

## CHAPTER 15

109 **"I got five of these Pontiacs"** The account of Smith's threat is from interviews with Wendell Scott Sr. and Frank Scott.

114 **"Jackie Robinson probably"** *Atlanta Journal*, July 23, 1977.

## CHAPTER 16

117 **"I will outrun Jarrett"** Unidentified newspaper clipping in Scott's personal scrapbook.

117 **more than twenty million dollars** *Sports Illustrated*, June 26, 1978.

118 **"I won $175"** Although Fielden's *Forty Years of Stock Car Racing* reported Scott's prize money as $425, Scott was adamant that he got only $175 in prize money and no deal money.

119 **"With those cars we had"** *Stock Car Racing*, October 2003.

120 **"You ought to have seen"** *Car and Driver* magazine, August, 1969.

121 **"The only way I can help"** *Stock Car Racing*, March 1968.

122 **"When they found out I was black"** *Atlanta Journal-Constitution*, March 15, 1986; *Circle Track*, October 1986.

123 **"he sometimes makes pit stops"** *Charlotte Observer*, May 7, 1962.

## CHAPTER 17

127 **"I needed $1,000 so bad"** *Fayetteville Observer*, October 21, 1977.

133 **"They took all the kick out of it"** *Roanoke Times*, December 4, 1963.

133 **"Everybody in the place"** *Charlotte News*, May 25, 1972.

133 **"Scott has the driving ability"** *Roanoke Times*, December 4, 1963.

## CHAPTER 18

136 **Lee Iacocca** Lee Iacocca declined to be interviewed for this book and did not respond to subsequent requests for comment.

138 **many angry letters** *Danville Commercial Appeal*, May 17, 1965.

138 **"He said the Ku Klux Klan"** *Atlanta Journal-Constitution*, November 6, 1989.

138 **France bailed one reporter out** Neal Thompson, *Driving with the Devil: Southern Moonshine, Detroit Wheels and the Birth of NASCAR* (Crown Publishers, 2006), p. 210.

139 **"I wrote the car companies"** *Charlotte News*, May 27, 1983.

141 **"He said, 'Wendell, tell Holman'"** *Stock Car Racing*, March 1968.

## CHAPTER 19

147 **"We wrote a couple of times"** Racing historians have written extensively about how technical inspections could be less than objective during NASCAR's early decades. For example, prominent racers such as Junior Johnson and Smokey Yunick were allowed to get flagrantly illegal cars into races because France wanted to please a manufacturer or to boost attendance in a slack period. France's sometimes questionable influence over inspections went back at least to the first Southern 500 in 1950. NASCAR tech officials spotted illegal parts on the winning car, but France

refused to allow them to take action. One official, Henry Underhill, resigned in protest. Many years later, author Al Pearce revealed in *The Illustrated History of Stock Car Racing* that Bill France was one of the owners of that car.

148 **"In my opinion Scott"** *Southern MotoRacing,* October 22, 1964.

148 **"the bright Fords"** *Charlotte Observer,* October 19, 1964.

151 **a "polite-but-no" conversation** Passino said he had no recollection of his meeting with Smith or of any conversations with other Ford executives or anyone else on the subject of financial support for Scott.

**CHAPTER 20**

152 **"was as great as that received"** *Danville Commercial Appeal,* May 17, 1965.

153 **"In his own way"** *Ibid.*

155 **"It was the guys who were racing"** *Atlanta Journal-Constitution,* March 15, 1986.

158 **"suddenly there was no deal"** Fielden, *Forty Years of Stock Car Racing,* vol. 3, p. 30.

159 **"Scott is not an angry man"** *Charlotte Observer,* May 16, 1965.

159 **"'This could be the best thing'"** *Charlotte News,* September 29, 1965.

159 **"didn't surprise anybody"** *Charlotte Observer,* October 18, 1965.

160 **"You should see the cards"** Newspaper Enterprise Association, July 11, 1966.

**CHAPTER 21**

163 **"shared the same deep"** Dan T. Carter, *The Politics of Rage: George Wallace, the Origins of the New Conservatism and the Transformation of American Politics* (Simon & Schuster, 1995), p. 11.

163 **In private conversations** *Ibid.,* pp. 236–7.

164 **"put the word out"** *George Wallace: "Settin' the Woods on Fire,"* PBS documentary, April 23–24, 2000.

164 **"Nothing came through Wallace's office"** Carter's biography of Wallace provides one of the more detailed accounts of his administration's corruption.

167 **Wallace immediately objected** Interview with Seymore Trammell Sr. by Carter, Emory University archives.

**CHAPTER 22**

170 **"Twenty years"** Actually Scott had been racing for fourteen years, since 1952, not for twenty years. The *NASCAR Newsletter* article repeated a fictional detail that Scott sometimes gave to writers — that he began racing in 1947, the same year Jackie Robinson joined the major leagues.

170 **"All I need is a little luck'"** *Ebony,* May 1966.

170 **"a good, consistent driver"** Newspaper Enterprise Association, July 11, 1966.

171 **"I just can't get"** Associated Press article, *Charlotte News,* May 25, 1966.

171 **"acting like children"** Fielden, *Forty Years of Stock Car Racing,* vol. 3, p. 62.

174 **"Man, they done closed the door"** *Stock Car Racing,* January 1968.

174 **Ford's decision-making process** Asked about the issue of sponsoring Scott, current Ford officials declined to comment. The company, which in the past has released many internal documents on its history, refused to make available any records on Ford's NASCAR program during Scott's career.

## CHAPTER 23

176 **"One leaf is for the highway"** *Stock Car Racing,* January 1968.

177 **carefully welded the crankshaft together** *Ibid.*

180 **"I can remember lots of times"** *St. Petersburg Times,* November 2, 1969.

181 **"because the Firestone man"** *Ibid.*

181 **"Sometimes I have been at a point"** This account of Scott's trip to Asheville is from David D. Ryan, "I Wonder Why I Keep Racing," *Emphasis on Virginians* magazine, August 1968.

183 **"stood silently as George Wallace"** *Charlotte Observer,* May 16, 1969.

183 **"I used to think about it"** *Atlanta Journal-Constitution,* March 15, 1986.

## CHAPTER 24

185 **part of Scott's business** After he retired from racing, Scott told writer Sylvia Wilkinson that "one of the mistakes I made was letting other folks drive my [spare] car when I should have let my boys drive it."

187 **"He ain't gonna make it"** *St. Petersburg Times,* July 6, 1969.

187 **a factory-sponsored Dodge** Householder could not be interviewed for this book; he died in 1972. A spokesman for Chrysler's motorsports program, Todd Goyer, said the company has no way of knowing why specific sponsorship decisions were made during the 1960s: "I can't give a company position on something that happened forty years ago."

188 **"Welcome to Bridgehampton"** This anecdote is from Brock Yates, *Sunday Driver* (Dell Publishing, 1972), p. 157.

188 **In a fury** *Charlotte Observer,* August 31, 1969.

## CHAPTER 25

195 **"After I won that race"** *St. Petersburg Times,* November 2, 1969.

195 **"Wreck it and we're out of business"** Associated Press, August 3, 1969.

## CHAPTER 26

197 **"The track is just too rough"** *Anniston (Alabama) Star,* September 13, 1969.

198 **more corporate dignitaries** *Anniston Star,* September 9, 1969.

198 **"The word was"** *Winston Cup Scene,* July 16, 1998.

198 **"Bill, how would you like"** Fielden, *Forty Years of Stock Car Racing,* vol. 3, p. 213.

198 **"There will be a race"** *Ibid.*

198 **"I needed to run it"** *Grand National Illustrated,* September 1983.

199 **"It had taken me a long time"** *Ibid.*

200 **"I was fixing to knock"** *Ibid.*

201 **"All my life"** Fielden, *Forty Years of Stock Car Racing,* vol. 3, p. 214.

201 **Ward got a letter** Actually, France's oldest son was not a junior — his name was William C. France. But he was known universally as Bill France Jr. and sometimes signed his name that way.

### CHAPTER 27

203 **"I had a good relationship"** *Southern MotorSports Journal,* October 17, 1980.

205 **five hundred dollars in deal money** In 1990, when Scott was suffering from terminal cancer, Wendell Scott Jr. said he pressed NASCAR for the $500, and it was paid.

205 **"Maybe because of what I went through"** *St. Petersburg Times,* November 2, 1969.

208 **help from France** *Stock Car Racing,* August 1997.

### CHAPTER 28

212 **used the gas** Earl Brooks declined to be interviewed for this book.

212 **"As usual, Wendell Scott"** *Charlotte News,* May 27, 1983.

### CHAPTER 29

214 **die of crash injuries** By 1972 the nine drivers, besides Friday Hassler, who had died from crash injuries during Scott's years in Grand National and Winston Cup were: Joe Weatherly, Riverside, 1964; Harold Haberling, Daytona, 1964; Fireball Roberts, Charlotte, 1964; Jimmy Pardue, Charlotte, 1964; Billy Wade, Daytona, 1965; Burren Skeen, Darlington, 1965; Harold Kite, Charlotte, 1965; Billy Foster, Riverside, 1967; and Talmadge Prince, Daytona, 1970.

216 **accept Lund as his friend** Tiny Lund was killed in a crash at Talladega in 1975.

216 **racial jibes and slurs** Carter, *The Politics of Rage,* p. 417.

216 **Wallace appointed France** During the late 1970s, suffering from chronic pain, Wallace experienced a religious rebirth and asked black people to forgive him for the wrongs he'd done as a segregationist. Many did, and Wallace won his last election for governor in 1982 with considerable black support. However, during the years when France aided Wallace's presidential campaigns, this repentance had not yet taken place.

216 **"were in close agreement"** Bledsoe, *The World's Number One,* pp. 59–60.

218 **"I feel sorry for Wendell"** *Charlotte News,* May 1, 1972.

218 **"It will be by far the best"** *Ibid.*

219 **"The press, if they need furniture"** Bledsoe, *The World's Number One,* pp. 171–2.

219 **with a prison record** President Ronald Reagan invited Junior Johnson to the Oval Office in 1985 and presented him with a full pardon for his bootlegging conviction.

220 **Howard paid eighteen thousand dollars** *Stock Car Racing,* September 1972.

220 **"rocket away"** Associated Press, May 24, 1972.

### CHAPTER 30

225 **"there wasn't an extra Chevrolet"** *Stock Car Racing,* September 1972.

225 **"racially prejudiced"** *Charlotte News,* May 25, 1972.

227 **"If I had only beat Petty"** *Charlotte News,* May 16, 1972.

231 **"the most humiliating experience"** *Stock Car Racing,* July 1973.

### CHAPTER 31

233 **"I couldn't get anybody"** *Stock Car Racing,* July 1973.

234 **NASCAR's underdogs** This account of the Darlington consolation race is from Bledsoe, *The World's Number One.*

236 **"just more or less a joke"** Sylvia Wilkinson, *Dirt Tracks to Glory: The Early Days of Stock Car Racing as Told by the Participants* (Algonquin Books, 1983), p. 66.

236 **"had almost reached the conclusion"** The rest of this chapter and all of the dialogue are from Bledsoe's book.

### CHAPTER 32

241 **"That's about 20 or 25"** *Charlotte News,* May 6, 1973.

243 **"I hope to hell France is happy"** *Anniston Star,* May 7, 1973.

### CHAPTER 33

247 **"On top of the sickness"** *Anniston Star,* May 13, 1973.

248 **"No other driver"** *Richmond Times-Dispatch,* June 22, 1977.

249 **payment on the Mercury** Scott said he paid more than two hundred dollars a month for nine years on his debt for the Mercury that was wrecked at Talladega, never missing a payment.

249 **"Everyone was truly happy"** *Grand National Illustrated,* September 1983.

### CHAPTER 34

260 **played an executive role** *AutoWeek* magazine, August 1, 1994.

### CHAPTER 35

263 **"quite impressive for a rookie"** *Stock Car Racing,* October 1973.

264 **"I'd dearly love"** *Stock Car Racing,* July 1973.

### CHAPTER 36

271 **"They didn't really ask my advice"** *Greensboro Daily News,* November 24, 1977.

272 **"The film seems to grow"** *Washington Post,* July 17, 1977.

272 **"I want to get rich"** *Norfolk Ledger-Star,* September 30, 1977.

272 **remembered as twenty-five thousand dollars** Leonard W. Miller, *Silent Thunder: Breaking Through Cultural, Racial and Class Barriers in Motorsports* (Red Sea Press, 2004), p. 49. A Warner Bros. spokeswoman, Susan N. Fleishman, declined to discuss whether *Greased Lightning* had made a profit. As a consultant to the film, Scott "was paid accordingly for the services he provided," she said. "Warner Bros. does not make public the terms of its contracts with private parties."

272 **"would ask me how I wanted"** *Circle Track,* October 1986.

273 **"but it hasn't taken us"** *Norfolk Ledger-Star,* September 30, 1977.

273 **"creates its own version of reality"** *New York Times,* April 13, 1990.

273 **"I thought it was going"** *Southern MotorSports Journal,* October 17, 1980.

273 **"My wife was showing the boy"** *Ibid.*

### EPILOGUE

287 **"Okay, NASCAR, it's your turn"** Associated Press, April 16, 2007.

# Index

*Note*: Numbers in **bold** refer to the insert.